Windows® Me
Millennium Edition
for Busy People

The Book to Use When There's No Time to Lose!

Ron Mansfield and Peter Weverka

OSBORNE

Osborne/**McGraw-Hill**

Berkeley / New York / St. Louis / San Francisco / Auckland / Bogotá
Hamburg / London / Madrid / Mexico City / Milan / Montreal / New Delhi
Panama City / Paris / São Paulo / Singapore / Sydney / Tokyo / Toronto

A Division of The **McGraw-Hill** *Companies*

Osborne/**McGraw-Hill**
2600 Tenth Street
Berkeley, California 94710
U.S.A.

For information on translations or book distributors outside the U.S.A., or to arrange bulk purchase discounts for sales promotions, premiums, or fund-raisers, please contact Osborne/**McGraw-Hill** at the above address.

Windows Millennium Edition for Busy People

1234567890 DOC DOC 01987654321

ISBN 0-07-213025-3

Publisher Brandon A. Nordin
Vice President & Associate Publisher Scott Rogers
Acquisitions Editor Roger Stewart
Project Editor Lisa Wolters-Broder
Acquisitions Coordinator Cindy Wathen
Technical Editor Andy Lardner
Copy Editor Sally Englefried
Proofreader Mike McGee
Indexer Valerie Robbins
Computer Designers Roberta Steele & Gary Corrigan
Illustrator Beth E. Young
Series Design Jil Weil
Cover Design Damore Johann Design, Inc.
Cover Illustration / Chapter Opener Illustration Robert deMichiell

This book was composed with Corel VENTURA™ Publisher.

For Marie, Noriko, and Tom

—P.W.

For Bivian Marr, N.P. and Dr. Amy Rosenman, M.D.
Your alertness and loving care saved Nancy's life.

—R.M.

About the Authors

Peter Weverka is the author of *Office 2000 for Busy People*, *Word 2000: The Complete Reference*, and 22 other computer books. Peter's humorous stories and articles have appeared in *Harper's*, *SPY*, and other grownup magazines.

Ron Mansfield is a microcomputer consultant and a critically acclaimed author. He has written more than a dozen best-selling computer books with over 2 million copies in print. Ron is a frequent lecturer at national computer seminars and has written hundreds of articles for industry magazines and newsletters.

CONTENTS

Acknowledgments

We are grateful to everyone at Osborne/McGraw-Hill for their excellent work on our book.

Thanks go especially to Roger Stewart and Cindy Wathen, who got the ball rolling and started the project along. We would also like to thank project editor Lisa Wolters-Broder and copy editor Sally Englefried for their hard work.

Andy Lardner poured over the manuscript to make sure that all the instructions on these pages are indeed accurate, and we thank him for that. Thanks as well go to indexer Valerie Robbins for her excellent work, to Jill Weil for her Busy People series design, and to Robert deMichiell for the witty pictures you will find on the pages of this book.

These Berkeleyites at Osborne/McGraw-Hill gave their best to this book, and for that we are very grateful: Roberta Steele, Beth Young, and Gary Corrigan.

We would be remiss if we didn't thank the editors who contributed so much to the previous editions of this book. Thank you Claire Splan, Stephane Thomas, Joanne Cuthbertson, Madhu Prasher, and Mark Karmendy.

Finally, thanks to the dynamic duo, Brandon Nordin and Scott Rogers, for their continuing support of the Busy People series.

CHAPTER 1

The Bare Essentials

INCLUDES

- Starting Windows Me
- Starting and quitting computer programs
- Switching back and forth between programs
- Opening, closing, saving, and naming files
- Minimizing and maximizing, moving, resizing, and scrolling in windows
- Shutting down Windows Me

Start Windows Me ➥ pp. 4–5

Flip the switch to turn on your computer or press CTRL-ALT-DEL. Network users and people who share their computers with others sometimes have to enter passwords to start Windows Me, but with luck you can press ESC or click OK in the Password dialog box and forge ahead.

Start a Computer Program ➥ pp. 7–10

- Click the Start button (or press CTRL-ESC) to open the Start menu, slide the pointer over Programs, and click the name of the program you want to start on the Programs menu or one of its submenus.
- Double-click a shortcut icon on the desktop.

Switch to Another Program You Are Running ➥ pp. 10–11

- Click a program button on the Taskbar.
- Press and hold down the ALT-TAB keys. Keep pressing TAB until, in the dialog box, the square appears around the program you want to switch to, then release the ALT and TAB keys.

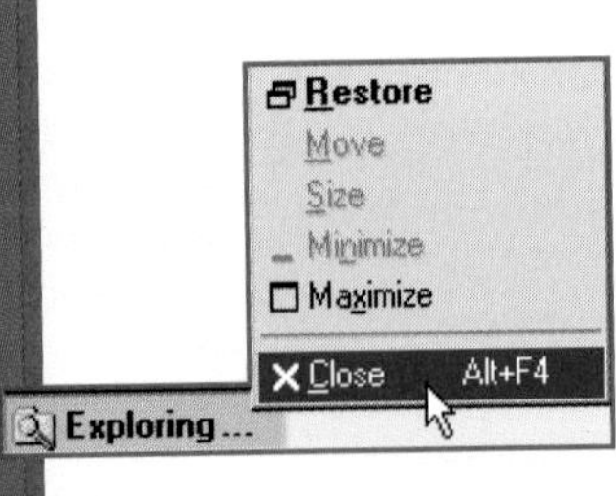

Quit a Program ➥ pp. 11–12

- Click the Close button (the X) in the upper-right corner of the program window.
- Choose File | Exit (or File | Close).
- Right-click a program button on the Taskbar and choose Close on the shortcut menu.

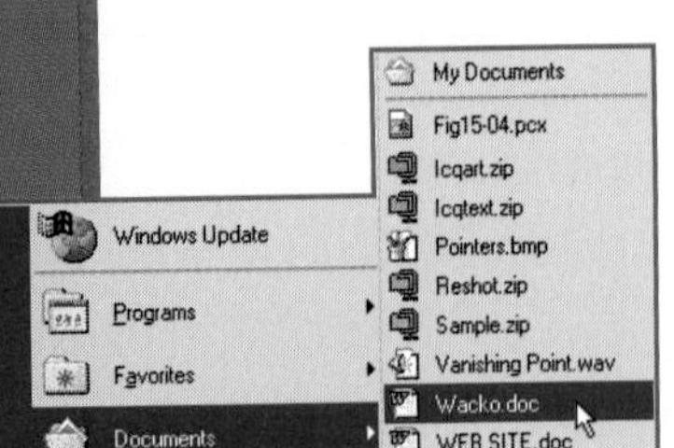

Open a File ➥ pp. 12–15

- Choose File | Open and, in the Open dialog box, find the folder in which the file is located, double-click the folder, click the name of the file, and click the Open button.
- Click the Start button, choose Documents, and click the file's name on the Documents menu.

Manipulate Program Windows Onscreen ➥ pp. 18–22

- Click the Minimize button to collapse a window onto the Taskbar, the Restore button to shrink a window to the size it was before you minimized it, the Maximize button to enlarge a window to full-screen size, or the Close button to close the program window and the program as well.
- To minimize all the windows on the desktop at once, click the Show Desktop button on the Quick Launch toolbar or right-click on the Taskbar and choose Minimize All Windows.
- To move a window, click its title bar and drag it elsewhere.
- To change the size of a window, move the mouse pointer over a border, and when the pointer changes into a two-headed arrow, click and drag.

Shut Down Windows Me ➥ pp. 22–25

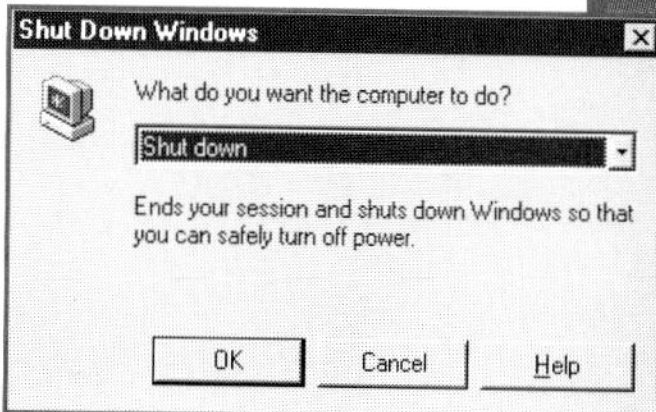

1. Click the Start button (or press CTRL-ESC) and choose Shut Down.
2. In the Shut Down dialog box, choose Shut Down.
3. Click OK.
4. After you see the "It's now safe to turn off your computer" message, turn off the computer's power switch and the monitor.

Windows Me is different from a standard computer program because you run Windows Me whenever you start your computer. To get technical about it, Windows Me is an *operating system.* Computer programs run on top of Windows Me and Windows Me, like a symphony conductor, runs the programs so that they work harmoniously. With Windows Me, you can run several programs at once, cruise the Internet, and print files all at the same time.

Chapter 1 explains the bare essentials of running Windows Me, the five or six things that you do whenever you sit at your computer. This chapter describes how to start Windows Me, start and stop computer programs, open and close files, manipulate windows, and shut down Windows Me.

Starting Windows Me

All you have to do to start Windows Me is turn on your computer, or, if your computer is turned on but asleep, press CTRL-ALT-DEL. If all goes well, you shortly see some technical gibberish, hear a "ta-da!" sound, see the Microsoft Windows Me opening screen, and then see the desktop. The Windows Me desktop looks something like Figure 1.1. In the figure, two programs have already been opened. Their names appear on buttons on the Taskbar along the bottom of the screen.

Besides a computer failure or your computer not being plugged in, two or three obstacles can keep the desktop from appearing right away. You might have accidentally left a floppy disk in the A drive or you might be connected to a network:

- **Disk in floppy drive** Try to start Windows Me when a disk is shoved in the floppy drive and you get a confusing "Non-system disk or disk error" message. The message says to "Replace and strike any key when ready." Translation: "Replace" means to eject the floppy disk. "Any" is not a particular key on the keyboard. Look for a key labeled Any and you will look in vain. Simply press any key whatsoever to make Windows Me start.

- **Connected to network** Network users have to enter a user name and password and sometimes a domain name as well. If you don't know or can't remember this important stuff, ask the network administrator. With luck, you can sometimes click OK or press ESC and start Windows Me without a password.
- **Shared computer** You might have to enter a password to start Windows Me if others share your computer or you are a member of a workgroup. Press ESC or click Cancel in the Enter Password dialog box.

"When People Share a Computer: Using User Profiles" in Chapter 5 explains how to handle passwords for different users.

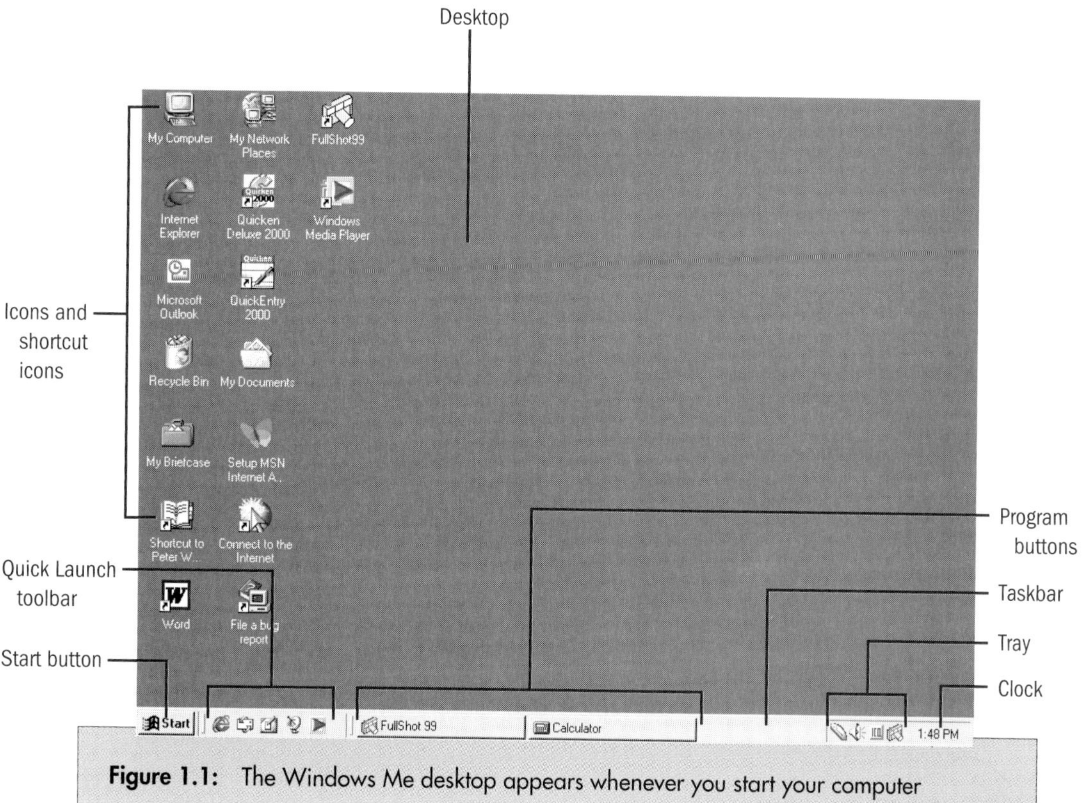

Figure 1.1: The Windows Me desktop appears whenever you start your computer

A Brief Geography Lesson

Before you take the leap of faith and start using Windows Me, you might as well look around and find out what's what. The following is a short geography lesson that explains the different parts of the screen. Glance at Figure 1.1 to find out precisely where the regions in this geography lesson are located.

Desktop *Desktop* is the catchall name for the part of the screen where all the work is done. When you open a program or file, it appears in a window on the desktop.

Shortcut Icons A *shortcut icon* is an image you can double-click to open a program, open a file, or even connect to a Web site. A handful of shortcut icons appear on the desktop automatically, and you can create shortcut icons of your own, as "Create the Shortcut Icons You Need" in Chapter 2 explains. A small arrow appears in the lower-left corner of shortcut icons.

TIP

If you can't see the Taskbar, someone has either dragged it offscreen or instructed Windows Me not to display it. See "Learn How to Handle the Taskbar" in Chapter 2.

Taskbar The Taskbar is the stripe along the bottom of the desktop. Names of computer programs that are running appear on buttons on the Taskbar, as do the Start button and the Quick Launch toolbar. You can burden the Taskbar with all kinds of stuff and change its size as well, as the following grotesque illustration shows.

Program Buttons The names of programs and files that are currently running or open appear on buttons on the Taskbar. To switch to a different program, click its button.

Quick Launch Toolbar The Quick Launch toolbar is one of several toolbars you can tack onto the Taskbar to either make your work go faster or make the Taskbar more crowded, depending on your point of view. A *toolbar* is a set of buttons. By clicking a button on a toolbar, you can perform a task or open a program.

Tray The *tray* is the area just to the left of the clock that is populated with small program icons. Sometimes when you install a new program on your computer, you discover a brand-new icon in the tray. Double-click an icon in the tray to run a program.

Clock The clock, located in the lower-right corner of the desktop, tells the time. And if you slide the mouse pointer over the clock, you can also find out today's date and the day of the week.

Sunday, August 05, 2001
2:19 PM

EXPERT ADVICE

To find out what something is in Windows Me, gently slide the mouse pointer on top of it. If you're lucky, a box appears with an oh-so-brief explanation of what the thing is. For example, slide the mouse pointer over the Start button and Windows tells you to "Click here to begin." Truer words were never spoken.

Starting, Closing, and Switching Between Programs

The desktop, the Taskbar, and all the other gizmos are nice, but what really matters is starting programs and getting down to work. To that end, the following pages explain how to start programs, close programs, and switch between the programs that are open. You will also learn how to run old-fashioned DOS programs, in case you still use those clunkers.

The Four Ways to Start a Computer Program

Windows Me offers no less than four different ways to start a program. Such an embarrassment of riches! You be the judge of which technique works best. The four techniques are:

- Clicking the name of a program on the Programs menu or one of its submenus
- Double-clicking a shortcut icon

In Chapter 5, "Starting a Program Each Time Windows Me Starts" explains how to start programs automatically each time you turn on your computer.

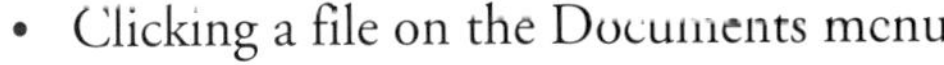

- Clicking a file on the Documents menu
- Using the Run dialog box

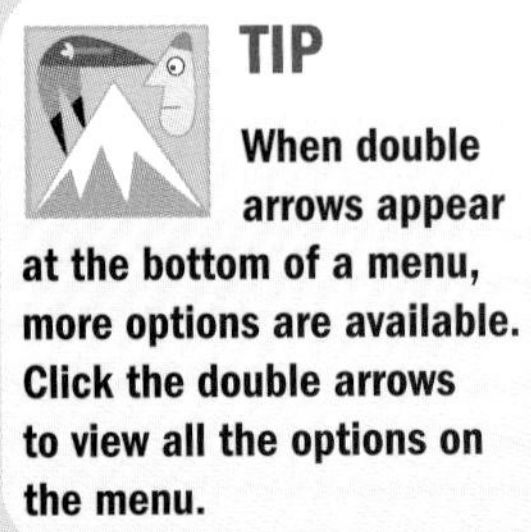

TIP

When double arrows appear at the bottom of a menu, more options are available. Click the double arrows to view all the options on the menu.

Figure 1.2 demonstrates the standard way to start a program—from the Programs menu. At the top of the Programs menu are submenu names, not program names. Notice the little arrows to the right of the submenu names. When you click or move the mouse pointer over a submenu name, another submenu appears beside the arrow. The program you want to open may be on a submenu. If it is, click it on the submenu to start it. When you move the pointer over a program name, you see either a description of the program or the name of the folder in which it is located on your computer.

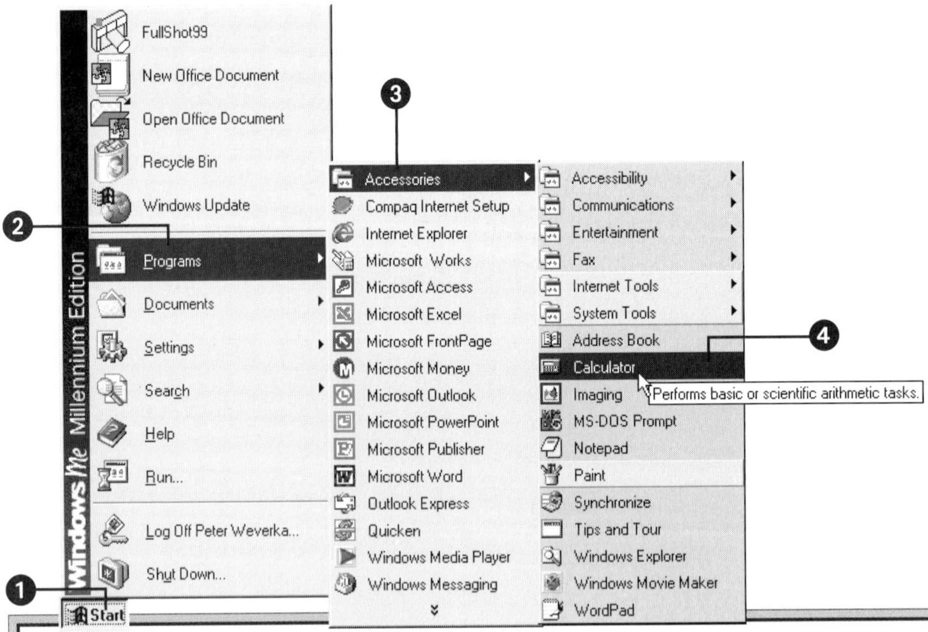

1 Click the Start button (or press CTRL-ESC).
2 Click or slide the mouse pointer over Programs, press the up arrow key to highlight the word *Programs*, or press the P key.
3 Slide the mouse pointer over the program you want to start (or press arrow keys to highlight the program's name).
4 If the program is on a submenu, slide the pointer onto the submenu. Click the mouse button (or press ENTER).

Figure 1.2: The standard way to open a program—from the Programs menu

Starting a Program with Its Shortcut Icon

Probably the fastest way to start a program is to double-click its shortcut icon. When you install a program, a shortcut icon is sometimes placed on the desktop as part of the installation procedure; sometimes you have to create the shortcut icon yourself. Anyhow, nothing could be easier or faster than double-clicking an icon to start a program (or clicking it if you opted for a "Web-style" Windows screen).

In Chapter 2, "Create the Shortcut Icons You Need" explains how to create your own shortcut icons.

Starting a Program from the Documents Menu

Another fast way to start a program is to click a filename on the Documents menu. The Documents menu is located on the Start menu. To see it, click the Start button (or press CTRL-ESC) and either click or slide the mouse pointer over the word *Documents*. The Documents menu lists the last 15 files that you worked on. By clicking a file, you not only reopen it, you also open the program with which it was created. In effect, you kill two birds with one stone when you open a program from the Documents menu.

Starting a Program from the Run Dialog Box

Finally, you can open a program by way of the Run dialog box. Use the Run dialog box as a last resort if the program you want to open isn't listed on the Programs menu or doesn't appear as an icon on the desktop. Follow these steps to start a program with the Run dialog box:

1. Click the Start button or press CTRL-ESC to see the Start menu.
2. Choose Run. You see the Run dialog box.
3. Click the Browse button. You see the Browse dialog box.
4. Using the same techniques you would use to find and open a file in the Open dialog box, find the program you want to start. To do so, you likely have to click the down arrow to open the Look In drop-down menu, choose the C drive, double-click a folder or two, and then click to select the .exe file of the program you want to open.
5. Click the Open button. Back in the Run dialog box, you see the path to the program you want to open.
6. Click OK.

In Chapter 5, "Adding a Program Name to a Menu" explains how to put stray programs on the Programs menu where you can find and start them without having to negotiate the Run dialog box.

Running a DOS Program

Not so long ago, PC users ran DOS programs, not Windows-based programs. Instead of clicking icons, you had to know and be able to type esoteric command names. Legions of nerds rose up to interpret and give DOS commands, but with the advent of Windows, the nerd legionnaires have become Web site developers.

If you are cursed and still rely on a DOS program, follow these steps to run it in Windows Me:

1. Click the Start button or press CTRL-ESC to see the Start menu.
2. Choose Programs.
3. Choose Accessories.
4. On the Accessories menu, choose MS-DOS Prompt. You see the black-clad screen and the familiar spindly letters:

5. Type a command or do whatever you have to do in DOS.
6. To close the MS-DOS window, click the Close button (the X) in the upper-right corner. You can always shut down a DOS program by typing **exit** and pressing the ENTER key.

Switching Between Programs

In Windows Me, you can run more than one program at the same time. In fact, you can run several programs. You can run as many programs as the memory in your computer allows. To switch to a new program, click its button on the Taskbar:

In the illustration shown here, Quicken is the active program. To switch to another open program, all you have to do is click its button on the Taskbar.

Laptop users and others who are fond of keyboard techniques can also switch between programs by pressing ALT-TAB and holding down the ALT key. When you press ALT-TAB, a box appears with icons that represent each program that is running. A square appears around the active program:

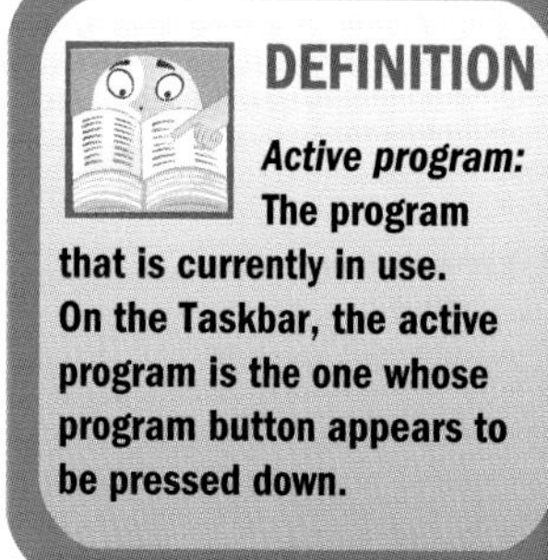

Still holding down the ALT key, press TAB until you can read the program's name and the square moves to the program that you want to switch to, then release the ALT key and the TAB key.

Closing Programs That Are Open

Windows Me offers as many ways to close programs as it does to start them. Let me count the ways to close a program:

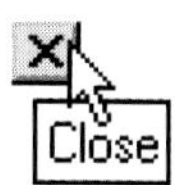

1. Click the Close button (the X) in the upper-right corner of the program window.
2. Choose File | Exit (or File | Close).
3. Press ALT-F4.
4. Right-click a program button on the Taskbar and choose Close from the shortcut menu.
5. Either double-click the Control menu icon in the upper-left corner of the window that the program is in (you'll find the icon to the left of the program's name), or click the icon to open the Control menu and then choose Close.

EXPERT ADVICE

If a program freezes and you can't close it, press CTRL-ALT-DEL. You see the Close Program dialog box and its list of open programs. Make sure that the program you want to close is highlighted in the list and then click the End Task button. Being a cynic, right after I encounter a program that has frozen, I like to gracefully close the other programs that are open and restart the computer.

Opening, Saving, and Closing Files

In computer land, nothing is more important than files. Computer programs are stored in files. Data is stored in files. To start working, you open a file. When you are finished working, you save and close your file. Following are instructions for opening, saving, closing, and naming files.

Different Ways of Opening Files

I have good news and bad news. The bad news is that opening a file can be difficult if you aren't sure where it is located on your computer. The good news is that Windows Me offers many shortcuts for opening files. Read on to learn the ins and outs of opening a file.

EXPERT ADVICE

Occasionally, when you try to open a file you see the Open With dialog box. This dialog box is Windows' way of saying, "I don't know which program was used to create that file. Which program should I use to open it?" In the list of programs in the dialog box, click the name of the program that can open the file, and then click OK. In Chapter 5, "Telling Windows Which Program Opens a File" explains how to specify once and for all which program opens a certain kind of file.

Speedy Ways to Open Files

First, the shortcuts. If you can use one of these techniques to open a file, go for it! Otherwise you have to use the dreary and forbidding Open dialog box, which is explained in the next section of this book. Here are the fastest ways to open a file:

- **Documents menu** The last 15 files you worked on are listed in alphabetical order on the Documents menu. To open one of these files, click the Start button (or press CTRL-ESC) and choose Documents on the Start menu. Then, on the Documents menu, click the name of the document you want to open.
- **My Computer** Double-click a filename in My Computer to open it. Doing so opens the file as well as the program with which it was created. "Rummaging for Folders and Files with My Computer" in Chapter 3 explains how to use the My Computer program.
- **Shortcut icon** Besides shortcut icons to start programs, you can create shortcut icons to open files. The icons lie on the desktop. All you have to do to open a file for which you've created a shortcut icon is double-click the icon. See "Create the Shortcut Icons You Need" in Chapter 2.

- **File menu** In many programs, names of the last four files you opened appear at the bottom of the File menu. To open one of these files, open the File menu and click the filename.
- **My Documents folder** When you choose File | Open, the Open dialog box appears and lists the files that are in the My Documents folder. One way to open files quickly is to keep the files on which you are currently working in the My Documents folder where you can get at them. See "Place Important Stuff in the My Documents and Favorites Folders" in Chapter 2 for further instructions.

EXPERT ADVICE

The Documents menu lists the last 15 files you opened, but suppose you don't want anyone to know what you've been doing with your computer? To keep Sherlock Holmes and other sleuths from finding out, empty the Documents menu: Click the Start button, choose Settings, and choose Taskbar and Start Menu. You see the Taskbar Properties dialog box. Click the Advanced tab and then the Clear button. You can also delete a filename on the Documents menu by right-clicking it and choosing Delete.

Opening Files with the Open Dialog Box

If you can't open a file by any other means, you have to resort to the Open dialog box. Follow these steps to locate a file and open it:

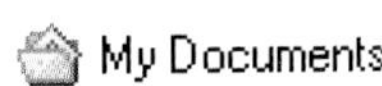

1. In the program in which you are working, choose File | Open or press CTRL-O. You see the Open dialog box. If you already opened a file since the last time you started your computer, the dialog box opens to the folder where the last file you opened is kept. Otherwise, the dialog box opens to the My Documents folder.

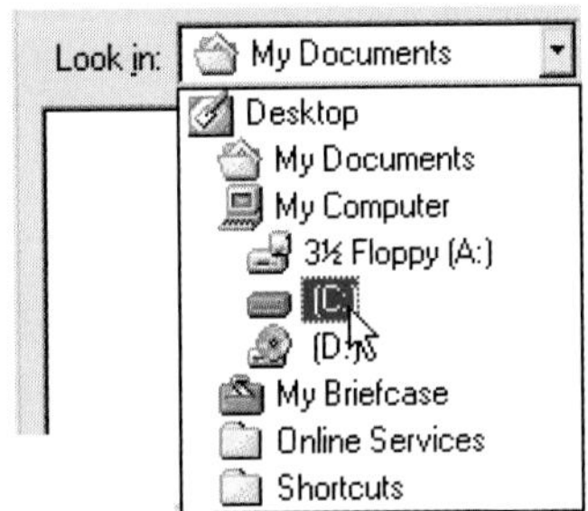

2. Find and select the folder in which the file is located. The Open dialog box offers strategies for doing so:
   - Open the Look In drop-down menu and choose a drive or folder. Go this route when you want to start looking from the top of the folder hierarchy downward. At the beginning of Chapter 3, "How the Folder Hierarchy Works" explains how folders and files operate in Windows Me.
   - Double-click a folder to open it and see its contents. As shown in Figure 1.3, the Open dialog box lists the folders and/or files in the folder you double-clicked. Keep double-clicking folders until you can see the file you want to open. The name of the folder you are looking in always appears in the Look In box.
   - Click the Up One Level button (or press BACKSPACE) to close a folder and move up the folder hierarchy.
3. Click to select the file you want to open.
4. Either double-click the file or click the Open button.

In Chapter 3, "Looking for Files and Folders with the Search Command" explains how to locate a missing file or folder.

If you have trouble finding the file you want to open, try these techniques for examining files in the Open dialog box:

- Click the Details button. As the next illustration shows, you see how large the files are, what type of file you are dealing with, and when you last modified the files.
- Open the Files of Type drop-down list and choose an option, as shown in the illustration. Choose files of a certain type to shorten

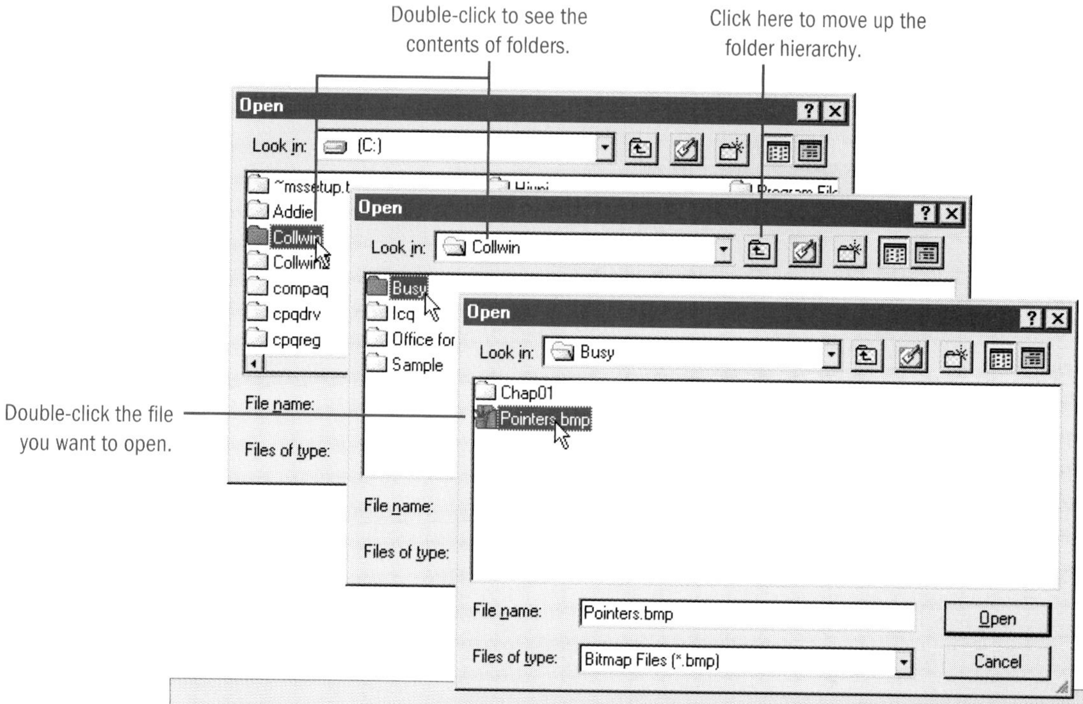

Figure 1.3: Windows offers many ways to help you find the file you want to open

the list, or choose All Documents (or All Files) to see all the files in the folder, no matter which program was used to create them.

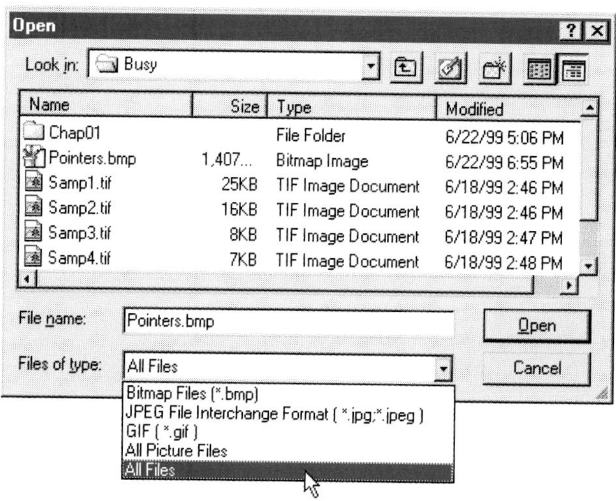

Saving a File

Saving the file from time to time as you do your work is essential. When you save a file, the program takes the work you did since the last time you saved the file and stores the work safely on the hard disk. Until you save your work, it rests in the computer's electronic memory (RAM), a tenuous place at best. If a power outage occurs or someone trips over the computer's power cord, you lose all the work you did since the last time you saved your file. Make it a habit to save files every ten minutes or so or when you complete a tedious task that you couldn't bear to do all over again.

Saving a file is pretty darn simple:

- Click the Save button.
- Choose File | Save.
- Press CTRL-S.

Saving a File for the First Time

When you save a file for the first time, a dialog box appears and invites you to give the file a name and to tell Windows Me which folder to keep it in. So the first time you save, you do two things at once—you save your work and name your file. Figure 1.4 shows how to save and name a file. Be sure to choose names that you will remember later. Filenames can be 255 characters long and can include numbers, characters, and blank spaces. However, the following characters cannot be part of a filename: / ? : * " < > |

TIP

Before you close a file, be sure to save it. Most programs offer a safeguard to keep you from closing a file without saving your work. Usually, a message box asks if you want to save the changes that you recently made to the file before closing it.

Closing a File

Congratulations! You finished working on your file, you saved it, and now you are ready to close it and go to lunch. Use any of these techniques to close a file:

- Choose File | Close.
- Double-click the Control menu icon in the upper-left corner of the file window. The icon is located on the title bar, to the left of the filename.
- Press ALT-F4.

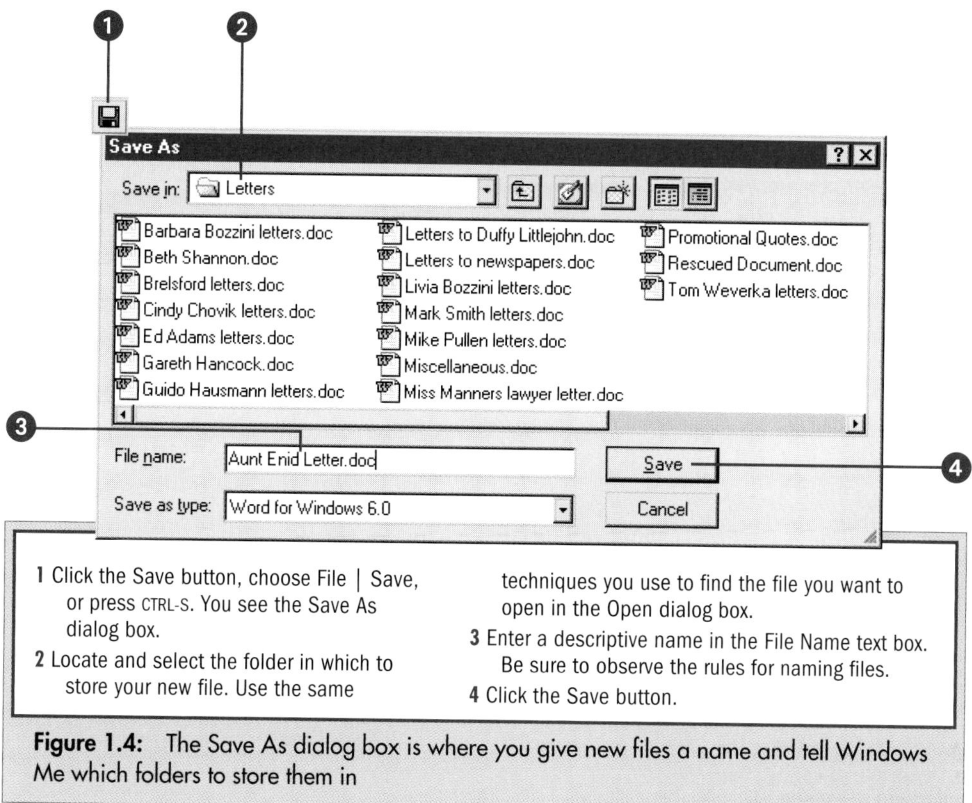

Figure 1.4: The Save As dialog box is where you give new files a name and tell Windows Me which folders to store them in

All About Windows

Windows are so important in Windows Me, Microsoft named the operating system after them. Clicking buttons is also important, but Microsoft rejected the name *Buttons* for its operating system. Buttons sounds like the name of a kitten or clown, whereas Windows has a futuristic ring and is appealing to voyeurs.

When you open a file or start a program, it appears in a window like the one in Figure 1.5. Learn how to manipulate windows on the desktop and you will go a long way toward working faster and better. On the following pages are instructions for minimizing and maximizing windows, arranging windows onscreen, moving windows, changing the size of windows, and scrolling in a window. Refer to Figure 1.5 if you get stumped by arcane window terminology.

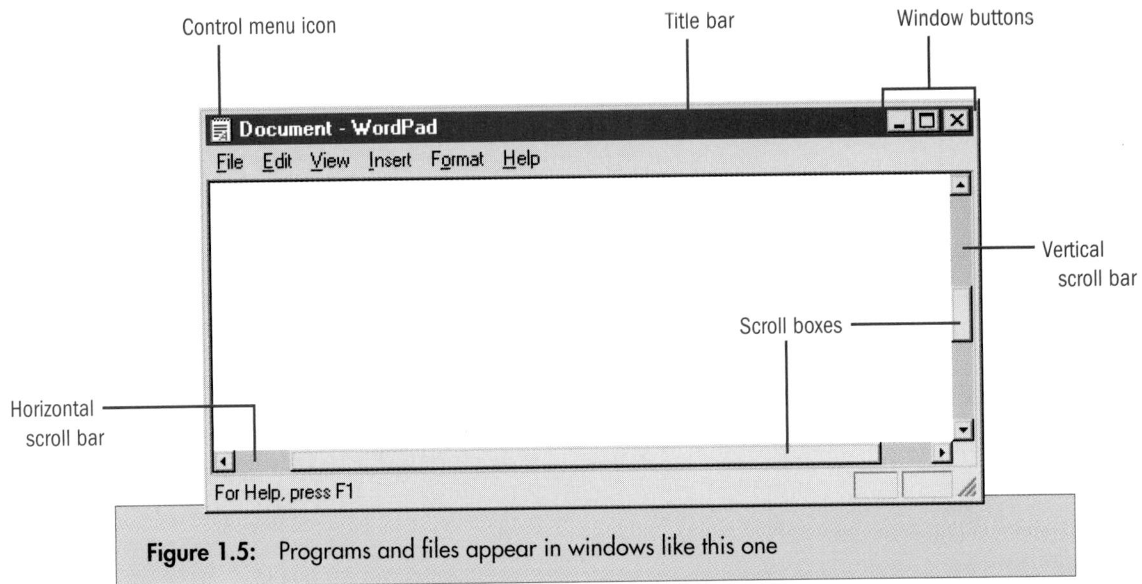

Figure 1.5: Programs and files appear in windows like this one

Minimizing, Maximizing, and Closing Windows

Slide the mouse pointer over the three square buttons in the upper-right corner of a window and you see the words Minimize, Restore (or Maximize), and Close. Clicking the window buttons is the cleanest and surest way to change the size of, or close, windows:

Minimize Button Collapses the window and makes it disappear. Clicking this button by no means closes the program. To see a program window after it has been minimized, click its button on the Taskbar or press ALT-SPACEBAR-N (pressing ALT-SPACEBAR opens the Control menu box, and pressing N chooses Minimize on the menu).

Restore Button Shrinks a window to the size it was before you maximized it last time. After you click the Restore button, it changes names and becomes the Maximize button. You can also double-click the title bar to restore a window or press ALT-SPACEBAR-R.

Maximize Button Enlarges a window to full-screen size. After you click the Maximize button, it changes names and becomes the Restore button. You can also double-click the title bar to maximize a window or press ALT-SPACEBAR-X.

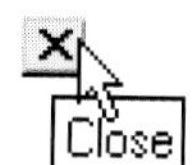

Close Button Closes the program window and the program as well. You can also press ALT-F4 to close the program window.

Besides minimizing, maximizing, restoring, and closing windows by clicking window buttons, you can also click the Control menu icon and choose Minimize, Maximize, Restore, or Close from the Control menu.

EXPERT ADVICE

To minimize all the open windows on the desktop at once, click the Show Desktop button on the Quick Launch toolbar. Click the button again to bring all the windows back. You can also minimize all the windows by right-clicking on the Taskbar and choosing Minimize All Windows on the shortcut menu. Right-click again and choose Undo Minimize All to see the windows.

Changing the Size and Location of Windows

Sometimes minimizing and maximizing windows is not enough and you have to change a window's size and position on your own. To really change the way that windows are arranged onscreen, you can try out two unusual commands, Cascade and Tile. Use these techniques to move and change the size of windows:

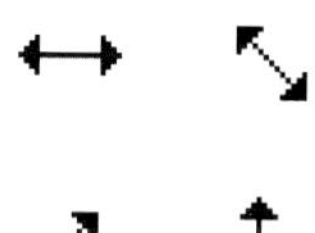

- **Changing a window's size** To make a window larger or smaller, move the mouse pointer over a border of the window. When the pointer changes into double-arrows, click and drag the border. The bare outlines of a new window show how large the window will be when you are done changing its size. When the window is just-so, release the mouse button.

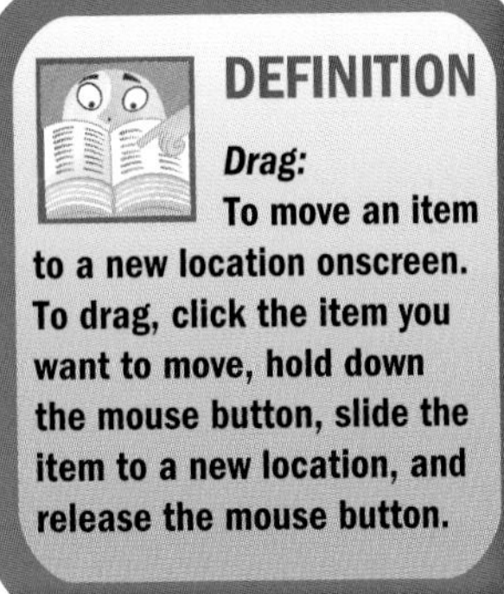

Drag a corner of the window to change its size but keep the window's proportions. Drag a side to make it wider; drag the top or bottom to make it taller or shorter.

- **Moving a window** To change the location of a window onscreen, click its title bar and start dragging. As this illustration shows, the bare outlines of a window appear. When the window outline is where you want the window to be, release the mouse button.

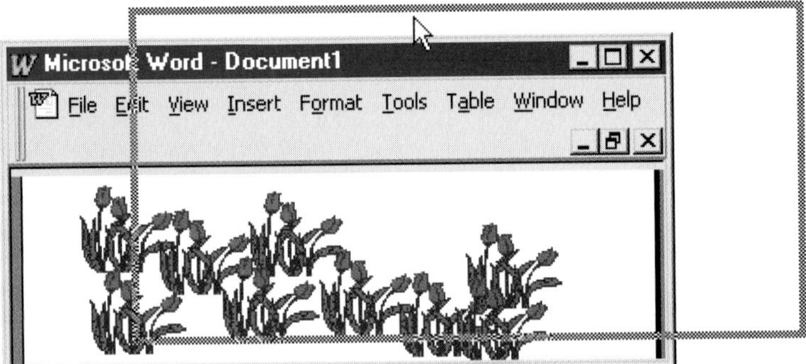

The Cascade and Tile commands are not for everybody and you can experiment with them as you will. To test these commands, right-click the Taskbar and choose Cascade Windows, Tile Windows Horizontally, or Tile Windows Vertically from the shortcut menu:

- **Cascade** The Cascade command puts all the open windows onscreen in a fan-like arrangement, as shown in Figure 1.6. To work on a particular file, click its title bar to move it to the front of the line.
- **Tile** The Tile commands open all the windows at once. You see a small portion of each open window. To make the window you want to work in fill the screen, click its Maximize button.

Right-click the Taskbar and choose Undo Cascade or Undo Tile if you regret choosing either command.

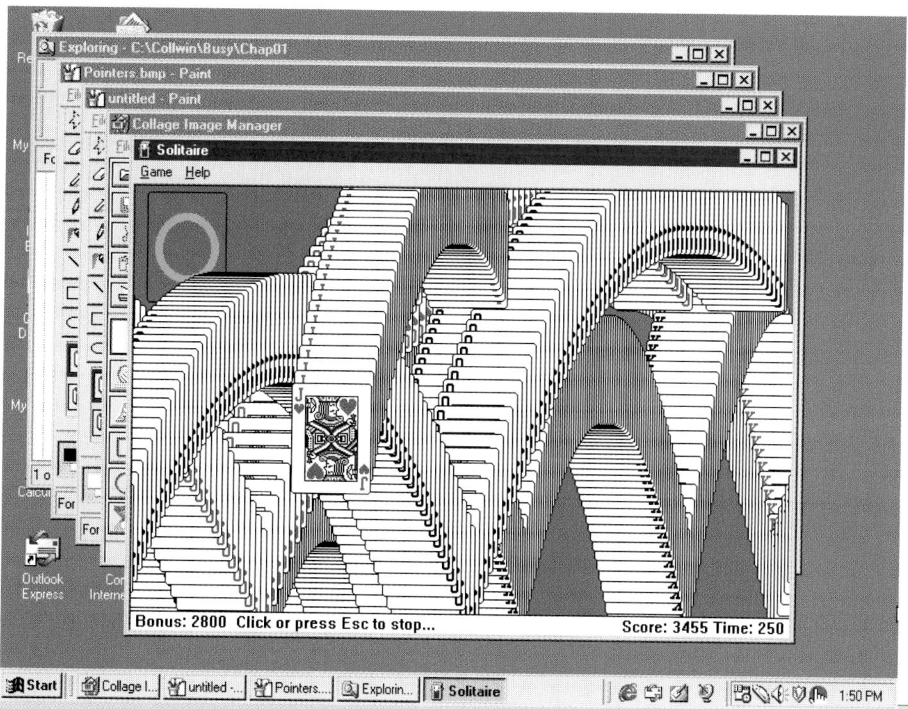

Figure 1.6: Right-click the Taskbar and choose Cascade Windows to see the title bars of all open windows. To win at Solitaire, keep trying!

Scrolling in a Window

By manipulating the scroll bars, you can change your view of a file. Use the scroll bar on the right side of the window (or press PAGE UP or PAGE DOWN) to move to the top or bottom of a file; use the scroll bar along the bottom to move from side to side. In the case of scroll bars, a figure is worth a thousand words. Figure 1.7 demonstrates how the scroll bars work.

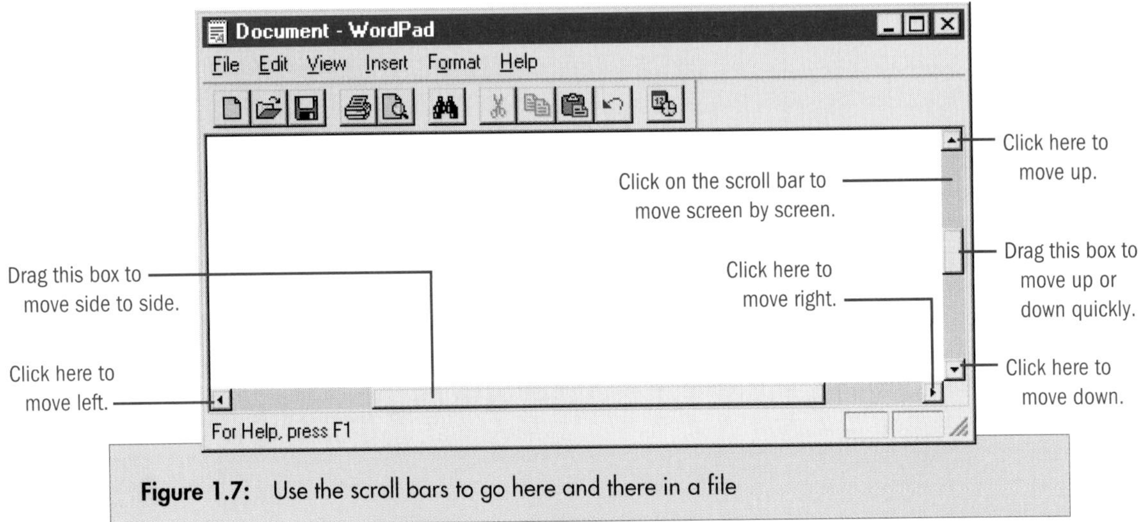

Figure 1.7: Use the scroll bars to go here and there in a file

Shutting Down Windows Me

Shutting down Windows Me is always a glorious moment. It means your work is done and you can go tree-topping or do whatever it is you like to do. However, you have to follow a specific procedure to shut down Windows Me. Read on to see how to shut down and what to do if your computer hangs and you can't shut down the proper way.

> **EXPERT ADVICE**
>
> **Whatever you do, don't close Windows Me simply by turning off your computer. Doing so can do serious damage to the hard disk. Be sure to follow the standard shutdown procedure. If worse comes to worst and your computer hangs, and turning off your computer proves the only way to shut down, wait a half-minute before turning your computer back on to allow the hard disk to stop spinning.**

Shutting Down the Right Way

Follow these steps to shut down Windows Me:

1. Click the Start button (or press CTRL-ESC) and choose Shut Down, the last command on the Start menu. You see the Shut Down Windows dialog box:

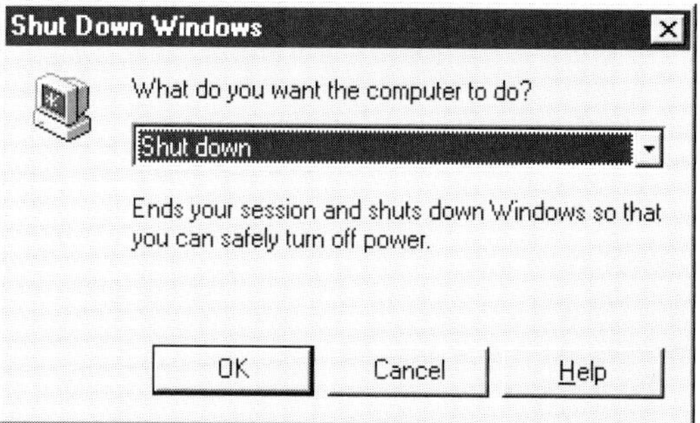

2. Choose a shutdown option (most likely the second):
   - **Shut Down** Shuts down Windows Me.
   - **Restart** Shuts down Windows Me and restarts the program right away. Choose this option when you are running low on memory or you have reconfigured your system. Restarting Windows Me clears the computer's memory banks and makes programs run faster. When you fiddle with display settings or install new software, you usually have to restart your computer.
   - **Stand By** Puts your computer in standby mode and shuts down the monitor and hard drive. To arouse your computer from its slumber, jiggle the mouse or press any key on the keyboard. (If you choose this option, do not follow step 5 and turn off your computer's power switch, or you'll

lose unsaved data in files that were open when you shut down.)

3. Click OK.
4. Stare patiently at the "Please wait while your computer shuts down" screen. *Do not* turn off the computer's power switch yet.
5. Turn off the monitor (and the printer and scanner and copy machine and coffee maker as well, if they are running). Even turn off your computer's power switch if you so choose.

EXPERT ADVICE

Many people simply leave their computers on, the idea being that turning a computer on and off too often sends electrical jolts through the system and can do damage. Decide for yourself whether or not to turn off the power when you are finished with your computer. Leaving a computer on uses electricity. And the hard disk and fan never get a rest, so they wear out faster. If you decide to leave your computer on, be sure to choose the Stand By option when you shut down—it saves electricity.

Shutting Down When the Computer Freezes Up

What happens if your computer goes berserk, freezes, and refuses to do anything more? When this happens, your only recourse is to try to gracefully shut down Windows Me and then restart your computer. And if you can't gracefully shut down, you have to clumsily shut down, lose unsaved data in the files you are working on, and risk doing damage to your hard disk.

Follow these steps to handle a stubborn computer that has stopped working:

1. Press CTRL-ALT-DEL. With any luck, you see the Close Program dialog box shown in Figure 1.8.
2. Click the name of the program that is "not responding."
3. Click the End Task button. Again, with any luck, the program you were working in when the computer froze shuts down. Save all open files, close all programs, and restart your computer.

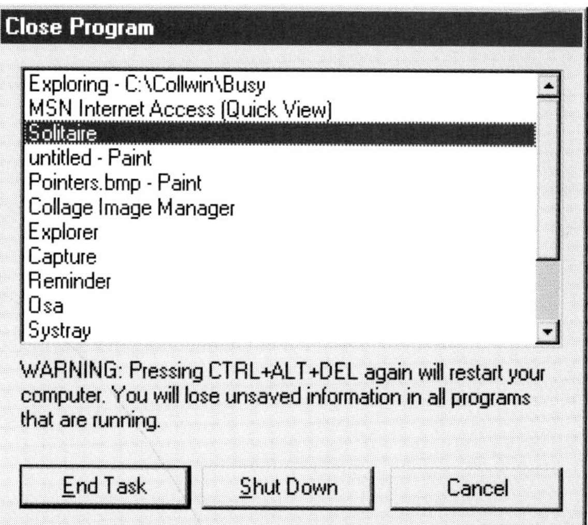

Figure 1.8: When your computer freezes, see if you can handle the problem in the Close Program dialog box

4. If your computer still doesn't budge, click the Shut Down button or press CTRL-ALT-DEL again. With any luck, your computer shuts down and restarts.
5. If you continue to suffer bad luck, turn off the computer's power switch.
6. Wait a full minute before turning your computer on again. If you turn it on before the platters stop spinning, you could harm the hard disk.

CHAPTER 2

Stuff to Do Once to Make Your Life Easier

INCLUDES

- Devising strategies for organizing and backing up files
- Viewing the files and folders inside of a window
- Deciding how to list filenames in windows and dialog boxes
- Getting the right look for the desktop
- Handling toolbars and the Taskbar
- Creating, moving, copying, and deleting shortcuts and shortcut icons
- Choosing a Web-style or classic-style desktop and folders

FAST FORWARD

Open a File Quickly in the My Documents Folder ➥ pp. 32–33

- Double-click the My Documents icon on the desktop.
- In the program you are using, choose File | Open to see the Open dialog box. If this is the first time you have opened a file since you started using the program, you see the contents of the My Documents folder. Double-click the name of the file you want to open.

Choose Classic-Style or Web-Style Folders ➥ pp. 34–35

1. Click the Start button and choose Settings | Control Panel.
2. Double-click the Folder Options icon in the Control Panel.
3. Under Web View on the General tab of the Folder Options dialog box, select the Enable Web Content in Folders option button or the Use Windows Classic Folders option button.

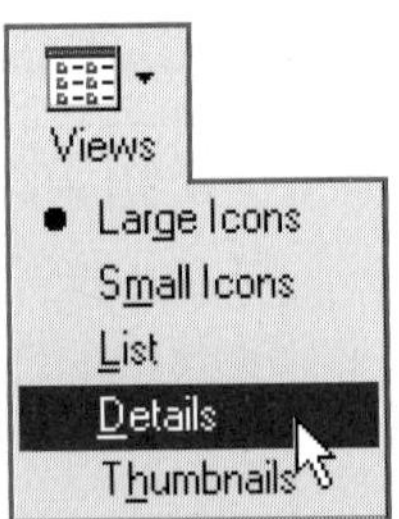

View Files in Different Ways ➥ pp. 36–37

- Click the down arrow next to the Views button and choose an option: Large Icons, Small Icons, List, Details, or Thumbnails.
- After choosing Details, click the Name, Size, Type, or Modified button to arrange files in alphabetical order by name, size, type, or date of modification.

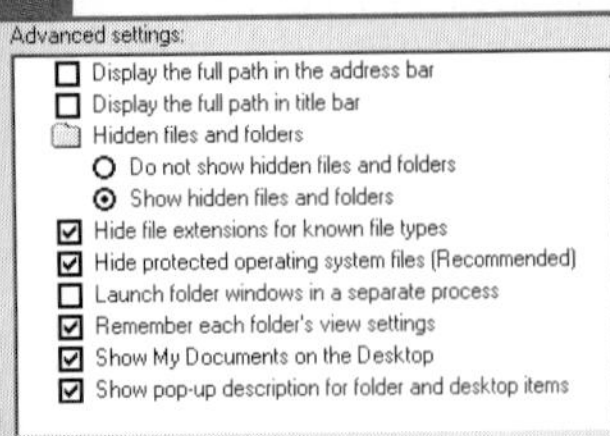

Decide How to List Files and Folders in Windows ➥ pp. 38–39

1. Click the Start button, choose Settings | Control Panel.
2. Double-click the Folder Options icon.
3. In the Folder Options dialog box, click the View tab.
4. Check or uncheck the Hide File Extensions for Known File Types check box to hide or display file extensions.
5. Select either the Do Not Show Hidden Files and Folders or the Show All Files and Folders option button to hide or display hidden file types.

Rearrange Icons on the Desktop ➥ p. 39

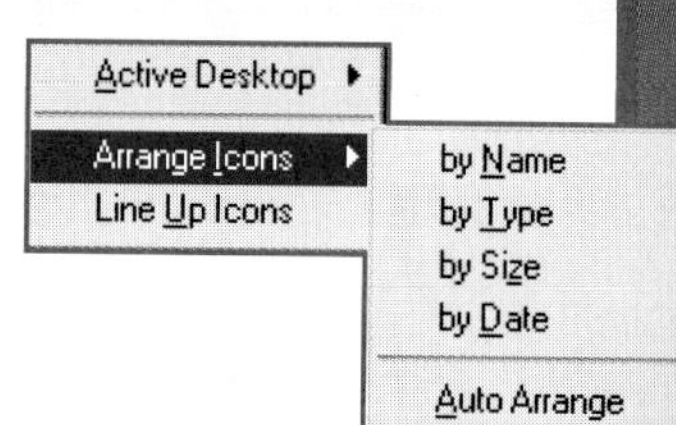

- Right-click and choose Arrange Icons to display icons with the same amount of space around each one.
- Right-click and choose Line Up Icons to put icons neatly in rows.

Remove or Display a Toolbar ➥ p. 42

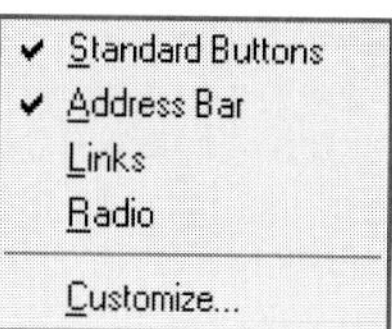

- Choose View | Toolbars and click the name of the toolbar you want to see or hide.
- Right-click anywhere on a toolbar or menu bar and click a toolbar name.

Create a Shortcut to a File, Program, Folder, Printer, or Whatnot ➥ pp. 46–50

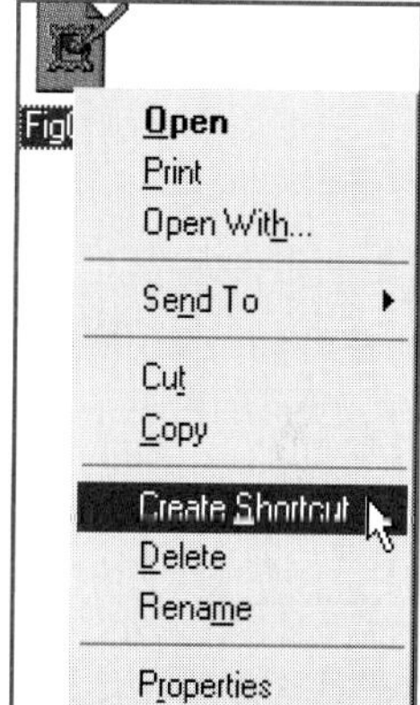

1. In My Computer, right-click the item you want to create a shortcut to and choose Create Shortcut.
2. Drag the shortcut item onto the desktop.
3. Right-click the icon, choose Rename, and enter a descriptive name.

Choose Whether to Show Web Content on the Desktop ➥ pp. 50–51

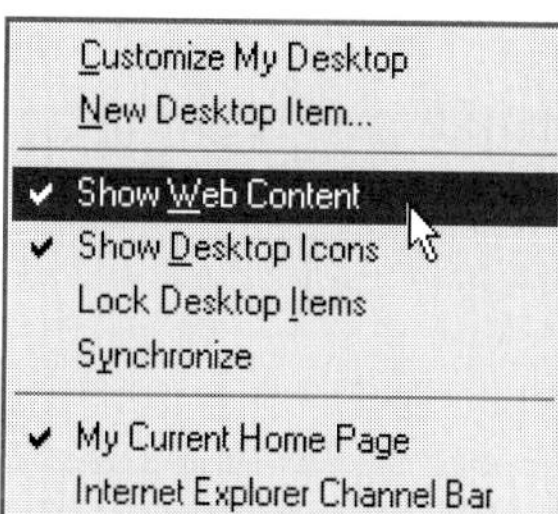

1. Right-click the desktop.
2. Choose Active Desktop | Show Web Content to select or unselect the Show Web Content command. When the Show Web Content command is selected, you can right-click, choose Active Desktop, and select options on the submenu to place your home page on the desktop as well as place the Channel Bar there.

In every computer program, you can put your best foot forward by learning to do three or four important things right from the start. Windows Me being an operating system, all the features are connected to one another. That means you can get a good start by doing a dozen or so things, not three or four.

This chapter explains the dozen things you can do in Windows Me to make the hours you spend at the computer more rewarding and enjoyable. You will learn strategies for organizing your work on disk, how you can save time by storing files in the My Documents folder, and why you should devise a strategy now for backing up your work. This chapter shows how to control what the screen looks like, how to handle toolbars, how to manipulate the Taskbar, and how to create shortcuts to the files and folders you want to work with. You also learn how to settle a few important Internet issues from the get-go and how to control the way that files are displayed in windows and dialog boxes.

Devise a Strategy for Storing Your Work on Disk

In Chapter 3, "How the Folder Hierarchy Works" explains how folders are stored in Windows Me. "Organizing and Managing Files and Folders" explains how to create and move folders.

Most people mistakenly believe that the files created with a program have to be stored on-disk either in the same folder as the program itself or in a nearby folder. Nothing could be further from the truth. Files created in Microsoft Word, for example, need not be stored deep in the folder hierarchy where the Microsoft Word program is. You can store Microsoft Word files and the files you create yourself anywhere you want. And you should store them in a convenient place where you can find them easily.

Figure 2.1 demonstrates one strategy for storing personal files on the hard disk. In this strategy, all personal files are stored directly on

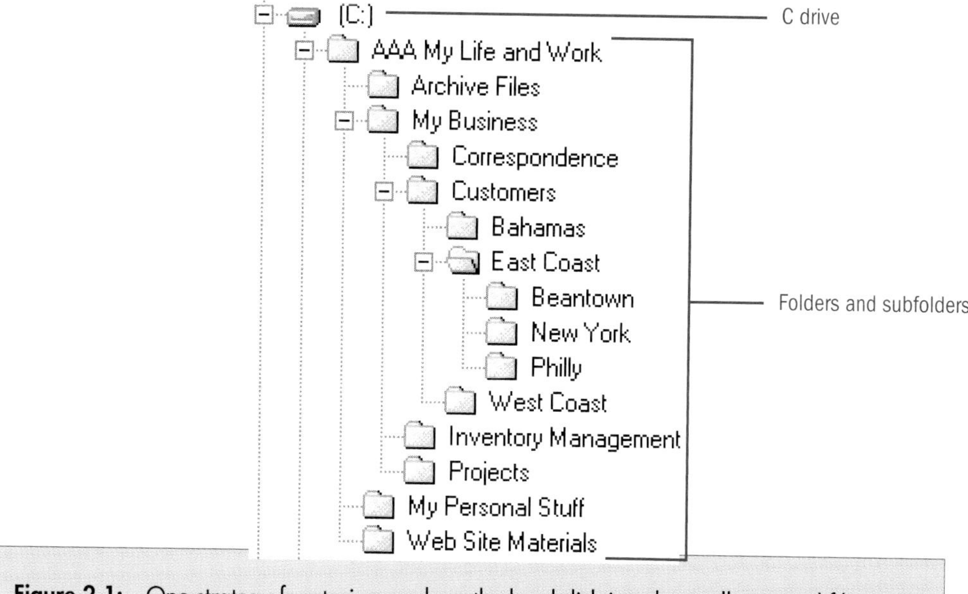

Figure 2.1: One strategy for storing work on the hard disk is to keep all personal files in a single folder where you can find them easily

the C drive in a folder called AAA My Life and Work and its subfolders. This user put the letters AAA in the name so that her personal folder would be first in the list of folders on the C drive, where she could find it easily. Inside the AAA My Life and Work folder are subfolders for storing archive files, files that pertain to a business, personal files, and Web site materials. Inside the My Business subfolder are more subfolders for storing files that pertain to various aspects of the business.

As a Windows Me user, one of your first jobs is to devise a strategy for storing your work on-disk. Create folders for the different kinds of work you do and arrange the folders on-disk in such a way that you can find them easily. When you want to create a link between files or open, back up, delete, move, or copy a file, you will know exactly where it is if you carefully devise a strategy for storing your work on disk.

Learn to Take Advantage of the My Documents Folder

Maybe the fastest way to open a file you are working on is to keep it temporarily in the My Documents folder. Instead of tunneling through the folder hierarchy to find and open a file, all you have to do is click a couple of times to open the My Documents folder, and then open the file from there. The My Documents folder is by far the easiest folder to open in Windows Me. Here are two methods for accessing the folder and opening a file:

- Double-click the My Documents icon on the desktop. My Computer opens to show the contents of the My Documents folder, as shown on the top of Figure 2.2. Double-click the file that you want to open.

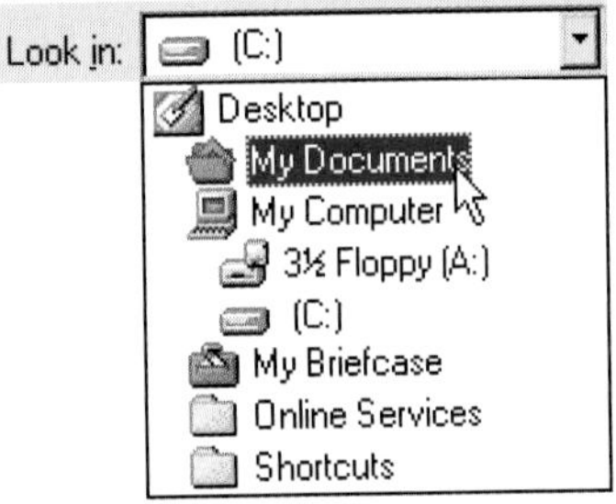

- In the program in which you are working, choose File | Open. As shown on the bottom of Figure 2.2, the contents of the My Documents folder appear in the Open dialog box. Select a file and click the Open button. (You don't see the My Documents folder if you previously opened files in a different folder. If the My Documents folder doesn't appear, open the Look In drop-down menu and choose My Documents.)

By the way, don't confuse the My Documents folder with the Documents option on the Start menu. When you click the Start button and choose Documents, you see a list of the last 15 files you worked on, not the contents of the My Documents folder. However, you can choose My Documents, the topmost option on the Documents menu, to open the My Documents folder in My Computer.

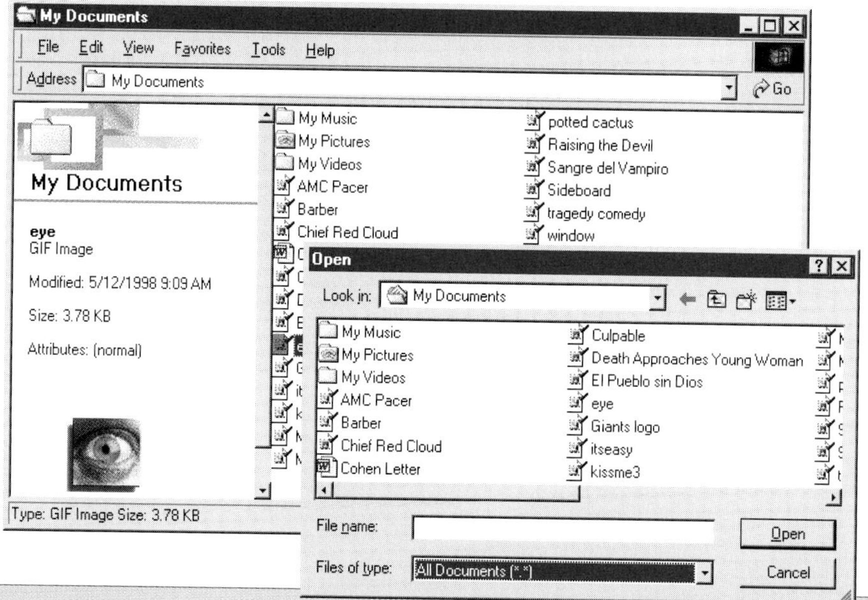

Figure 2.2: Double-click the My Documents icon on the desktop to open the My Documents folder in My Computer (left), or choose File | Open to see the My Documents folder in the Open dialog box (right)

Decide When and How to Back Up Files

Computers are fabulous machines until they break down. A broken computer is worse than useless. The data stored on the hard disk is trapped inside and will never be of use to anyone. Unless someone had the foresight to back up the data, no one will ever be able to see or use it again.

In computer lingo, *backing up* means to make a second copy of a computer file and store it in a safe place where nothing can harm it (how to back up a file to a floppy disk is explained in Chapter 3). For now, you need to devise a backup plan. Answer these questions to get started:

- *Which of my files are important or irreplaceable and therefore need to be backed up?* Losing a client database, an address list, or a novel-in-progress is gut-wrenching and can have tragic consequences.
- *How often should I back up my important files—daily, weekly, monthly?* The answer depends on how much trouble reconstructing a file is. If reconstructing a file is any trouble whatsoever, back it up often.
- *How should I back up my files?* To back up a few small files, copy them to floppy disks. To quickly back up many hundreds of files, copy them to a tape drive or Zip drive.
- *Where should I store the backup copies of the files?* Store disks or tapes where they are safe from floods, wildfires, earthquakes, power outages, burglars, disk failures, and children with grubby hands or glasses of apple juice. Since no such place exists, do your best under the circumstances.

Decide Whether You Like Classic-Style or Web-Style Folders

Windows Me offers two ways to view folders in My Computer, the Recycle Bin, the Search Results window, and other places where folders and their contents are displayed—classic style or Web style. Web style gives you the advantage of being able to click a file and get a thumbnail picture of what's in it, as shown in Figure 2-3. What's more, you can glance at the left side of the window to learn what kind of file you are dealing with, the file's size, and when it was created.

In Chapter 3, "Organizing and Managing Files and Folder" explains how to copy and move files and folders.

The advantage of classic-style folders is that you can see more folder contents in the window. Moreover, copying and moving files is easier in a classic-style folder window, because you don't have to drag the files over the thumbnail image and other stuff on the left side.

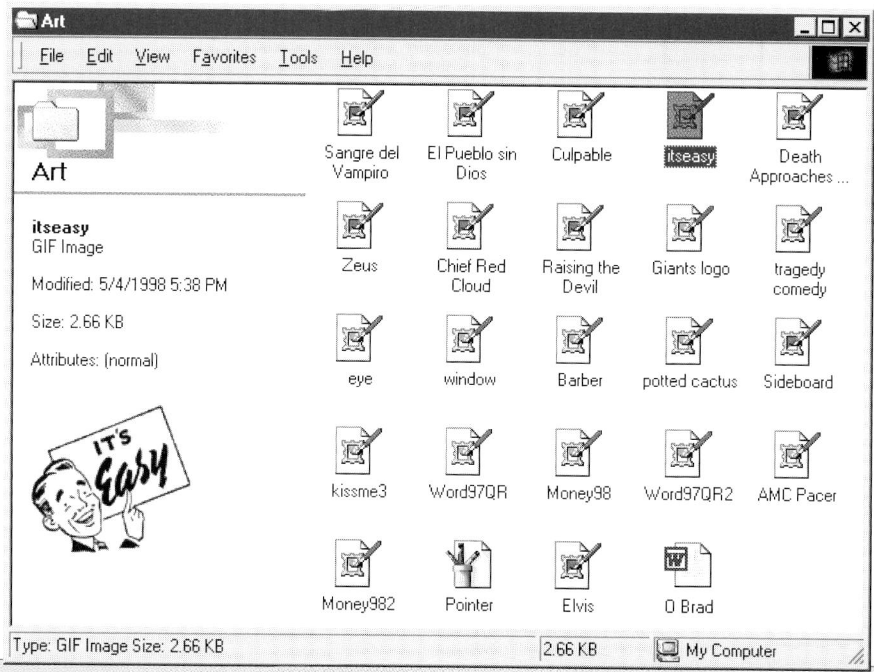

Figure 2.3: In a Web-style folder window, you can click a filename to learn what's in a file and when it was created

Follow these steps to tell Windows Me whether you want Web-style or classic-style folder windows:

1. Click the Start button and choose Settings | Control Panel. The Control Panel opens.
2. Double-click the Folder Options icon (if you don't see this icon, click the View All Control Panel options hyperlink). The Folder Options dialog box appears.

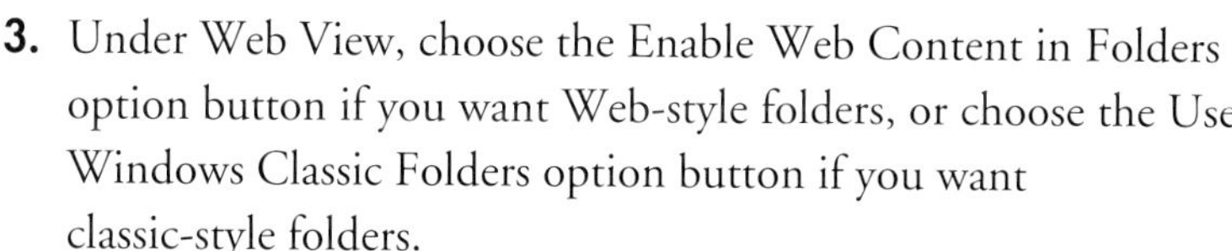

3. Under Web View, choose the Enable Web Content in Folders option button if you want Web-style folders, or choose the Use Windows Classic Folders option button if you want classic-style folders.

4. Click OK.

Learn the Ways to View Folders and Files

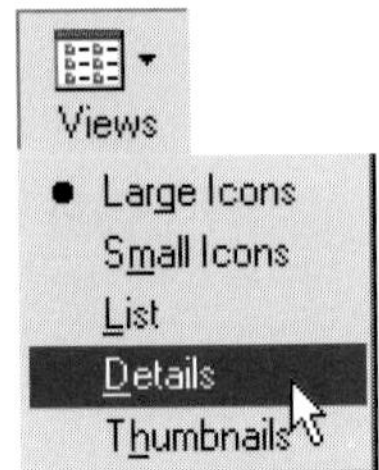

Because finding the folder or file you want to open can be difficult, Windows offers different ways of viewing folders and files. No matter where you go in Windows—My Computer, the Recycle Bin, the Open dialog box, the My Documents folder, or the Search Results window—you can choose a View menu option to get a better idea of what is in the folder you are rummaging through. Folders and files can appear as large icons, as small icons, in a list, in a detailed list, or as thumbnails. And if you opt for a detailed list, you can arrange the list by name, file type, size, or the date on which the file was last saved.

Figure 2.4 shows different ways of viewing folders and files. Follow these steps to change views:

1. Either click the down arrow next to the Views button to see the Views menu or click Views on the menu bar.
2. Choose an option: Large Icons, Small Icons, List, Details, or Thumbnails.

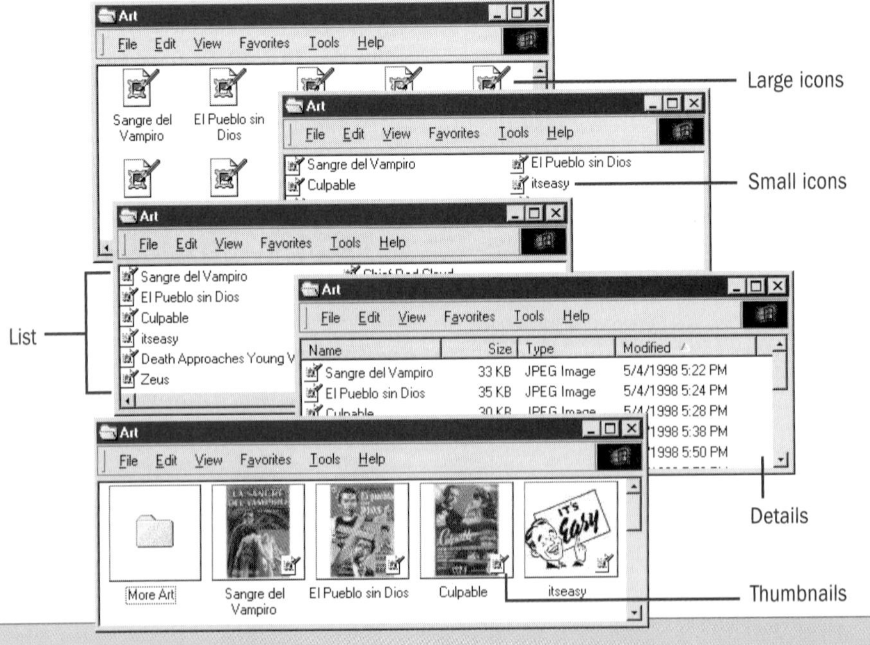

Figure 2.4: Large Icons, Small Icons, List, Details, and Thumbnails

Figure 2.5 shows how to rearrange files and folders in Details view so you can find what you're looking for. If I were you, I would fold down the corner of this page. These same techniques work in My Computer, the Recycle Bin, the Open dialog box, the Search Results window, and other places where files are sometimes hard to locate.

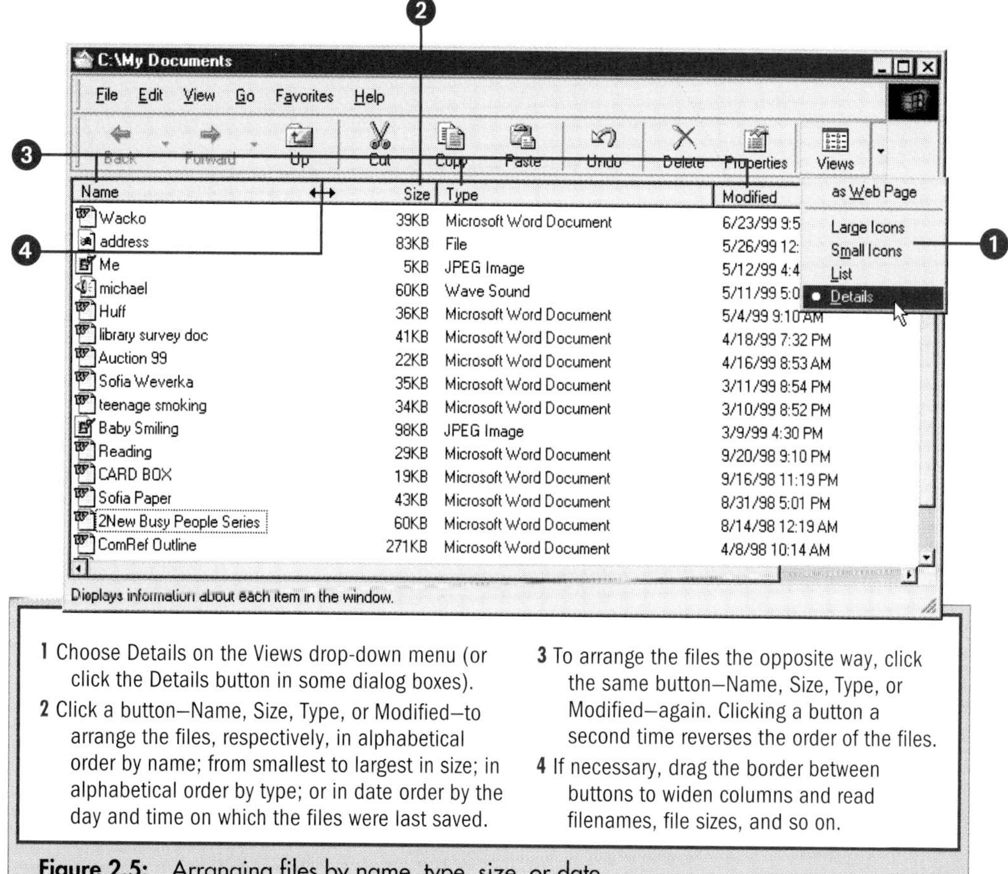

1 Choose Details on the Views drop-down menu (or click the Details button in some dialog boxes).

2 Click a button—Name, Size, Type, or Modified—to arrange the files, respectively, in alphabetical order by name; from smallest to largest in size; in alphabetical order by type; or in date order by the day and time on which the files were last saved.

3 To arrange the files the opposite way, click the same button—Name, Size, Type, or Modified—again. Clicking a button a second time reverses the order of the files.

4 If necessary, drag the border between buttons to widen columns and read filenames, file sizes, and so on.

Figure 2.5: Arranging files by name, type, size, or date

EXPERT ADVICE

The four columns you see in Details view aren't the only columns you can see in a folder window. Choose View | Choose Columns to include an Author, Title, Subject, or one of 18 other columns. In the Columns Settings dialog box, select the columns you want and click OK.

Decide How to List Files in Folders and Dialog Boxes

DEFINITION

File extension: **A three-letter designation at the end of a filename that describes what type of file the file is. The extension comes after the filename and is separated from the name by a period. Paint.exe, for example, is an .exe (or executable) file, also known as a program file. Sunset.gif is a .gif file, a kind of graphics file.**

Unless you tell it otherwise, Windows does not show file extensions in dialog boxes and folder windows. Hidden files are not shown either. But not being able to see file extensions can be a handicap when you are working with different types of files because the extension identifies the kind of file you are working with. In graphics and desktop publishing programs, where files of different types are often jumbled together, being able to identify files by their three-letter extensions is a must.

Follow these steps to tell Windows Me how to display filenames in windows and dialog boxes:

1. Click the Start button and choose Settings | Control Panel. The Control Panel opens.
2. Double-click the Folder Options icon (if you don't see it, click the View All Control Panel Options hyperlink). The Folder options dialog box appears.
3. Click the View tab.
4. Under Files and Folders, check or uncheck the following options, and then click OK:
   - **Display the Full Path in Title Bar** Lists the path to the file you are working on in the title bar. I find this option very nice. In My Computer and other windows where files are manipulated, all you have to do is glance at the title bar to see precisely where files are located on your computer:

DEFINITION

Path: **A list of the successive folders in which a file is located.**

C:\AAA My Life and Work\My Business\Customers\East Coast\Philly 

   - **Hidden Files and Folders** Check the first option, Do Not Show Hidden Files and Folders, to keep the background files that programs need from appearing in windows and dialog boxes. Check the second option, Show Hidden Files and Folders, if you need to see hidden files and folders.

Hide File Extensions for Known File Types Uncheck this box if you want to see file extensions as well as filenames in windows and dialog boxes where files appear.

EXPERT ADVICE

The only drawback to displaying file extensions is that you have to know and enter an extension whenever you save and name a file. For example, instead of naming a Microsoft Word file Addresses, **you have to type** Addresses.doc **in the Save As dialog box, "doc" being the three-letter extension for Word files.**

Make the Desktop Look Just So

Since you have to stare at the Windows Me desktop as you work, you might as well stare at a pretty face rather than an ugly one. The next few pages explain how to display and rearrange icons on the desktop, pick a screen saver, and choose a screen size and screen resolution for your monitor.

In Chapter 5, "Making the Screen Easier to Look At" explains other ways to change the appearance of the screen.

Displaying Icons on the Desktop (and in Folders)

Icons on the desktop and file icons in folder windows tend to jumble together when you do a lot of moving and copying and pasting. To prevent icons from jumbling together, right-click a blank place on the desktop or in a folder window and choose one of these commands:

- **Arrange Icons | Auto Arrange** Arranges icons in military fashion, with the same amount of space around each one.
- **Line Up Icons** Lines up the icons in rows but does not close empty space between icons.

Later in this chapter, "Keeping Shortcuts in a Desktop Folder" explains a technique to keep the desktop from getting crowded with shortcut icons.

EXPERT ADVICE

To make desktop and folder icons larger so you can see them better, right-click a blank place on the desktop and choose Properties. In the Display Properties dialog box, click the Effects tab, check the Use Large Icons check box, and click OK.

Selecting a Screen Saver

In the old days of computer technology, monitors suffered from burn-in if they were left on too long. The onscreen image would eat into the monitor's phosphorous lining and damage it. To prevent burn-in, screen savers were developed.

Although screen savers aren't necessary anymore since they don't save the screen from damage, they are fun and worth using if only because they burst onscreen when you've been idle too long and remind you to go back to work. Figure 2.6 shows how to select a screen saver of your very own.

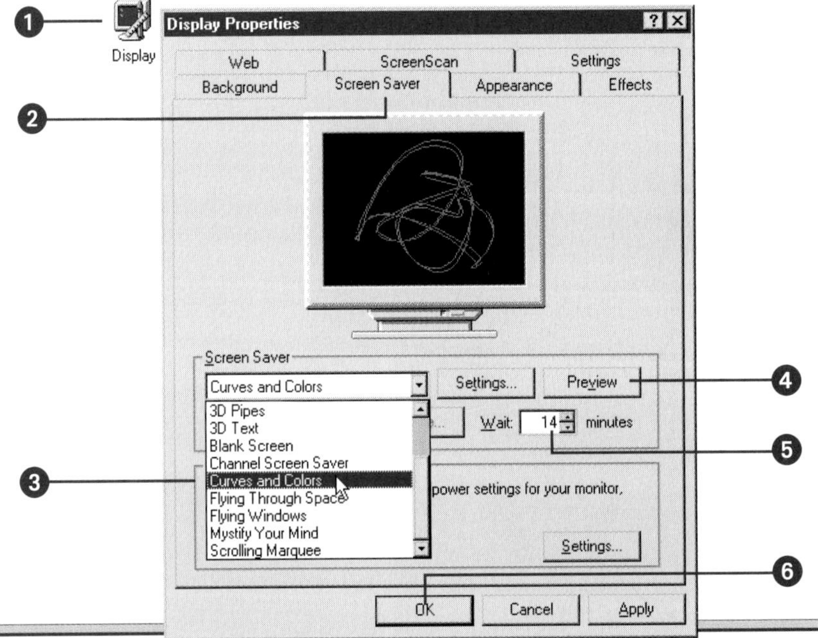

1 Either click the Start button, choose Settings | Control Panel, and double-click the Display icon, or right-click an empty part of the desktop and choose Properties from the shortcut menu.

2 Click the Screen Saver tab in the Display Properties dialog box.

3 From the Screen Saver drop-down menu, choose a screen saver and glance at the sample monitor to see what it is.

4 Click the Preview button. The screen saver fills the screen. Jiggle the mouse to see the Display Properties dialog box again.

5 In the Wait box, enter how many minutes should elapse before the screen saver kicks in. If you're lazy, enter **1**—the screen saver will burst onscreen after every minute you waste by dreaming.

6 Click OK.

Figure 2.6: The screen saver you choose in the Display Properties dialog box will appear onscreen if you neglect to touch the computer for a certain number of minutes

Choosing a Screen Size and Screen Resolution

In computer lingo, *resolution* describes how clearly images and letters appear onscreen. Resolution is determined by the number of colors, 16 or 256, that are used to display images and the size of the screen in pixels. The more pixels, the larger the screen appears to be. The more colors used in a display, the clearer the pictures look. If you work with graphic images or photographs, you owe it yourself to display pictures in 256 colors. At 16 colors, everything is a smudge.

Figure 2.7 describes how to choose a screen size and screen resolution. Depending on which option you choose, you might have to restart your computer before the settings take effect.

DEFINITION

Pixel:

A dot in a grid of thousands of dots that, together, make an image. On a monitor screen, the image you see is composed of thousands of pixels. The term stands for "picture element."

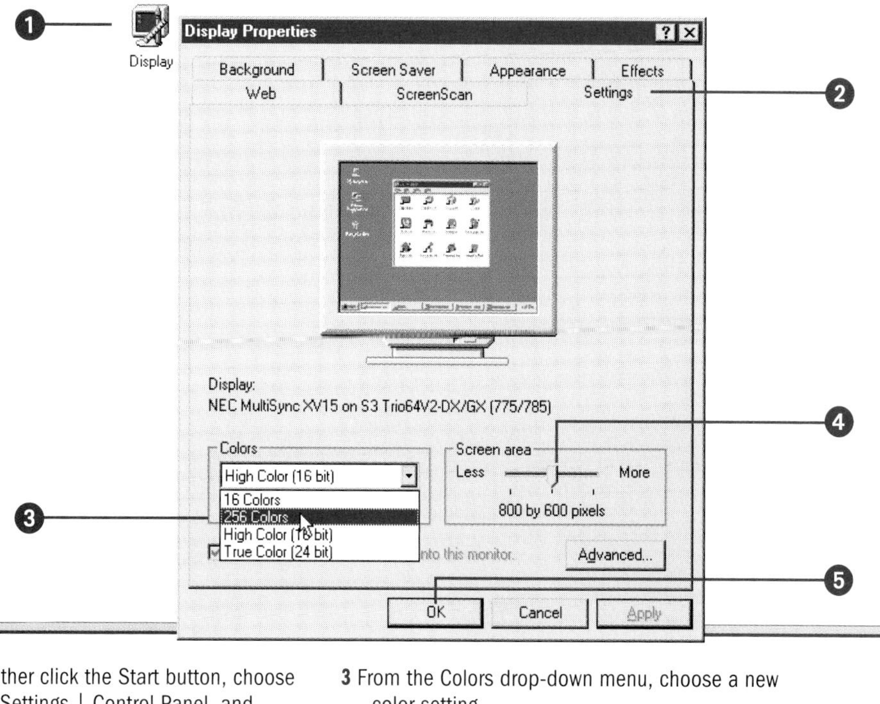

1 Either click the Start button, choose Settings | Control Panel, and double-click the Display icon, or right-click a blank spot on the desktop and choose Properties.

2 In the Display Properties dialog box, click the Settings tab.

3 From the Colors drop-down menu, choose a new color setting.

4 Under the Screen area, drag the slider to 640 by 480 pixels, 800 by 600 pixels, 1,024 by 768, 1,600 by 1,200 pixels, or another size. The sample monitor gives an inkling of what these settings look like onscreen.

5 Click OK.

Figure 2.7: Experiment with the Screen Area and Colors settings until you concoct a screen you are happy with

EXPERT ADVICE

Some monitors can't display at 1,024 by 768 or 1,600 by 1,200 pixels. Other monitors do not offer 256 colors. If you choose a setting in the Display Properties dialog box and nothing happens, blame it on your monitor or video card, not on Windows Me.

Learn How Toolbars Work

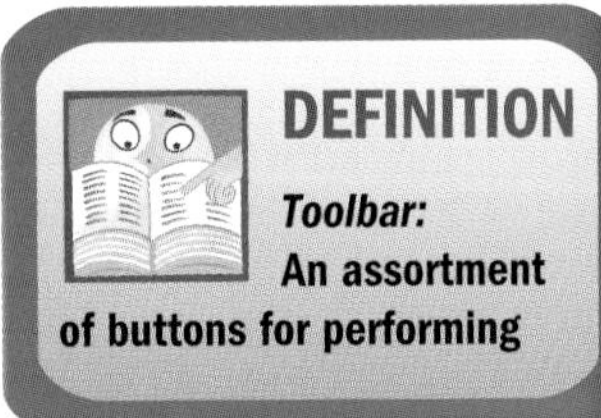

Knowing how to display and remove toolbars is worthwhile, because toolbars take up valuable space onscreen. Fortunately, removing them and getting them back is as easy as right-clicking or choosing options from the View menu, as the next illustration shows. A check mark next to a toolbar's name on a menu means that the toolbar is displayed. Display or remove toolbars as you need them.

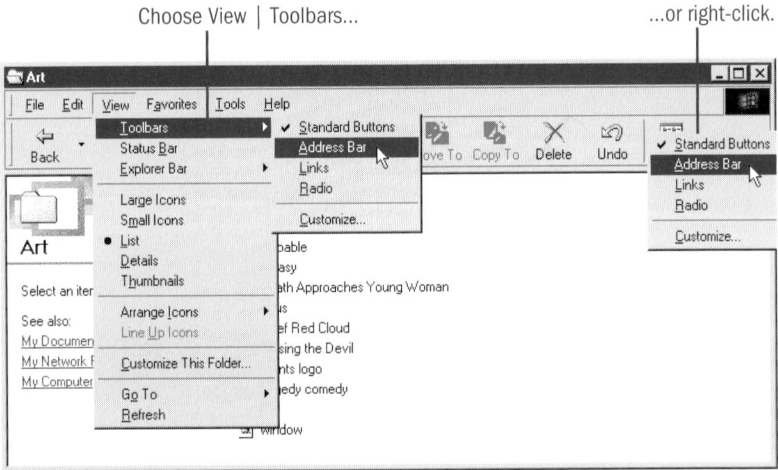

Do the following to display or remove toolbars:

- **With the View Menu** Choose View | Toolbars and click the name of the toolbar you want to see or hide.
- **By Right-Clicking** Right-click anywhere on a toolbar or the menu bar and click a toolbar name.

Learn How to Handle the Taskbar

In Windows Me, Microsoft has burdened the Taskbar with additional cargo, so learning how to pilot the Taskbar is worthwhile. These pages explain how to change the position and size of the Taskbar, handle the toolbars on the Taskbar, and remove and display the Taskbar.

DEFINITION

Taskbar: **The stripe along the bottom of the screen. The Start button and the names of programs that are running appear on buttons on the Taskbar.**

Techniques for Managing a Crowded Taskbar

As you surely know, Windows puts a new button on the Taskbar when you open a new program. By clicking a Taskbar button, you can start working in a different program. That's fine and dandy, except when six or eight programs and a toolbar are open, the Taskbar gets very crowded, and you can't tell what's what:

TIP

The next section in this chapter explains Auto Hide, a technique for making the Taskbar appear onscreen only when you click the bottom of the screen.

One way to solve the overcrowding problem is to enlarge the Taskbar. Gently move the mouse pointer over the top of the Taskbar, and when you see the double arrows, click and drag the Taskbar up the screen. You can make the Taskbar as large as you want, and when you want to shrink it down to size, move the pointer over the top of the Taskbar again, and click and drag—but this time drag down the screen.

To move a toolbar, slide its border.

Click to see more buttons.

When Windows can't display all the buttons or toolbars, double arrows and slider-borders appear on the Taskbar. Click a double arrow to see more buttons. To move a toolbar left or right on the Taskbar, drag its slider-border left or right.

Some people solve the crowded toolbar problem by dragging the toolbar from the bottom of the screen to the side of the screen. To take this drastic measure, click a blank space on the Taskbar, drag toward the upper-right or upper-left corner of the screen, and release the mouse button. Do the opposite to return the Taskbar to its home port along the bottom of the screen.

Auto Hide: Playing Hide and Seek with the Taskbar

Don't panic if the Taskbar disappears. It disappeared because somebody turned on the Auto Hide option, you shrunk the Taskbar to minuscule proportions, or someone has instructed Windows to put the Taskbar behind open windows. To find out where the problem lies, move the mouse pointer to the very bottom of the screen:

- If the Taskbar suddenly reappears, Auto Hide has been turned on.

  The Auto Hide option is a very convenient way of grabbing more room for programs onscreen. When Auto Hide is turned on, the Taskbar does not appear. To see it, move the mouse pointer to the very bottom of the desktop—the Taskbar comes out of hiding, ready for you to click a button. Figure 2.8 explains how to turn on Auto Hide.
- If you see the top half of a double arrow, you shrunk the Taskbar. Click and drag upwards to see the Taskbar again.
- If nothing happens, the Always on Top option that tells Windows to place the Taskbar in front of open windows has been turned off. Click the Start button and choose Settings | Taskbar and Start Menu. Then check the Always on Top option in the Taskbar and Start Menu dialog box (refer to Figure 2-8).

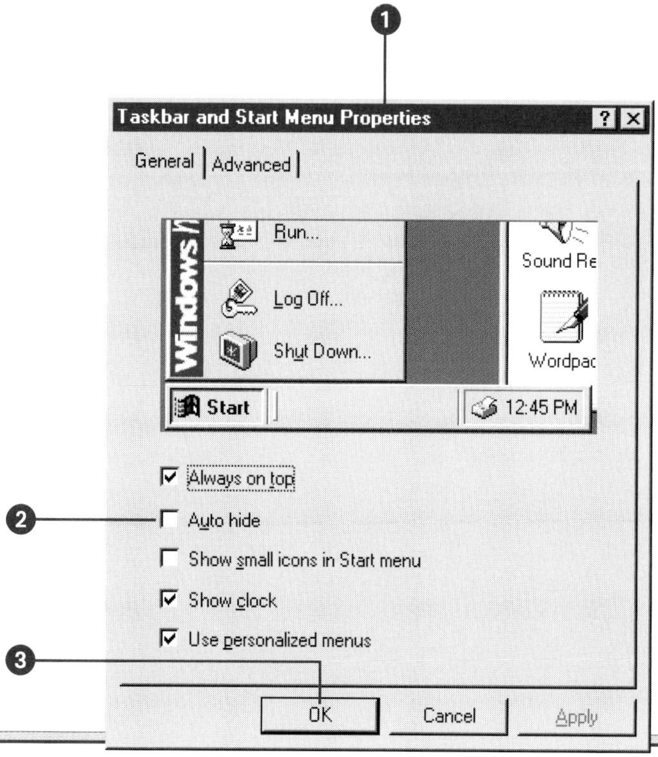

1 Either right-click an empty place on the Taskbar and choose Properties or click the Start button and choose Settings | Taskbar and Start Menu.

2 Check or uncheck the Auto Hide check box.

3 Click OK.

Figure 2.8: Turning the Auto Hide option on or off

Introducing the Toolbars on the Taskbar

As if the Taskbar isn't crowded enough, you can place a total of four different toolbars on the Taskbar. To display or remove a toolbar, right-click a blank space on the Taskbar (search carefully to find it if you must), choose Toolbars on the shortcut menu, and click a toolbar name:

Earlier in this chapter, "Learn How Toolbars Work" explained how to remove and display toolbars.

- **Links Toolbar** Puts buttons for each Internet site you bookmarked on the Taskbar so you can click a button and go to a favorite Web site. The Links toolbar gets its buttons from the C:\Favorites\Links folder.

- **Address Toolbar** Presents a text box so you can type Internet addresses. Either type an address or click the arrow to see addresses you entered in the past and perhaps choose one. Press ENTER to start Windows Explorer and either display a Web page onscreen or go on the Internet and retrieve a Web page.
- **Desktop Toolbar** Collects all the icons and shortcut icons on the desktop in a toolbar. Don't bother with this one. If you need to see desktop icons in a hurry, simply click the Show Desktop button on the Quick Launch toolbar.
- **Quick Launch Toolbar** Offers the all-important Show Desktop button and buttons for quickly connecting to the Internet.

EXPERT ADVICE

You can launch your favorite programs from the Quick Launch toolbar. To do so, create a shortcut icon for each program you want to launch. Then drag the shortcut icons onto the Quick Launch toolbar—that's right, simply drag them on. To remove an icon from the Quick Launch toolbar, drag it onto the desktop.

Create the Shortcut Icons You Need

In my opinion, shortcuts are one of the best things going in Windows Me. Instead of burrowing into the Programs menu to open a program, you can double-click its shortcut icon. Create a shortcut to a printer and all you have to do to print a file is drop it on the shortcut icon. You can create shortcuts to your favorite folders to open them quickly in My Computer. And creating shortcuts is easy.

Probably one or two shortcuts are already on your desktop. To distinguish a shortcut icon from an icon, look for the little arrow in the lower-left corner. The arrow tells you that the icon is a shortcut icon. When you double-click a shortcut icon, a program, file, folder, printer, or network location opens onscreen. Herewith are directions for creating shortcuts, naming shortcut icons, and deleting, moving, and copying shortcuts. You also learn how to tidy the desktop by keeping all shortcut icons in a desktop folder.

Creating a Shortcut Icon

Figure 2.9 demonstrates how to create a shortcut icon. Figure 2.10 shows how to create a shortcut icon for an item on a Windows Menu. Some Windows Menu items—the Calculator, for example—deserve shortcut icons, since opening them from the Windows Menus is such a chore.

In Chapter 3, "Rummaging for Folders and Files with My Computer" explains how to find items in that program.

If I were you, I would double-click shortcut icons after creating them to make sure they take you where you want to go. If you ever doubt where a shortcut leads, right-click it and choose Properties. The Shortcut tab of the Properties dialog box lists the path to the file, folder, or whatever.

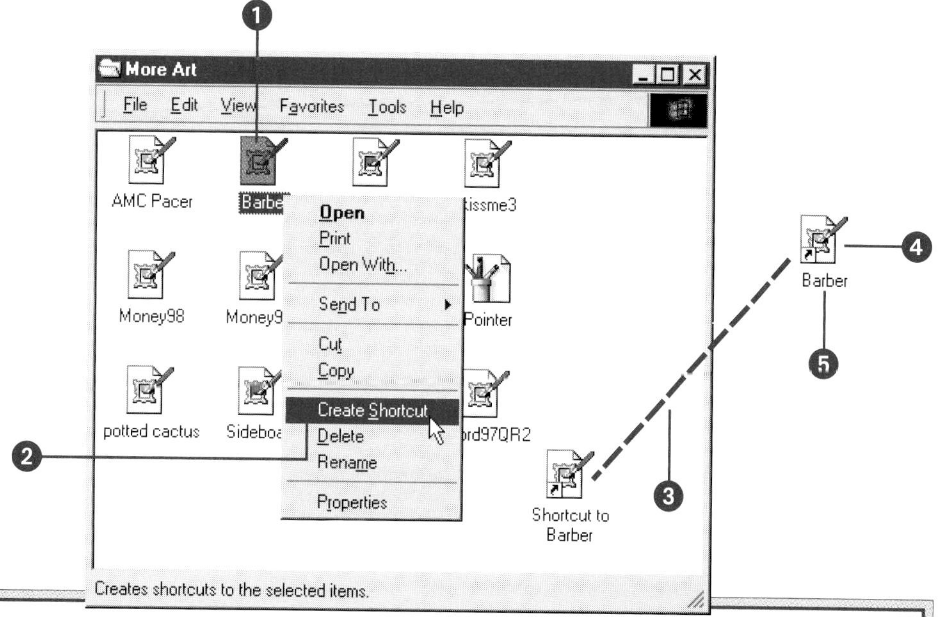

1 In My Computer, find the item to which you want to create a shortcut–the program file, file, folder, URL address, or whatever–and click to select it.

2 Right-click the item and choose Create Shortcut (you can also choose File | Create Shortcut). A shortcut icon with the words *Shortcut to* appears at the bottom of the window.

3 Drag the shortcut icon out of the My Computer window and onto the desktop. (If necessary, click the Restore button in the upper-right corner of the window to shrink the window onscreen before you start dragging your new shortcut icon.)

4 Right-click the shortcut icon and choose Rename.

5 Enter a descriptive name for your new shortcut icon and press ENTER.

Figure 2.9: To create a shortcut, find the item in My Computer, right-click it, and choose Create Shortcut

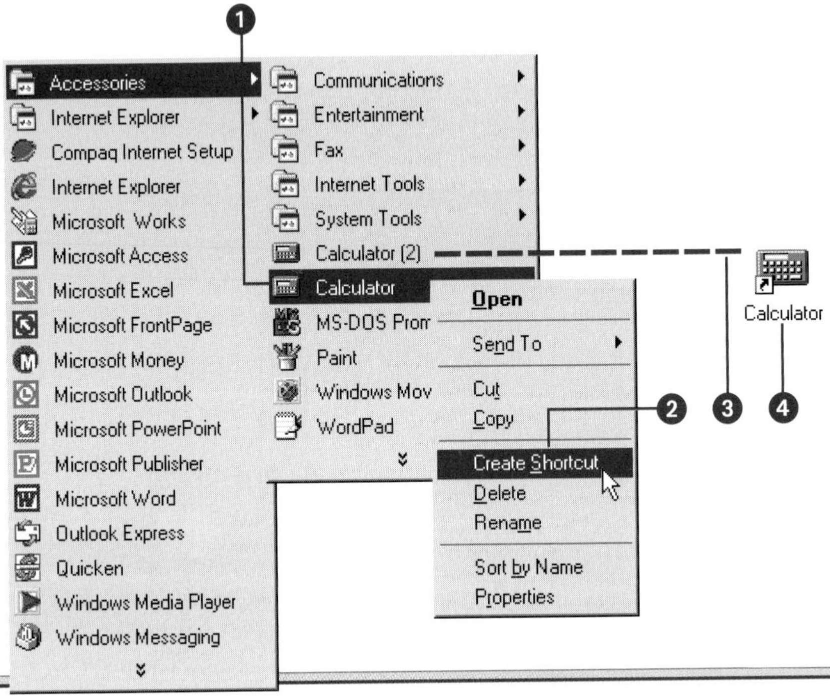

1 On the menu, select the item you want to make a shortcut to, but *don't* click to open the item.

2 Right-click the item and choose Create Shortcut. Directly above the item, you see a shortcut item with the number 2 after its name.

3 Drag the number 2 item off the menu and onto the desktop to create the shortcut icon.

4 Right-click the icon, choose Rename, and remove the (2) from the name.

Figure 2.10: Creating a shortcut icon for an item on a Windows Menu

Copying and Moving Shortcuts

After you've created a shortcut, you can move or copy it here, there, and everywhere. Some shortcut icons beg to be put in several different places. For example, shortcuts to your favorite programs belong on the desktop and on the Quick Launch toolbar. A shortcut to your favorite folder belongs in the My Documents folder. Here's how to copy or move a shortcut icon:

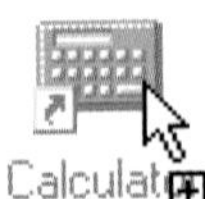

- **Copying** Hold down the CTRL key as you drag the icon to a new location—into a folder window or onto the desktop, for example. As you drag, a plus sign appears below the pointer so you know that you are copying the shortcut, not moving it.

You can also right-click the shortcut icon, choose Copy from the shortcut menu, and then right-click where you want to place the copy and choose Paste.

- **Moving** Drag the shortcut icon to a new location. You can also right-click the shortcut icon, choose Cut from the shortcut menu, and then right-click where you want to move the shortcut icon and choose Paste.

Another way to move or copy a shortcut icon is to drag it while holding down the right mouse button. When you release the mouse button, a menu appears with options called Move Here and Copy Here. Choose one or the other.

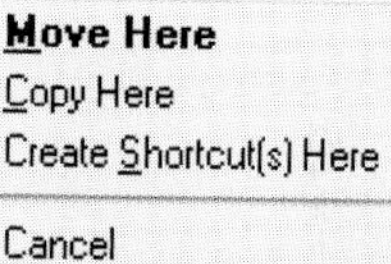

Deleting Shortcuts

Deleting a shortcut icon is easy: Right-click it and choose Delete from the shortcut menu. Then click Yes when Windows asks if you really want to delete your shortcut icon. Don't worry about deleting the file or folder that the shortcut goes to—you are merely deleting a shortcut when you delete a shortcut icon. To delete several shortcut icons at once, hold down the CTRL key and click them before you right-click and choose Delete.

Shortcuts, like files and folders, land in the Recycle Bin after they have been deleted. You can revive a shortcut if that proves necessary (see "Recycle Bin: Recovering Deleted Files and Folders" in Chapter 3).

Keeping Shortcut Icons in a Desktop Folder

The Windows desktop can get mighty crowded with shortcut icons. One way to practice crowd control is to create a desktop folder and put shortcut icons inside it. When you want to take a shortcut, double-click the desktop folder to see the shortcut icons inside and then double-click a shortcut icon. Desktop folders stay on the desktop beside My Computer, My Documents, and the other major-league icons.

Follow these steps to create a desktop folder for your shortcut icons:

1. Right-click a blank place on the desktop and choose New | Folder. A new folder appears.

2. Type a name for your folder (I suggest "My Shortcuts") and press ENTER.
3. Double-click your new desktop folder to open it in My Computer.
4. Drag the shortcut icons that litter the desktop into your new folder.

When you need to double-click a shortcut icon, you will know where to find it—in your Shortcuts folder on the desktop.

To Show (or Not to Show) Web Content on the Desktop

In Chapter 6, "Eight Ways to Surf the Internet Faster" explains how to choose a home page—the first Web site you see when you launch Internet Explorer and go on the Internet.

For fans of the Internet, Windows Me offers a way to bring the Internet right onto your doorstep. As shown in Figure 2-11, you can make the Windows desktop into a kind of Web browser by putting your home page on the desktop. And while you're at it, you can make the Channel Bar appear there, too. Putting Web content on the desktop crowds the desktop a bit, but it makes connecting to the Internet easier.

Follow these steps to show Web content on your Windows Me desktop:

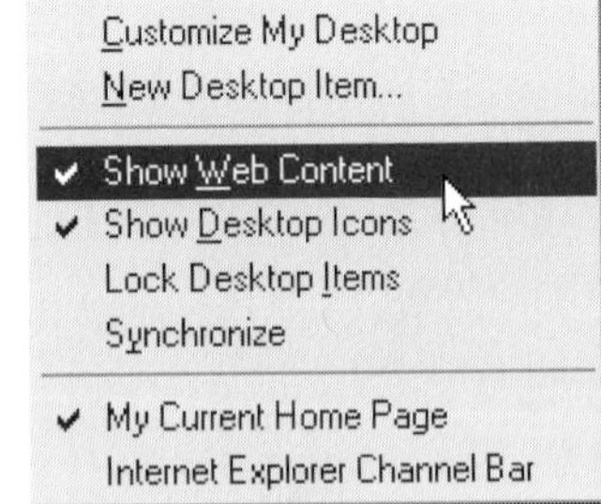

1. Right-click the desktop.
2. Choose Active Desktop on the shortcut menu.
3. Choose the Show Web Content command.

After the command is chosen, you can right-click the desktop, choose Active Desktop, and then choose these commands on the submenu to turn your copy of Windows into a beehive of Internet activity:

- **My Current Home Page** Puts your home page on the right side of the desktop (refer to Figure 2-11).

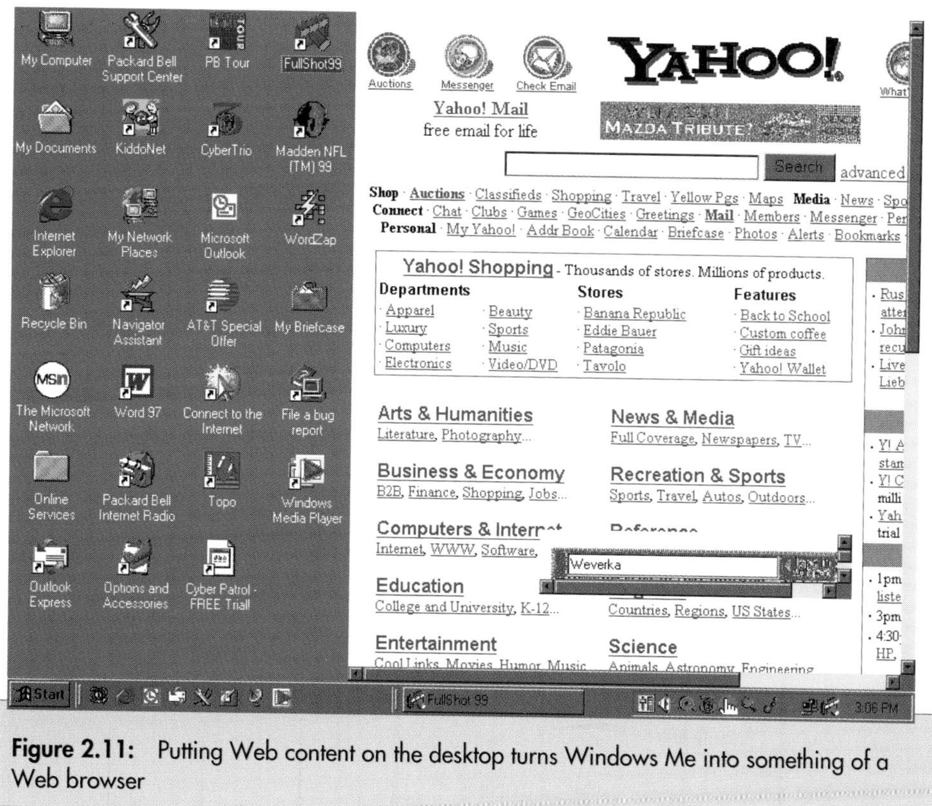

Figure 2.11: Putting Web content on the desktop turns Windows Me into something of a Web browser

- **Internet Explorer Channel Bar** Places the Channel Bar on the desktop. Click a button to visit one of the Web sites that is listed on the Channel Bar.

Create an Emergency Startup Disk

When you installed Windows Me, you created an emergency startup disk. Do you still have it? Floppy disks have a habit of disappearing, but keeping an emergency startup disk on hand is absolutely necessary. If something evil this way comes and your computer dies, put the emergency startup disk in the A drive and push the computer's reset button. With luck, your computer will start in MS-DOS mode. From there the neighborhood computer guru might be able to fix your computer.

Follow these steps to create an emergency startup disk if yours has run away:

1. Put an empty disk with at least 1.2MB of disk space in the floppy drive.
2. Click the Start button and choose Settings | Control Panel.
3. In the Control Panel, double-click the Add/Remove Programs icon.
4. Click the Startup Disk tab in the Add/Remove Programs Properties dialog box.
5. Click the Create Disk button.
6. Follow the onscreen directions.

When the deed is done, label the disk and put it in a safe place.

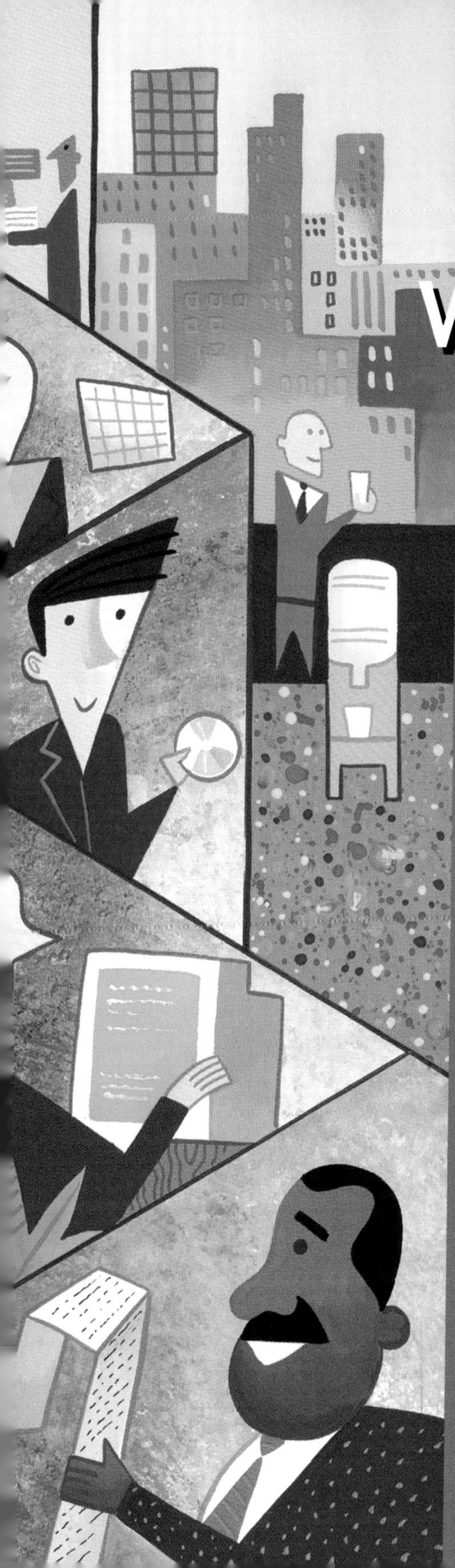

CHAPTER 3

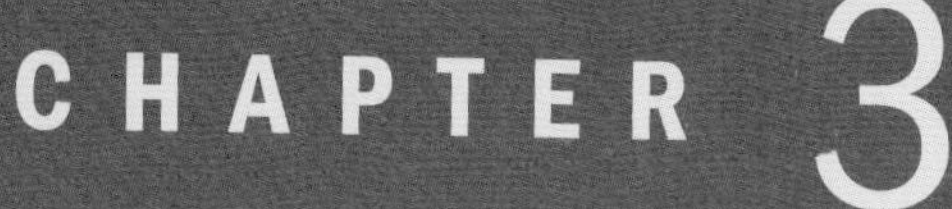

Working with Files and Folders

INCLUDES

- Peering into a computer with My Computer
- Finding a folder or file with Windows' Search command
- Selecting, creating, renaming, copying, moving, and deleting files and folders
- Recovering files you deleted
- Copying and moving data from file to file

FAST FORWARD

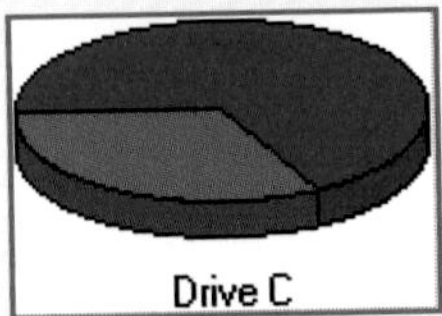

Find Out How Much Free and Used Space Is on Your Hard Disk ➥ pp. 60–61

1. Open My Computer and click the (C:) drive icon.
2. Choose File | Properties.

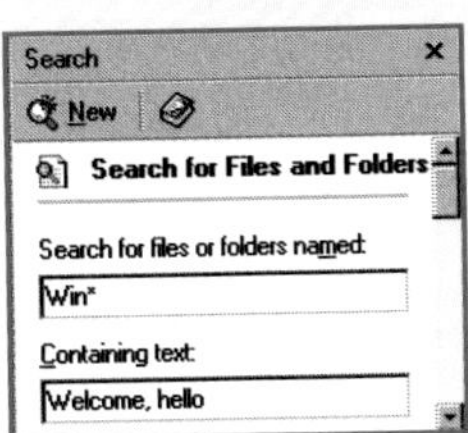

Search for a File or Folder with the Windows Search Command ➥ pp. 61–65

1. Click the Start button and choose Search | For Files or Folders.
2. Enter criteria for the search in the Search Results dialog box.
3. Click the Search Now button.

Create a New Folder ➥ p. 66

1. In My Computer, locate and select the folder in which to put your new folder.
2. Choose File | New | Folder, type a name for the new folder, and press ENTER.

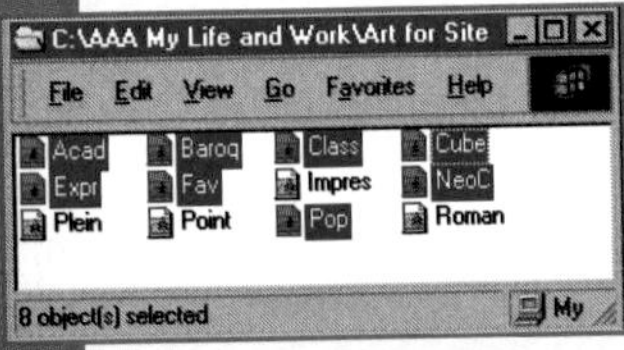

Select Files in My Computer ➥ pp. 66–67

- CTRL-click to select various files.
- Click the first file, then SHIFT-click the last file to select neighboring files.
- Press CTRL-A or choose Edit | Select All to select all the files in the folder.

Move or Copy Files to New Folders ➥ pp. 68–69

1. Open My Computer; then locate and select the files you want to move or copy.
2. To copy the files, click the Copy button, choose Edit | Copy, or press CTRL-C; to move the files, click the Cut button, choose Edit | Cut, or press CTRL-X.
3. Display and click the folder that is to receive the files or folders.
4. Click the Paste button, choose Edit | Paste, or press CTRL-V.

Rename a File or Folder ➥ pp. 72–73

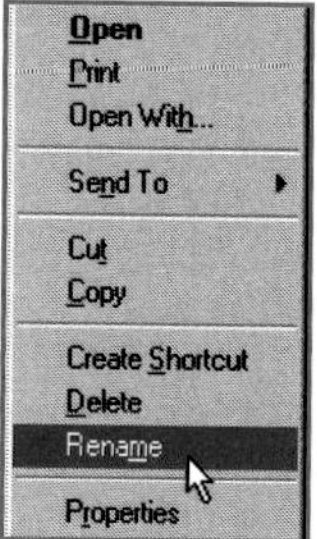

1. In My Computer or the Open dialog box, find and click the file or folder you want to rename.
2. Right-click and choose Rename from the shortcut menu.
3. Type a new name and press ENTER.

Delete Files or Folders ➥ p. 73

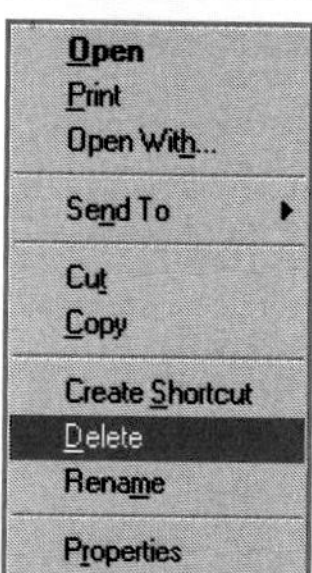

1. In My Computer or the Open dialog box, find and select the folder(s) and file(s) you want to delete.
2. Press the DEL key, choose File | Delete, or right-click an item you selected and choose Delete from the shortcut menu.
3. Click Yes in the message box that asks if you want to delete the items.

Recover a File You Deleted Accidentally ➥ pp. 73–75

1. Double-click the Recycle Bin icon on the desktop.
2. Select the files and folders you want to restore and choose File | Restore.

In this installment of the Windows Me saga, you discover how to peer into your computer. You learn how to find out precisely what's inside and rearrange it, if you want to. You learn the various and sundry ways to manage and organize files and folders with Windows Me.

This chapter starts by demystifying the folder hierarchy by which folders and files are stored. Then it describes a handy gadget that you can use to inquire into your computer system—My Computer. You will learn how to locate files and folders and how to select, copy, move, rename, and delete them. For the mistake-prone, this chapter explains how to recover a file or folder that was deleted accidentally. And you will also learn how to copy and move data from one file to another.

How the Folder Hierarchy Works

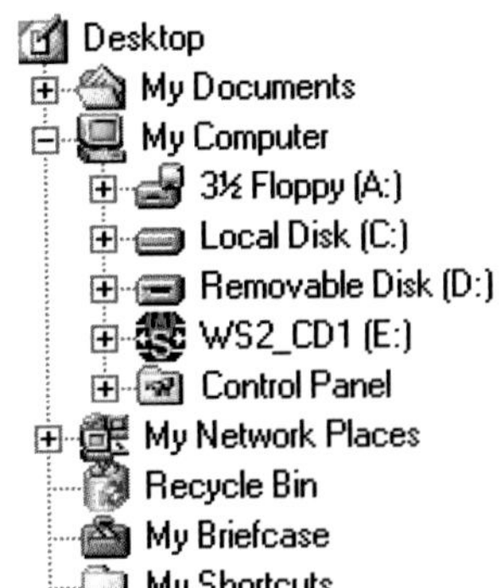

By now you must have noticed that your computer system is littered with folders. Files are kept in folders. Sometimes folders hold other folders. When you save a file for the first time, you are asked which folder to save it in. When you install new software, the installation program informs you that your new software will be kept in the such-and-such folder.

What you may not realize is that Windows maintains a structure, or hierarchy, for folders so that data is well organized and easy to get at. Yes, there is method to this madness. At the top of the hierarchy is the Desktop folder. Inside it are the A drive, C drive, D drive—the *root directories*—and the other major-league folders. As you dig deeper into the hierarchy, you encounter more folders.

Figure 3.1 shows where customer information files—Bronx, Brooklyn, Queens, and Manhattan—are kept on a computer. The files are stored five layers deep—five folders deep—on the C drive in a folder called New York. In Figure 3.1, I used a Windows program called My Computer to locate the files, which appear on the right side of the window.

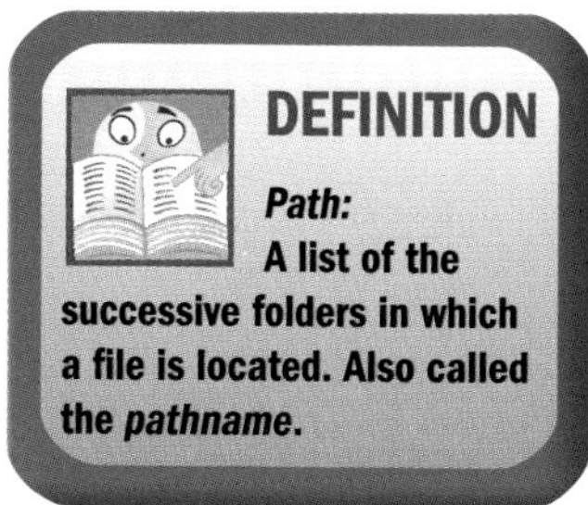

Path: **A list of the successive folders in which a file is located. Also called the *pathname*.**

Altogether, the five folders add up to the *path* that is shown in the Address bar in Figure 3.1: C:\AAA My Life and Work\My Business\Customers\East Coast\New York. By organizing folders this way, you can open files quickly. When you want to move, delete, or copy a file, you know precisely where to find it. Throughout this chapter, you learn how to locate, manipulate, and organize the files and folders on your computer. As you manage your files and folders, remember how the folder hierarchy works.

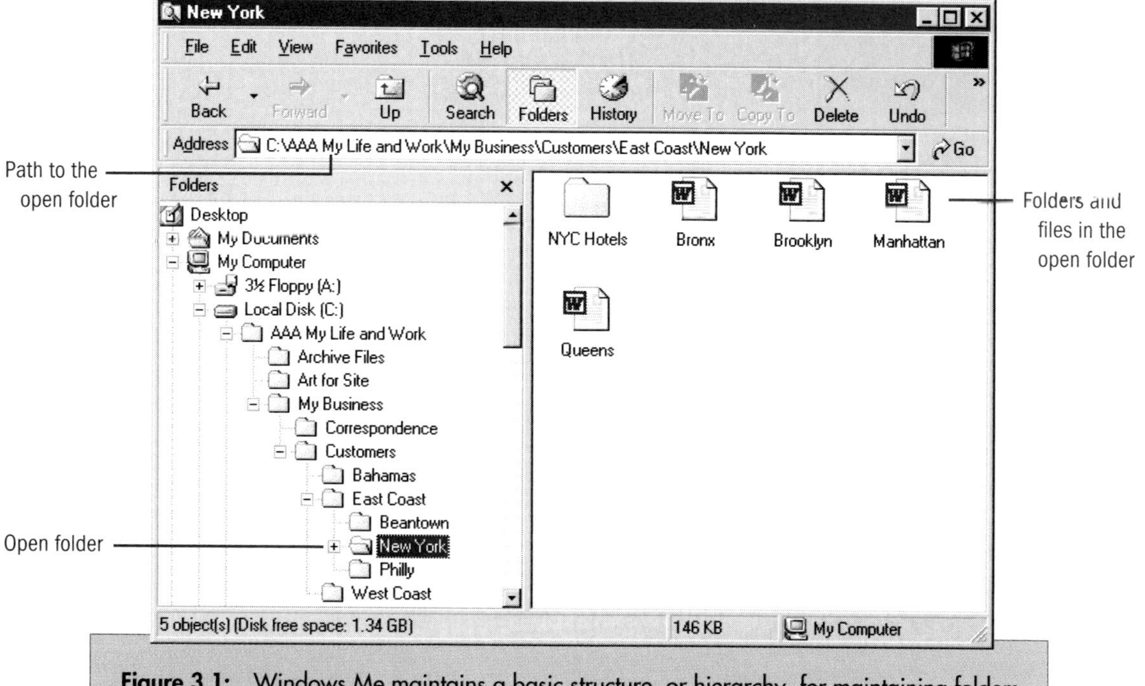

Figure 3.1: Windows Me maintains a basic structure, or hierarchy, for maintaining folders and files. You can use My Computer to see where folders and files are located

Exploring Your Computer System

In Chapter 2, "Learn the Ways to View Folders and Files" explains different ways of displaying stuff in folder windows, including the My Computer window.

Before you can arrange, delete, move, or copy files and folders, you have to find them. Before you can create a new folder, you have to find the folder in which to put the new one. To create a shortcut icon, you have to find the file to which the shortcut goes. Windows Me users spend a lot of time rummaging in their computers. Knowing what's there is essential, so Windows Me offers a special program called My Computer for peering inside a computer.

The following pages introduce My Computer and explain how to use it to get from folder to folder, as well as how to find out how much disk space you have.

My Computer: Peering into Your System

The My Computer program is for locating folders and files on your computer. To start My Computer, double-click the My Computer icon on the desktop. The top-level drives and folders on your computer appear in the My Computer window, as shown at the top of Figure 3.2. By clicking a drive icon or folder, you can display the

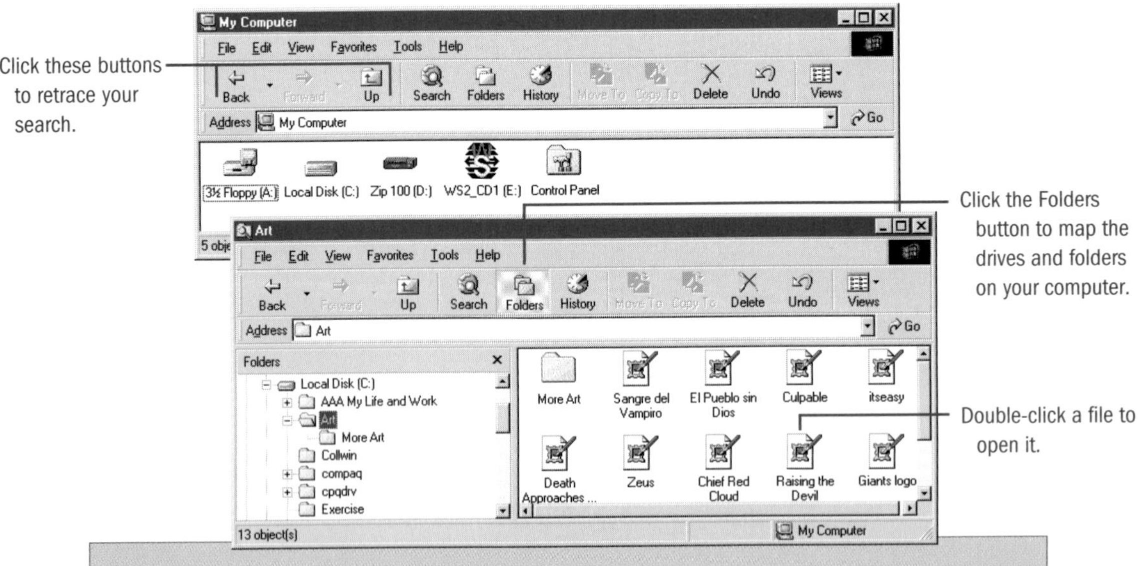

Figure 3.2: Click folders and drive icons in the My Computer window to burrow into your computer and locate folders and files

contents of the drive or folder in the My Computer window. Folders and files are listed in alphabetical order. To get a better sense of where you are going inside your computer, click the Folders button. Drive icons and folders appear in the window pane on the left; the window pane on the right shows the folders and files in the folder you are currently visiting, as shown on the bottom of Figure 3-2.

Follow these instructions to use the My Computer program to search for a folder or file that you want to open, move, copy, delete, or torture somehow:

- **Finding Folders in the Hierarchy** Click the Folders button. The drives and folders on your computer appear in the window pane on the left side of the My Computer window. Click the plus sign (+) next to a drive or folder you want to investigate. The folders inside that folder appear below it. Click a minus sign (–) to keep the folders inside a folder from being displayed. (You can drag the boundary between the two sides of the My Computer window to give more room to either window pane.)
- **Seeing the Contents of a Folder** Double-click a folder's icon or name. The files and folders in the folder you double-clicked appear on the My Computer Screen. After you click the Folders button, you can click a folder's icon or name (not the plus sign beside the icon or name) on the left side of the My Computer screen to see the folder's contents on the right side. See "Learn the Ways to View Folders and Files" in Chapter 2 to learn how to change the way in which folders and files are displayed in a window.

My Computer also offers a bunch of toolbar buttons for going from folder to folder, as described in Table 3.1.

EXPERT ADVICE

A quick way to learn more about a file or folder is to right-click it in My Computer and choose Properties from the shortcut menu. In the Properties dialog box, you see how large the folder or file is, when it was created, and when it was last accessed, among other juicy facts.

Navigation Technique	Description
Back	Click the Back button (or press ALT-LEFT ARROW) to revisit a folder you saw earlier. You can also click the down arrow beside the button to see a list of the folders you visited and click a folder's name to visit it again.*
Forward	Click the Forward button (or press ALT-RIGHT ARROW) to return to a folder you viewed earlier. You can also click the down arrow to see a list of folders and click a folder's name.
Up	Click the Up button (or press BACKSPACE) to climb a step higher in the folder hierarchy.
History	Click the History to open a window pane on the left side of the window that shows, by day or week, the folders you visited and files you opened. Click a folder or file to preview it on the right side of the My Computer screen.

** If you don't see the Back, Forward, Up, or History button, choose View | Toolbars | Standard Buttons.*

Table 3.1: Going from Folder to Folder in My Computer

Seeing How Much Space Is on the Hard Disk

In Chapter 9, "Disk Cleanup: Uncluttering the Hard Disk" explains how to remove superfluous files from the hard disk and acquire more disk space.

Sooner or later, everyone has to answer the question, "How much disk space do you have?" You need to know before installing new software. Maybe your hard disk doesn't have enough room to install new software. Maybe the family next door has more disk space than you. To keep up with the Joneses, you might need a new hard disk. Figure 3.3 explains how, in My Computer, you can find out how much free and used disk space is on your hard disk.

When you enable the Web Content in Folders option, you can tell how much used and free space is on the hard disk merely by opening My Computer and selecting the C drive icon. See "Decide Whether You Like Classic-Style or Web-Style Folders" in Chapter 2.

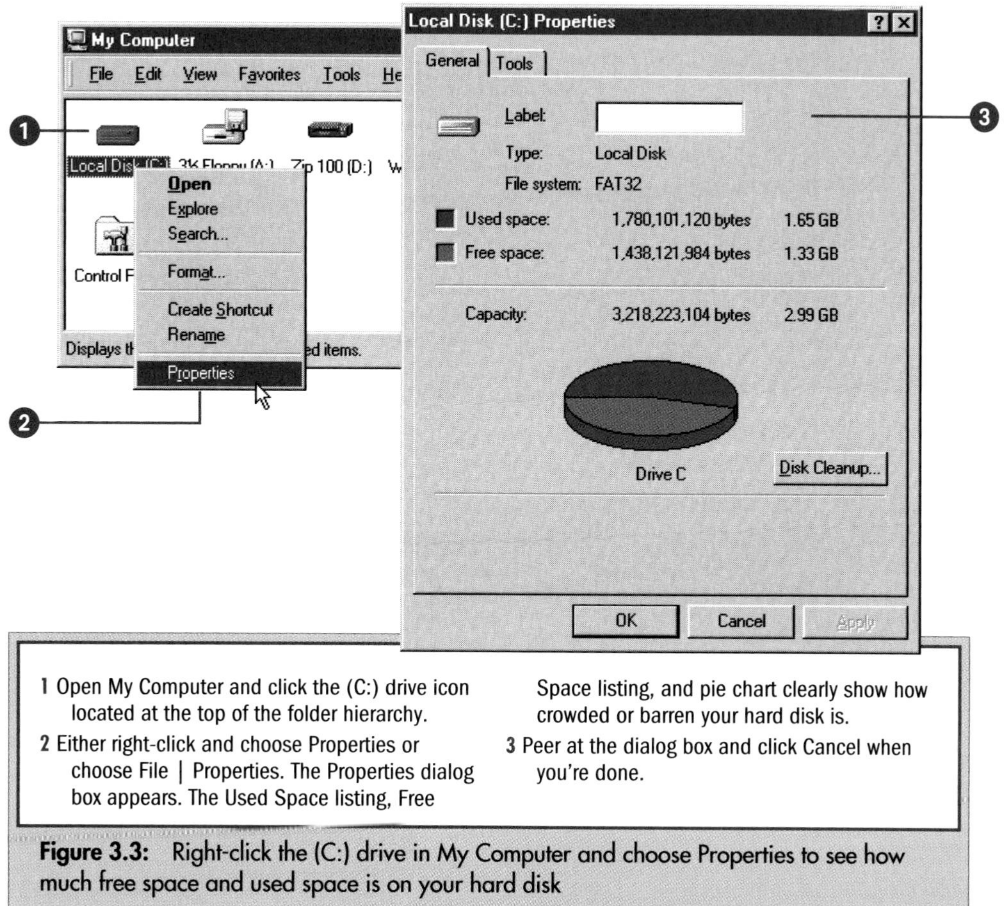

Figure 3.3: Right-click the (C:) drive in My Computer and choose Properties to see how much free space and used space is on your hard disk

Looking for Files and Folders with the Search Command

So far, this chapter has explained how to look for folders and files with My Computer. But what if you try your hardest yet simply can't find a folder or file? In that case, you have to abandon My Computer and ransack your computer with the Windows Me Search command.

The next few pages explain this powerful command and how to review the results of a search. Meanwhile, ask yourself these questions. The answers will help aid the search.

TIP

If you deleted a file accidentally, you can still recover it. See "Recycle Bin: Recovering Deleted Files and Folders" later in this chapter.

- Where was I last working? In which folder, disk, network device?
- Was I using my desktop machine or my portable? Is the file on the machine I think it is on?
- Did I misspell the name of the file when I saved it?
- Could I have moved the file accidentally into the wrong folder?
- Did someone who also uses my machine rename or move my file?
- Did I incorrectly change the file's three-letter extension?
- When I tried to open the file with the Open dialog box, did I display the wrong file type in the dialog box?
- Did I delete the file?

Conducting the Search and Reading the Results

Before you learn the nitty-gritty of entering search criteria (described shortly), you should know how to conduct a simple search and read its results. Follow these steps:

TIP

If the file you are looking for appears right away, or if the search drags on too long and you suspect that either nothing will come of it or it will yield too many files and folders, click the Stop Search button.

1. Click the Start button (or press CTRL-ESC).
2. Choose Search | For Files or Folders. You see the Search window shown in Figure 3.4. In the figure, a search has already been undertaken.
3. Enter criteria for the search (the next section explains how). You don't have to fill in all the boxes or make use of all the Search options
4. Click the Search Now button. The results of the search appear on the right side of the dialog box. (If no files or folders turn up, you see the words "Search is complete. There are no results to display.") The lower-left corner reports how many files were found.

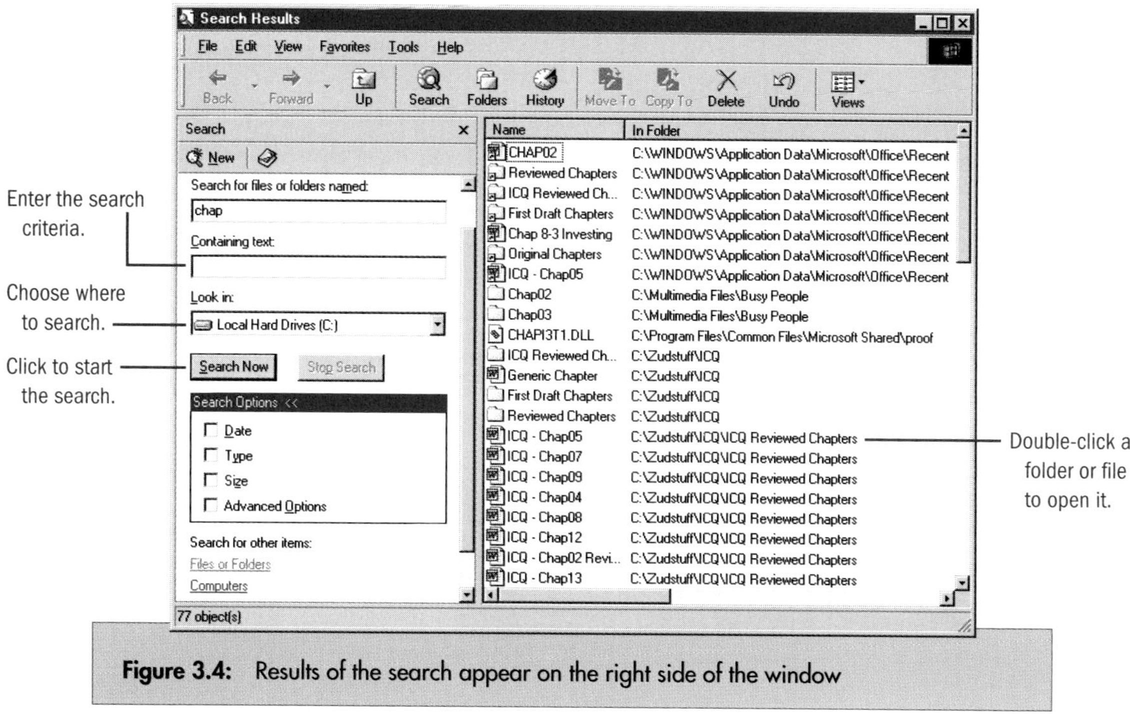

Figure 3.4: Results of the search appear on the right side of the window

5. To examine the search results, avail yourself of these opportunities:
   - **Open a Folder or File** Double-click a folder to open it in My Computer; double-click a file to open it in the program in which it was created.
   - **Sort the Files** In Detail view (choose View | Details), you can rearrange the files in the window by clicking the Name, Size, Type, or Modified button at the top of a column. The Name and Type buttons arrange the files in alphabetical order in one of those respective categories, the Size button arranges the files by size, and the Modified button arranges the files by date of last modification. Click the button a second time to reverse the order of the folders and files.
   - **Start a Different Search** Click the New button to erase the search criteria, enter new criteria, and embark on a different search.

In Chapter 2, "Learn the Ways to View Folders and Files" explains how to arrange files in windows and thereby locate them more easily.

Entering the Search Criteria

Locating files and folders with the Search command is a bit like searching the Internet. The more criteria you can enter to aid the search, the quicker and more accurate the search is. The Catch-22, however, is that entering many different criteria for a search increases the chances of making an error.

When you enter search criteria, you needn't make use of all the tools in the Search Results window. To pinpoint a folder or file, accurately enter the information that you know. And if at first you don't succeed, try, try, try again by changing the criteria and clicking the Search Now button.

TIP

To be specific about capitalization in the files and folders you are looking for, select the Advanced Options check box and then the Case Sensitive check box. With the Case Sensitive option selected, entering chap finds chap01, chaplain, and Schapstuckle, but not Chap or Chapter 9.

Entering a Name and Location for the Search

Enter the name of the folder or file you are looking for in the Search for Files or Folders Named text box. Or, if you vaguely remember the name, enter the part of the name that you can remember. For example, entering **chap** finds *Chap*, *chap01*, *Chapter 9*, *chaplain*, and *Schapstuckle*. If you know that somewhere inside the file itself is a specific word or name, enter it in the Containing Text box. Be sure to pick an obscure word, not one that is found in most files. Entering a telephone number or fax number is a good way to find a file. These numbers fall in the "one of a kind" category and do not produce many files in search results.

SHORTCUT

To save yourself the trouble of choosing a folder in the Look In drop-down menu, locate the folder you want to search in My Computer. Then right-click the folder and choose Search. The Search Results window opens with the folder you chose in the Look In box.

In the Look In drop-down menu, choose an option to tell Windows Me where to look for the files or folders. If you want to look in a specific folder and its subfolders, choose Browse at the bottom of the drop-down menu. You see the Browse for Folder dialog box. Find and select the folder you want to look in, and then click the OK button. The path to the folder you chose appears in the Look In box.

Search Options <<

- Date
- Type
- Size
- Advanced Options

Entering More Search Options

The Search options—Date, Type Size, and Advanced Options—are for pinpointing the file or folder you are looking for. When you click a check box, options appear to help with the search.

Click the Date check box to describe when the file was last modified, when it was created, or, in the case of .html files, when it was last accessed. Choose an option from the first drop-down menu and then enter the date. You can do that either by entering a number in an In the Last *x* Months or Days box, or by entering inclusive dates in the bottom two text boxes.

Date
files Modified
in the last 1 months
in the last 1 days
between 7/23/2000
and 8/22/2000

Click the Type check box if you know what type of file you are looking for. Choose the file type from the drop-down menu.

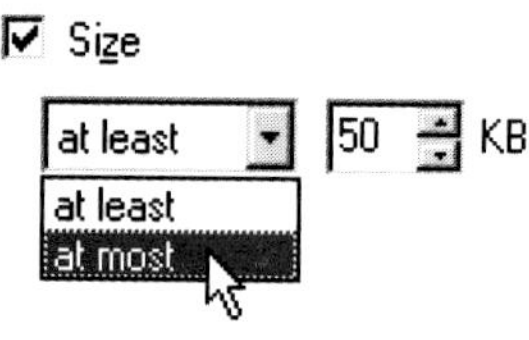

Click the Size check box if the file or folder you are looking for is a definite size. Choose At Least or At Most and enter a number in the KB box to describe in kilobytes the smallest or largest files to search for. One megabyte (MB) equals roughly 1,000 kilobytes (KB). To search for files larger or smaller than 1MB, enter **1000** in the KB box.

By default, Windows Me searches subfolders as well as folders, but if you want to search only in a particular folder, click the Advanced Options check box and uncheck the Search Subfolders check box.

Organizing and Managing Files and Folders

So far in this chapter, you have had a jolly good time learning how to locate files and folders with My Computer and Windows' Search command. Having learned to locate files, you can start managing them. You can copy them, move them, and rename them. You can delete them, and, if you want, resuscitate them. These exciting tasks are explained in this part of the chapter, where you learn to organize and manage files and folders.

Creating a New Folder

See "Devise a Strategy for Storing Your Work on Disk" in Chapter 2 for advice about storing your work so you can find it easily.

Create a new folder when you start a new project or begin an undertaking that requires new files. You need a folder to store the new files so you always know where they are. Create new folders in My Computer.

Follow these steps to create a new folder for storing files or other folders:

1. In My Computer, locate and select the folder in which to put your new folder. In other words, find the folder in the hierarchy to which the new folder will be subordinate. Earlier in this chapter, "My Computer: Peering into Your System" explains how the program works.
2. Choose File | New | Folder or right-click the folder and choose New on the shortcut menu. A folder icon and the words "New Folder" appear.

3. Type a name for the folder. The name you type replaces the words "New Folder." Be sure to choose a descriptive name. The same rules that apply to filenames apply to folders—255 characters (but don't get carried away), spaces allowed, the following characters not allowed: / \ ? ; : " < > * |
4. Either press ENTER or click elsewhere on the desktop.

"Keeping Shortcut Icons in a Desktop Folder" in Chapter 2 explains how to create a folder on the desktop for shortcut icons. One or two desktop shortcut folders can help prevent crowding on the desktop.

Selecting Files and Folders

Learn the various and sundry ways to select files and folders and you will make the time pass quickly in Windows Me. In order to move, copy, delete, or rename a file or folder, you have to select it. And

Windows Me offers numerous ways to select several files or folders so you can move, copy, or delete several at once.

To select files or folders, display them in My Computer. Selecting one file or folder is easy enough—just click it. Instructions for selecting more than one are given in the following list. Don't be afraid to open the Views drop-down menu and experiment with different views as you select files and folders. Depending on how you select files and how many you want to select, some views are better than others.

- **To Select Various Items** Hold down the CTRL key and click files and folders. As you click, the files are highlighted. After items have been selected, you can CTRL-click to unselect them.

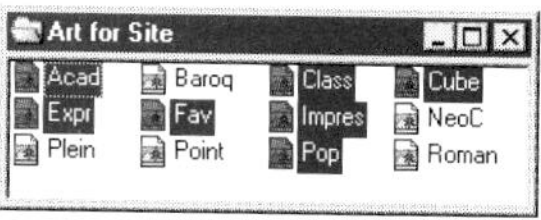

- **To Select Neighboring Items** Click the first file or folder, then hold down the SHIFT key and click the last. Use this technique in List and Detail view when the items you want to select are next to one another. In Chapter 2, "Learn the Ways to View Folders and Files" explains how to change views of a folder.

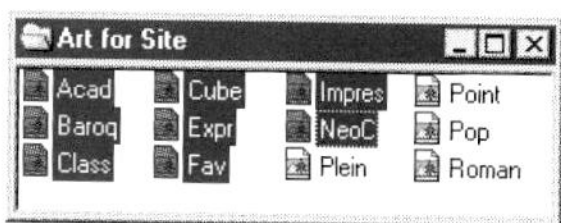

- **To Select a Group of Items** Click (but not on an icon or item name) and drag to form a box around the items you want to select. Use this technique in Large Icons, Small Icons, or Thumbnails view to select files that are found beside one another.

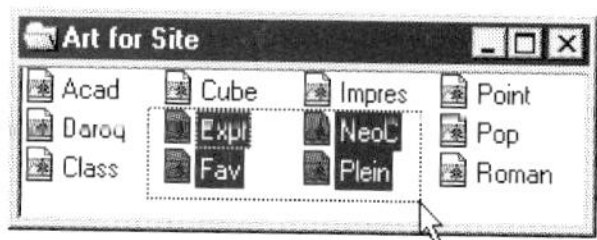

- **To Select All the Items** Press CTRL-A or choose Edit | Select All. All the items in the folder are highlighted. CTRL-click if you want to unselect a few of them.

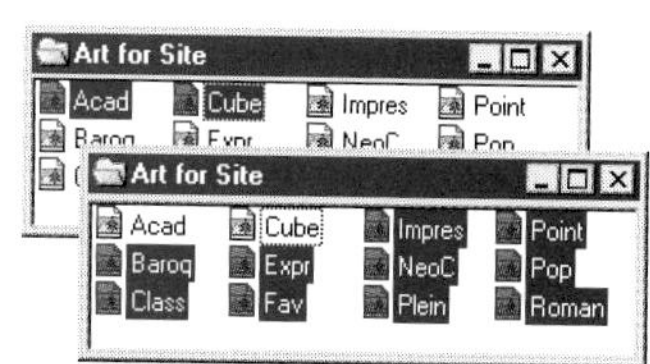

- **To Select All But One or Two Items** Click the items you *don't* want and then choose Edit | Invert Selection when you want to select all but one or two items in a folder. Instead of laboriously CTRL-clicking a dozen items, using this technique saves a lot of time.

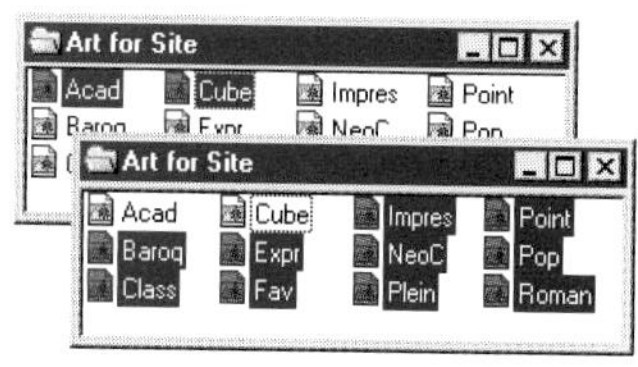

Copying and Moving Files and Folders

Except for the fact that Windows Me offers so many different techniques for copying and moving files and folders, copying and moving is easy. The problem is finding the technique that suits you. Personally, I like the dragging method, but people who aren't adept with the mouse prefer cutting, copying, and pasting. In the spirit of democracy, all techniques are described here. By the way, when you copy or move a folder, you copy or move all the folders and files inside it as well.

> **EXPERT ADVICE**
>
> **You can't move or copy a file that is open. Try to do that and you see an "Error Moving File" message box. Click OK in the message box, close the file, and then move or copy it. After a file or folder is moved, all shortcut references to it are rendered invalid. Hyperlinks and OLE links to it are invalid as well. And you can't open it from the Documents menu or the bottom of the File menu in the Open dialog box. The moral: Think twice before moving important files and folders, or else plan carefully where to put them in the first place.**

Copying and Moving with the Copy, Cut, and Paste Commands

Figure 3.5 explains how to copy and move files and folders with the Copy, Cut, and Paste commands. If you have copied or moved text or data in a computer program with the Copy, Cut, and Paste commands, you will be delighted to know that copying and moving files and folders works exactly the same way.

> **EXPERT ADVICE**
>
> **Usually, but not always, My Computer presents an accurate picture of what is in a folder. But suppose you minimize a folder window, fool with its contents, and then maximize the window later on. What you see will be inaccurate. A folder might have been moved. A file might have been deleted. The files might not be in alphabetical order. To see what's really in a folder, choose View | Refresh. Choose this command when you suspect that all is not what it seems in a My Computer window.**

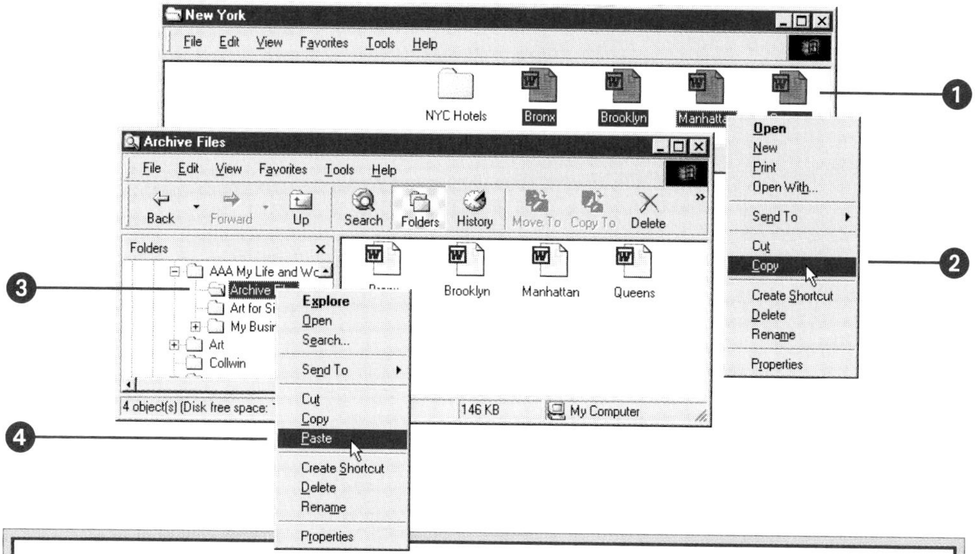

1 Open My Computer, locate the file(s) or folder(s) to copy or move, and then select the files or folders. Earlier in this chapter, "Selecting Files and Folders" explains how to do just that.

2 Choose a Copy or Move command. To copy, choose Edit | Copy, press CTRL-C, or right-click and choose Copy. To move, choose Edit | Cut, press CTRL-X, or right-click and choose Cut.

3 Display and click the folder that is to receive the files or folders. If you click the Folders button in My Computer, you can simply display and click a folder on the left side of the screen without doing anything in the right side.

4 Choose Edit | Paste, press CTRL-V, or right-click and choose Paste.

Figure 3.5: Moving and copying files and folders with the Cut, Copy, and Paste commands

Copying and Moving with the Copy To and Move To Commands

My Computer offers two commands to make copying and moving files and folders a little easier: The Copy To and Move To commands. Select the files or folders you want to copy or move, and then either click the Copy To or Move To button, or choose Edit | Copy to Folder or Edit | Move to Folder. You see the Browse for Folder dialog box. Select the folder where you want to move or copy the files or folders and click the OK button.

Dragging to Copy and Move Files and Folders

Dragging files and folders to copy or move them requires skill with the mouse. You have to display both the folders and files you are copying or moving as well as the folder you will copy or move them to. To complicate matters further, sometimes you have to press a key while you drag to copy or move files and folders. Oh well, it's easy when you get the hang of it.

Follow these steps to copy or move files and folders by dragging them:

1. In My Computer, locate and select the file(s) and folder(s) that you want to move or copy. Earlier in this chapter, "Selecting Files and Folders" explained how to do that.

2. Click the Folders button, if necessary, and display the folder that will receive the file(s) or folder(s) you want to move or copy. If you need help finding files or folders, see "My Computer: Peering into Your System" earlier in this chapter.
3. Locate and select the file(s) and folder(s) that you want to move or copy. Earlier in this chapter, "Selecting Files and Folders" explained how to do that.

4. Drag the files and folders to the destination folder, and then release the mouse button. As you drag, ghostly images of the files or folders appear onscreen so you know where to drop them.
   - **Copying** Hold down the CTRL key as you drag, unless you are copying files or folders to a different drive (3½ Floppy [A:], for example). You don't have to press CTRL when copying to a different drive because a copy is made automatically. A plus sign (+) appears below the pointer as you drag.
   - **Moving** Simply drag the files or folders. To move them to a different drive, hold down the SHIFT key as you drag. Without pressing SHIFT, the files are copied to the other drive, not moved there.

4. To be on the safe side, open the folder to which you copied or moved the files and folders to make sure that they landed in the right place.

Choose Edit | Undo Move or Edit | Undo Copy (or press CTRL+Z) if you accidentally move or copy a file to the wrong location. Choosing the Undo command reverses your latest action, whatever it happened to be.

EXPERT ADVICE

Folders get crowded when new files and folders are moved into them. You can prevent overcrowding in a folder by right-clicking an empty space inside its window and choosing Line Up Icons or Arrange Icons | Auto Arrange from the shortcut menu. These commands arrange icons in a strict military fashion so you can read and find them.

Making Backup Copies to a Floppy Disk

On the subject of copying files, Windows Me offers a special command for backing up files and folders on the C drive to the A drive. Figure 3.6 explains how to make simple backup copies of important files or folders to a floppy disk.

By the way, if your computer has an A and B floppy-disk drive, you can very quickly copy all the files on one floppy disk to another floppy disk. To do so, put the disk whose contents you want to copy in one of the drives, put an empty disk in the other, open My Computer, right-click one of the drive icons, and choose Copy Disk from the shortcut menu. The Copy Disk dialog box appears. In the Copy To box, click the second drive's icon and then click the Start button. Be sure to use an empty disk. This command copies a disk's entire content, including blank space!

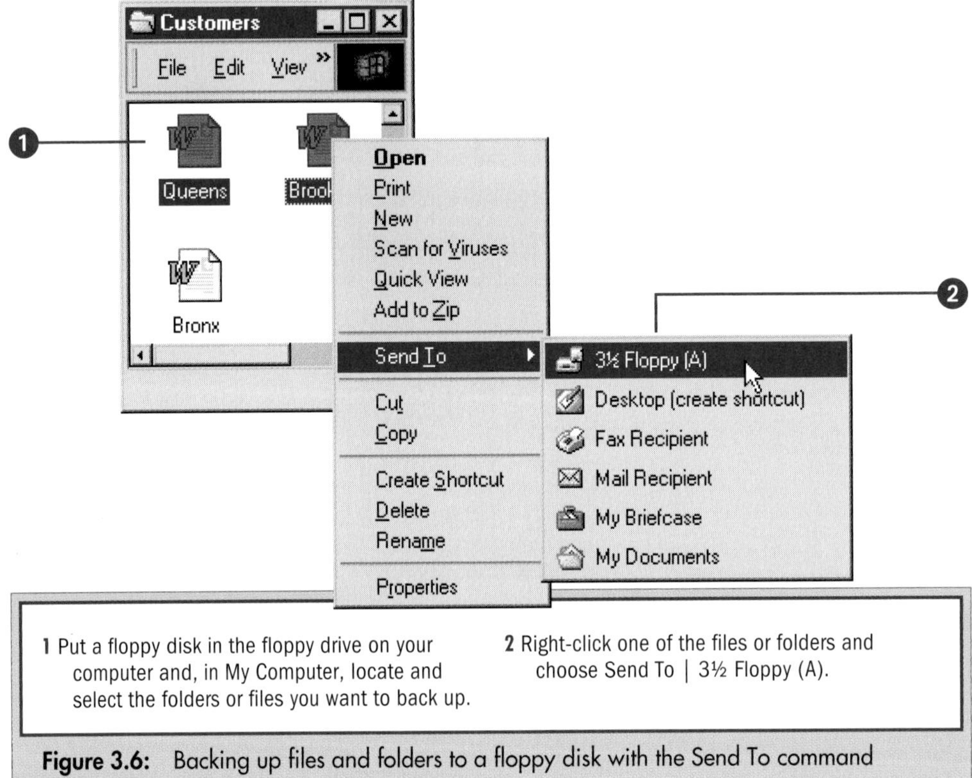

Figure 3.6: Backing up files and folders to a floppy disk with the Send To command

Renaming a File or Folder

Few things could be easier than renaming a file or folder. You can do it in My Computer or while you are opening a file in the Open dialog box. Follow these steps to give a file or folder a new name:

> **SHORTCUT**
> If you're in a hurry to rename a file, from My Computer or the Open dialog box, click the file you want to rename, wait a second, and click the name again. Then type in the new name.

1. In My Computer or the Open dialog box, find the file or folder you want to rename.
2. Select the file or folder.
3. Right-click and choose Rename from the shortcut menu, choose File | Rename, or press F2.
4. Type the new name. Be sure to keep the same file extension, if the file extension appears. You can click in the name that is

already there and press BACKSPACE or DELETE to delete one or two letters before you start adding letters of your own.

5. Press ENTER or click elsewhere.

Deleting Files and Folders

Deleting files and folders is easy. And you can delete several at once. If only the same could be said for cockroaches and radio talk show hosts. Follow these steps to delete files and folders:

1. In My Computer or the Open dialog box, find and select the folder(s) and file(s) you want to delete.
2. Press the DELETE key, choose File | Delete, or right-click an item you selected and choose Delete from the shortcut menu.
3. Click Yes (or No if you get cold feet) in the box that tells you how many files and folders will be deleted and asks if you want to go through with it.

For the mouse-inclined, the fastest way to delete a file or folder is to drag it from its present location in My Computer window and drop it over the Recycle Bin icon on the desktop.

If you delete a file or folder accidentally, you can resuscitate it. The next section in this chapter explains how. In Chapter 9, "Disk Cleanup: Uncluttering the Hard Disk" explains how to remove unnecessary files from your computer.

Recycle Bin: Recovering Deleted Files and Folders

Bottles, cans, and newspapers aren't the only items that can be recycled. You can also put the files, folders, and shortcut icons you deleted back in circulation with the Recycle Bin. This utility retains most files and folders that were deleted in case you regret deleting them. Files from DOS programs and a handful of other kinds of programs do not land in the Recycle Bin when you delete them. Read on to learn how to restore a file or folder from the Recycle Bin, purge files, and tell Windows Me how many deleted files and folders to keep on hand.

Restoring a File You Deleted Accidentally

Figure 3.7 shows how to examine the files and folders in the Recycle Bin and maybe put one or two back in circulation. After you restore a file, it returns to the folder from which it was deleted. By the way, Details view is the best way to view files in the Recycle Bin window. In Details view, you can see the original location of each item and the date it was deleted. Choose View | Details to switch to Details view.

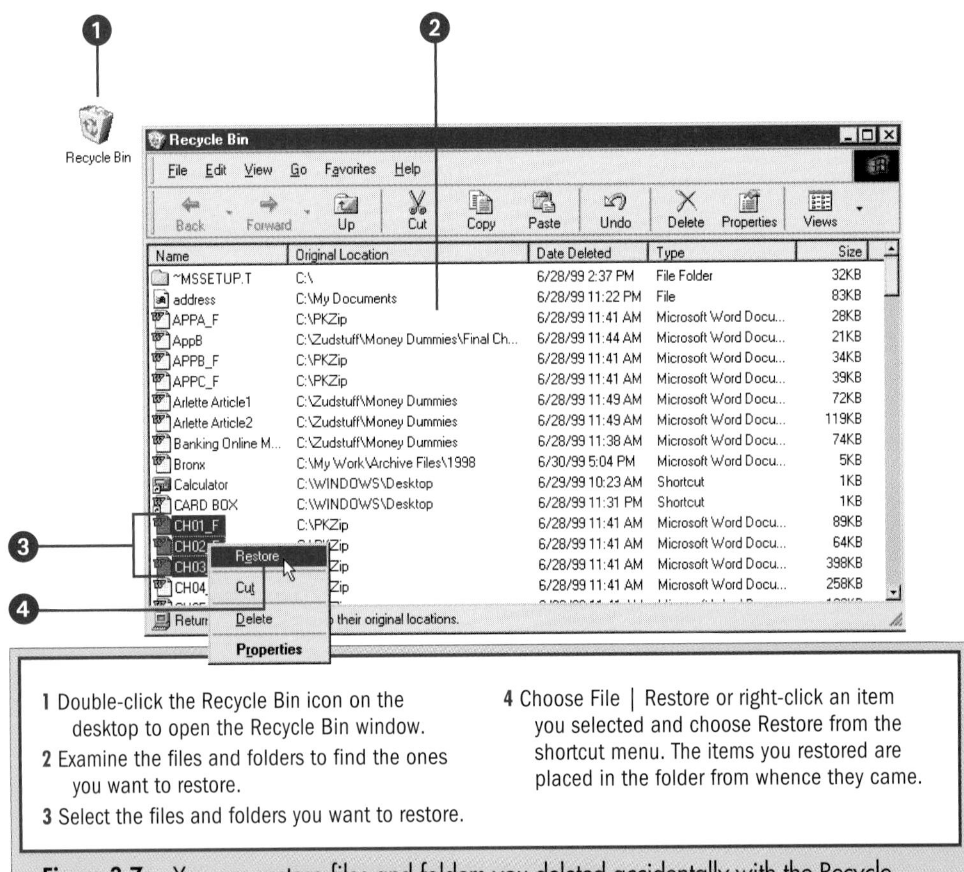

Figure 3.7: You can restore files and folders you deleted accidentally with the Recycle Bin utility

Purging Files from the Recycle Bin

If you are absolutely, positively, unmistakably certain that all files and folders in the Recycle Bin have no value, you can get rid of them all at once by right-clicking the Recycle Bin icon on the desktop and choosing Empty Recycle Bin from the shortcut menu. You can also choose File | Empty Recycle Bin in the Recycle Bin window. But do you really want to discard all the files? Maybe one or two are worth keeping.

A better strategy is to periodically open the Recycle Bin and remove only the files and folders that you know are useless. To do that, double-click Recycle Bin on the desktop, examine the files and folders in the Recycle Bin, select the ones that deserve deleting, press DELETE or choose File | Delete, and click Yes in the message box.

By the way, if you are no fan of the Recycle Bin and you want to delete files permanently when you give the Delete command, press SHIFT-DELETE to delete files. Or else right-click the Recycle Bin icon, choose Properties from the shortcut menu, and click the Do Not Move Files to the Recycle Bin check box, as shown in Figure 3.8.

EXPERT ADVICE

To begin with, 10 percent of the hard disk is devoted to storing deleted files in the Recycle Bin. When the 10 percent capacity is reached, the oldest files in the Bin are automatically erased. If you work with multimedia programs whose files can be very large, you might consider increasing the 10 percent capacity. And if you are running low on disk space, you might consider decreasing it to allow more room for files. To change the Recycle Bin's capacity, right-click the Recycle Bin icon and choose Properties. In the Recycle Bin Properties dialog box, shown in Figure 3.8, drag the Maximum Size slider and click OK.

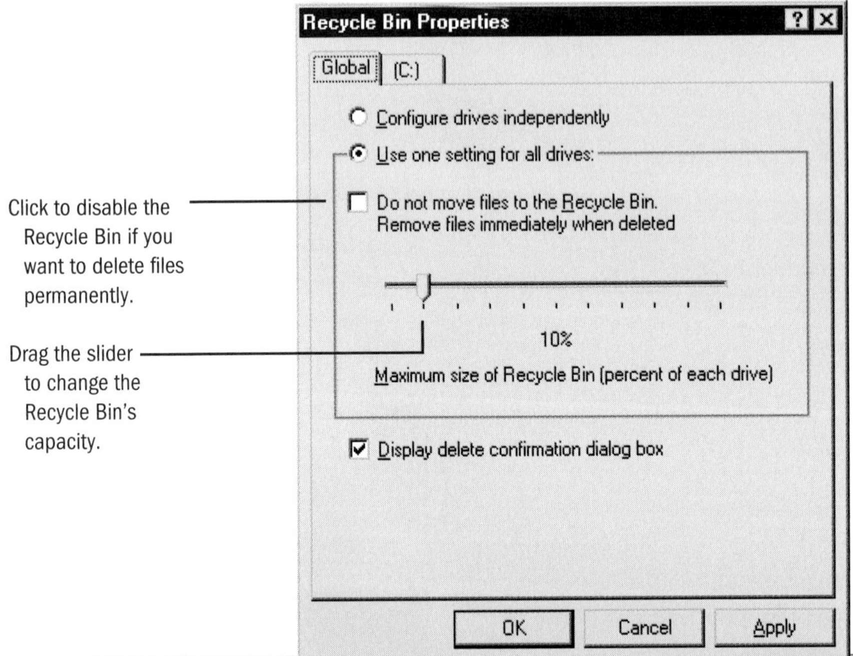

Figure 3.8: Drag the slider to increase or decrease the Recycle Bin's capacity for storing deleted files

Sharing Data Between Files

In my opinion, one of the best things going in Windows Me is being able to copy and move data from one file to another. The thank-you letter to Aunt Ida, with a few small changes, can be used as a thank-you letter to Uncle Bert. The Address database table, with a bit of luck and a tweak here and there, can be used as a table in a word processing file. You can even *link* two files so that changes made to part of one file are made automatically to a corresponding part in another file.

When you copy or move data, it is placed in an electronic holding tank called the Clipboard. The data stays there until you cut or copy new data and the new data takes the place of the old. These pages explain three methods for copying and moving data between files, how to create links between files, and how to open a handy device called the Clipboard Viewer for seeing what's on the Clipboard.

CAUTION

To successfully copy or move data, you almost always have to pass the data between files of the same type. Copying a graphics file into a word processing file, for example, can be problematic. And you can make guacamole out of a perfectly good spreadsheet by copying it into a graphics program. Test and retest before you commit yourself to copying and especially moving data.

Moving and Copying Data from File to File

Copying data leaves the original stuff intact, but moving uproots the data for good. Following are three methods for shuttling data between programs—cut and paste, drag and drop, and scraps. You be the judge of which method works best.

Using the Cut, Copy, and Paste Commands

Follow these steps to copy or move data from place to place with the Cut, Copy, and Paste commands:

1. Select the data you want to copy or move. Different programs offer different techniques for selecting data, but you can almost always select it by clicking and dragging.
2. Move or copy the data to the Clipboard:
   - **Moving** Choose Edit | Cut, click the Cut button, right-click and choose Cut, or press CTRL-X.
   - **Copying** Choose Edit | Copy, click the Copy button, right-click and choose Copy, or press CTRL-C.
3. Click where you want the data to go.
4. Choose Edit | Paste, click the Paste button, or press CTRL-V.

TIP

Press the PRINT SCREEN key (sometimes labeled PRINT SCRN and located to the right of F12) to take a snapshot of your computer screen and copy it to the Clipboard. Press ALT-PRINT SCREEN to take a snapshot of the active window, not the entire screen.

Dragging and Dropping

Figure 3.9 explains a second, slightly speedier but more trying way to move or copy data. With the *drag-and-drop* method, you select data in one place and drag it to another (don't confuse the term with "drop and drag," which in deer-hunting circles means to kill the game and bring it to camp).

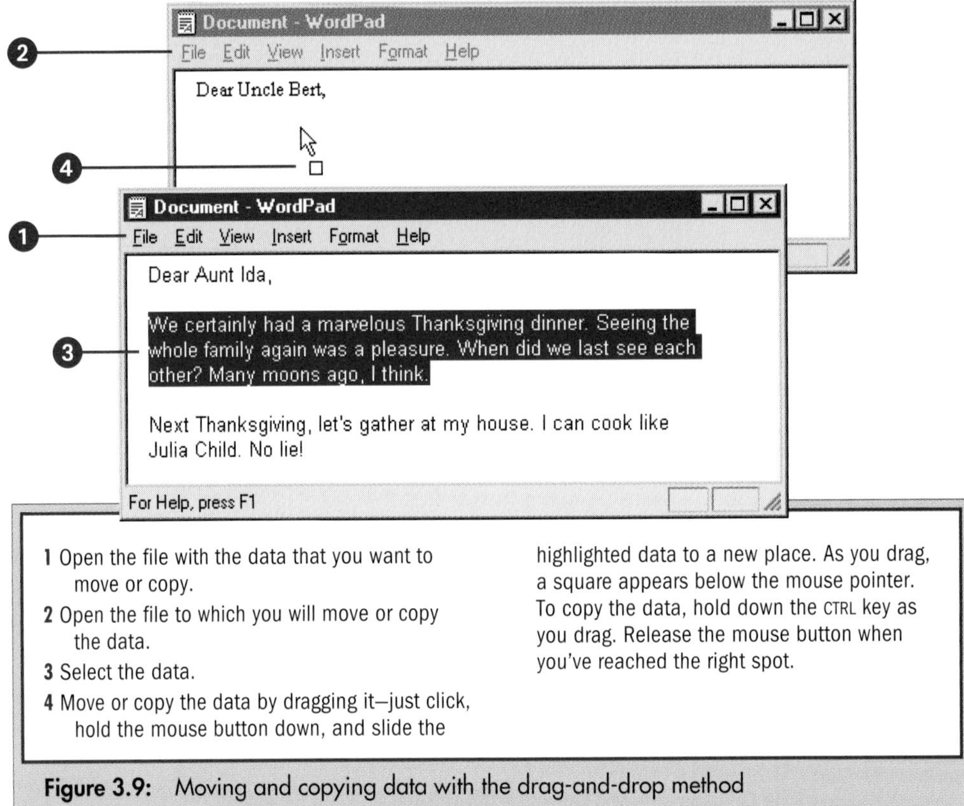

1 Open the file with the data that you want to move or copy.

2 Open the file to which you will move or copy the data.

3 Select the data.

4 Move or copy the data by dragging it—just click, hold the mouse button down, and slide the highlighted data to a new place. As you drag, a square appears below the mouse pointer. To copy the data, hold down the CTRL key as you drag. Release the mouse button when you've reached the right spot.

Figure 3.9: Moving and copying data with the drag-and-drop method

Copying Data with the "Scraps" Technique

Yet another drag-and-drop technique is to create *scraps* on the desktop. Use this technique to copy text from many different files and then assemble the text in a single file. With this method, you open files one at a time or several at once, select text in each file, and drag it onto the Windows desktop to form a scrap. Then, with the scraps arranged neatly on the desktop, you drag them one at a time into a single file. Follow these steps to copy data by creating scraps:

1. One by one or several at once, open the files from which you want to copy data.

2. Select text in one file.
3. Drag it out of the window and onto the desktop to make a scrap—an icon with a picture of a torn page or picture along with cryptic words that describe where the scrap came from and what it is.
4. Repeat steps 1 through 3 until you've assembled all the scraps on the desktop.
5. Open the file to which you will copy the data scraps.
6. One by one, drag the scraps into the file.

SHORTCUT

To get rid of the scraps that litter the desktop, hold down the CTRL key and click each one. Then press DELETE.

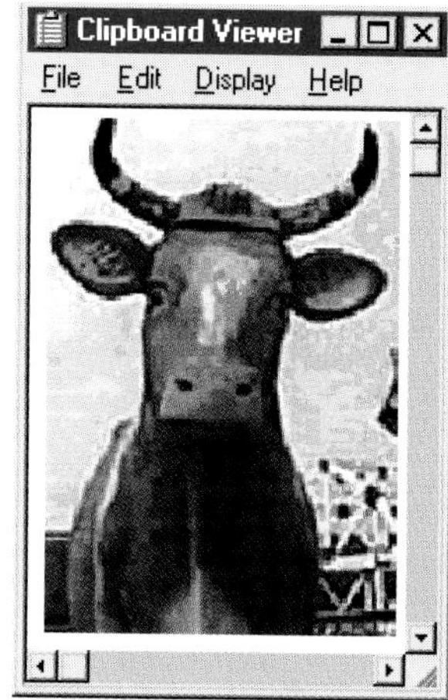

Clipboard Viewer: Seeing or Saving What's on the Clipboard

If you doubt what's on the Clipboard, want to get a better look at what's there, or want to save what's on the Clipboard to a file, open the Clipboard Viewer by following these steps:

1. Click the Start button and choose Programs | Accessories | System Tools | Clipboard Viewer. You see whatever is on the Clipboard in the Clipboard Viewer window.
2. To save what's on the Clipboard, choose File | Save As and fill in the Save As dialog box.
3. Click the Close button to close the Clipboard Viewer.

CAUTION

OLE links are broken when files are renamed or moved. If you are disciplined and know how to plan ahead, go ahead and make OLE links between files. But if you often move and rename files, object linking and embedding is more trouble than it's worth. Very carefully create or choose folders for storing OLE files. For practical purposes, you can't move these files after you create them.

Linking Data Between Files with OLE

Besides conventional ways of copying text, you can link two files so that changes made in the original are made to its copy automatically. Windows calls this ability *object linking and embedding* (OLE). If a list in a file you are working on happens to be useful in the annual report, you can link the files so that updates made to the list are made immediately in the annual report as well.

In linking and embedding, the original file from which the copy is made is called the *source file*. Its cousin, which gets updated when the source file changes, is called the *destination file.* Follow these steps to create a dynamic link between files so that changes made to the source file are made automatically in the destination file:

1. Open the source file, or master copy, whose changes will affect the other file.
2. Select the part of the source file that you will copy to the destination file.
3. Choose Edit | Copy, click the Copy button, or press CTRL-C.
4. Open or switch to the destination file and place the cursor where you want the copy to go.
5. Choose Edit | Paste Special. You see the Paste Special dialog box.

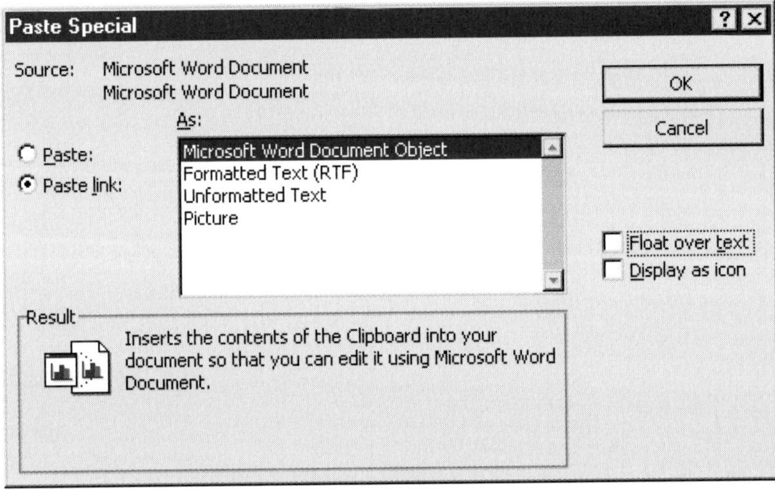

6. Choose Options in the Paste Special dialog box:
   - **As** Windows Me should already have made a correct choice here. The As box describes the type of information you are copying—a document or picture, for example.
   - **Paste *or* Paste Link** Choose the Paste Link option button to create a link between the files and be able to update the destination file automatically. If you choose the Paste option button, a copy is placed in the destination file, but it isn't updated automatically. However, you can open the program

with which the copied data was created and edit the copied data merely by double-clicking the copied material in the destination file.

7. Click OK to close the Paste Special dialog box.

In the destination file, you can tell where the link is because it turns gray when you click it. Changes made to the source file are made automatically to the destination file if both files are open, or as soon as the destination file is reopened.

Suppose you want to break a link, you suspect that a link isn't up to date, you moved the source file, or you want to open the source file and make changes there. Better follow these steps:

1. In the destination file, click the link and then choose Edit | Links. You see the Links dialog box.
2. Click a button in the dialog box:
   - **Update Now** Click this button to update the link.
   - **Open Source** Click this button to open the source file so you can make editorial changes there.
   - **Change Source** Click this button if you moved the source document to a new folder. In the Change Source dialog box, find the source file, click it, and click Open to reestablish the link.
   - **Break Link** Click this button to break the link between the source file and the destination file.
3. Click OK.

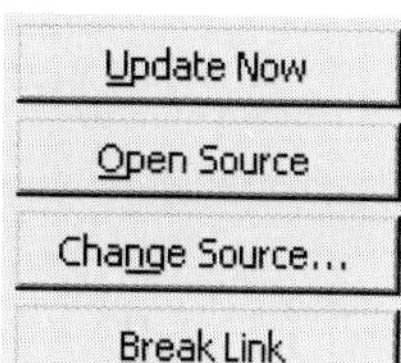

CHAPTER 4

Doing the Setup Work

INCLUDES

- Installing and removing software programs
- Installing a new hardware device
- Installing a new printer on your system
- Loading fonts and viewing fonts
- Resetting the clock, date, and time zone
- Connecting your computer to the Internet

FAST FORWARD

Install New Software ➥ pp. 87–91

1. Click the Start button and choose Settings | Control Panel.
2. In the Control Panel, double-click the Add/Remove Programs icon.
3. Click the Install button.
4. Insert the CD or floppy disk with the program you want to install, click the Next button, and follow the setup program's instructions for installing the new software.

Please wait while each of the following components is removed...

✔ Shared program files...

✔ Standard program files...

✔ Folder items...

Enlist Windows' Help to Remove a Program ➥ p. 91

1. Click the Start button and choose Settings | Control Panel.
2. Double-click the Add/Remove Programs icon.
3. On the list of programs at the bottom of the dialog box, find and click the name of the program you want to remove.
4. Click the Add/Remove button and click Yes in the "Are you sure?" message box.

Install a New Hardware Device on Your System ➥ pp. 92–95

- To install a plug-and-play device, turn off the computer and install the hardware. When you turn on the computer, Windows notices the new hardware device and installs a driver to make it run successfully.
- To install a device that isn't plug and play, click the Start button, choose Settings | Control Panel, and double-click the Add New Hardware icon. In the Add New Hardware Wizard dialog boxes, keep making choices and clicking the Next button.

Install a New Printer ➥ pp. 97–99

1. Click the Start button, choose Settings | Printers, and double-click the Add Printer icon.
2. Click Next, and, if the next dialog box asks whether to install a local or network printer, choose one or the other and click Next again. In the second Add Printer Wizard dialog box, click the name of the company that made your printer and the model name of your printer. Then click Next.
3. Choose the port for your printer, probably LPT1, click Next, and click the Yes option button if you want your new printer to be the default printer.

Find Out Which Fonts Are Available on Your System ➥ pp. 100–102

1. Click the Start button, choose Settings | Control Panel, and double-click the Fonts shortcut icon.
2. In the Fonts folder, double-click the font that you want to examine.

Reset the Clock, Date, and Time Zone ➥ pp. 104–106

1. Double-click the clock in the lower-right corner of the screen.
2. Enter the correct date and time, and click OK.

Set Up an Internet Connection to Your ISP ➥ pp. 106–112

1. Click the Start button and choose Settings | Control Panel, and double-click the Internet Options icon.
2. In the Internet Properties dialog box, click the Connections tab, and then click the Setup button to start the Connection Wizard.
3. Answer the questions in the Connection Wizard dialog boxes.

In the bad old days, a chapter like this about installing software and hardware on a computer might require dozens and dozens of pages. But times have changed for the better. Instead of skirmishing, software and hardware manufacturers realized that the mere mortals who operate computers would be happier if standard procedures for installing software and hardware were developed. This chapter explains what those standard procedures are and how to uninstall a program that you don't want anymore.

You'll also find advice for installing software or hardware for which there isn't a standard setup program that Windows Me can read. Installing and uninstalling software and hardware like that can be tricky. Equally tricky is making a connection between your computer and the Internet. This chapter tackles that subject, too.

You also discover how to load and unload *fonts,* the typeface designs that come with Windows Me, and how to tell Windows Me the correct date and time. You want the clock in the lower-right corner of the screen to tell the right time, don't you? For cosmopolitan globetrotters, this chapter also explains how to change regional settings.

Installing and Uninstalling Software Programs

Appendix A explains how to install and uninstall Windows Me or its various components.

Software that's worth anything comes with an installation program. All you have to do is tell the installation program to go to work, click a few buttons, and make a cup of tea while the software loads itself. When the time comes to uninstall the software because you no longer require it, all you have to do is run the software's uninstall program.

Old programs and programs from second-rate developers, however, do not come with uninstall programs. The only way to remove an old program is to practice a scorched-earth policy of deleting the folders in which it is stored. Installing a program for which there isn't an installation program is also a clumsy and rough undertaking. Read on to find out how to install software programs, uninstall them, and upgrade to a newer version of software that is already loaded on your computer.

Installing New Software

Before you try to install a new software program, find out whether the software comes with an installation program. If it does, you can rely on the installation program to do most of the work. Do the following to see if an installation program is on the CD or floppy disk that the software comes on:

- **CD** In some computers, the installation program starts automatically as soon as you slide the CD in the CD-ROM or DVD drive. If the installation program doesn't start, open My Computer, click the CD-ROM drive icon (probably [D:]), and look for a file called setup.exe or install.exe. (If you are having trouble telling which setup or install file is the right one, choose View | Details and look in the Modified column for the word *Application.* Setup and install files are applications in their own right whose job it is to install a program.)
- **Floppy Disk** Put Disk #1 in the floppy drive, open My Computer, click the floppy drive icon (probably [A:]), and look for a setup.exe or install.exe file.

CAUTION

Before you install a program, especially a public domain program or one you acquired online, study its Readme files. A *Readme file* provides last-minute compatibility news, instructions, tips, and caveats that don't appear in the instruction manual. To open a Readme file, look for a file called Readme, Read_me, or some such on the CD or floppy disk and double-click it in Windows Explorer or My Computer.

If you don't see a setup.exe or install.exe file, you're on your own. You have to install the file yourself. Following are instructions for installing software with the help of a program and installing software yourself. Be sure to quit running all other programs before you install new software.

Installing Software with an Installation Program

If you just finished investigating whether the CD or floppy disk has an installation program and you are staring at a setup.exe or install.exe file in My Computer, double-click the .exe file to start the installation program. You can skip the following steps, which explain how to get

Windows' help to locate and start installation programs. To begin at the beginning, follow these steps:

1. Close all the files and computer programs that are open.
2. Click the Start button and choose Settings | Control Panel. You see the Control Panel window.
3. Double-click the Add/Remove Programs icon. The Add/Remove Programs Properties dialog box shown on the left side of Figure 4.1 appears.

4. Click the Install button. You see the Install Program From Floppy Disk or CD-ROM dialog box.
5. Insert the CD in the CD-ROM drive or, if you are installing the program from a floppy disk, insert the first disk in the floppy drive.
6. Click the Next button. If all goes correctly, the dialog box changes names to Run Installation Program, as shown on the right side of Figure 4.1, and SETUP.EXE or INSTALL.EXE appears in the Command line box. If for some reason a filename doesn't appear, click the Browse button, and, in the Browse dialog box, locate the installation file, click it, and click the Open button to make it appear.
7. Click the Finish button.

What happens next depends on the program you want to install, how big it is, and how many settings it requires you make. Usually, a bunch of dialog boxes appear, you make choices in each dialog box, and then the ordeal ends. When you are done, a new program name is added to the Programs menu, and, in some cases, a new shortcut icon lands on the desktop.

Most installation programs do the following as part of the installation procedure:

- Ask you for a code number to prove you really purchased the software

- Check for sufficient space on the hard disk
- Check the computer for compatibility problems
- Create new folders for the new software
- Prompt you, if you are installing the program from floppy disks, to insert new disks
- Make changes to your computer's system files
- Add new fonts and drivers
- Tell you when the installation is over and whether it was successful

Installing Software on Your Own

The program you want to install doesn't come with its own installation program? Don't fret—worse things have happened. To install the program, create a new folder for it on your computer and copy the program's folders and files into the folder you created. The trick is to copy all the folders and files, including the hidden files. To

At the end of Chapter 2, "Decide How to List Files in Folders and Dialog Boxes" explains the vagaries of listing three-letter file extensions and hidden files in dialog boxes, Windows Explorer, and My Computer.

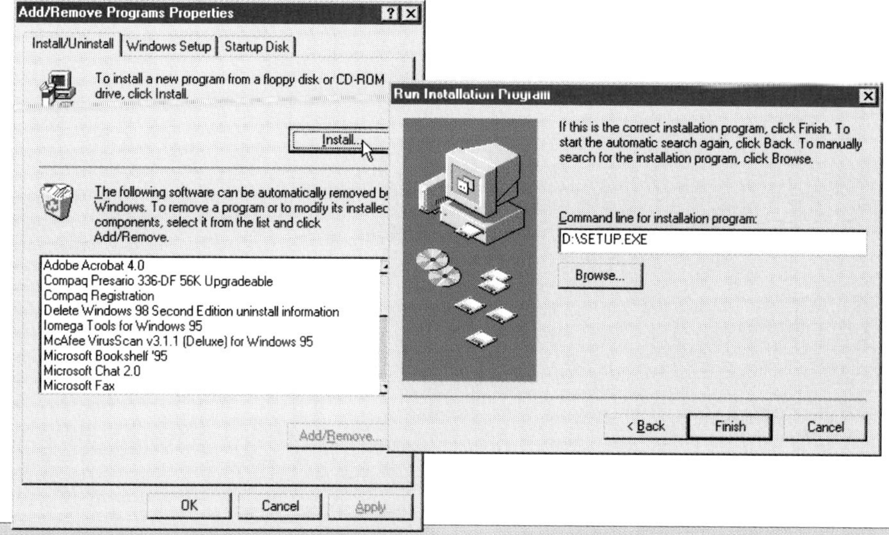

Figure 4.1: Getting Windows' help to locate and launch an installation program

TIP

To put a program you installed yourself on the Programs menu, see "Adding a Program Name to a Menu" in Chapter 5. "Create the Shortcut Icons You Need" in Chapter 2 explains how to create a shortcut icon for a program.

Appendix A explains how to install Windows Me and what happens when you upgrade from Windows 95/98.

make sure you copy the hidden files, follow these steps before you start copying:

1. Click the Start button and choose Settings | Control Panel.
2. Double-click the Folder Options icon (if you don't see it, click the View All Control Panel options hyperlink).
3. Click the View tab in the Folder Options dialog box.
4. Under Hidden Files and Folders, check the Show All Files and Folders option button if a check mark isn't already there.
5. Click OK.

When you install a program on your own, its name isn't entered on the Programs menu. Officially, it isn't even loaded on your computer or entered in the Windows Registry (the file in which Windows keeps information about computer programs), although you can run your new program easily enough.

Upgrading to a Newer Version of a Program

Upgrading to a newer version of a program is simply a matter of installing the newer version. Everything is done in the background, as the installation program notices the older version of the software on

EXPERT ADVICE

Before you upgrade, find out if files created in the new version of the program can be read by the old version. Coworkers and friends who have the old version of the program might not be able to read the files you create with the new one. Fortunately, almost all programs provide a means of saving a file so that it can be read by older versions. If the old version of the program can't read files created in the new version, be sure to save files in a format that the old version can read before you pass the files to coworkers and friends who are stuck with the old version.

your computer and installs the newer version over the older one. If the software is worth anything, the personal settings you made in the last version of the software—such as screen colors and the default font you like so well—are retained when the new version is installed.

CAUTION

As you remove a program, the Remove Shared File? message box appears if you try to delete a shared file. A *shared file* is a file that several programs rely on, not just the program whose files you are deleting. Removing shared files may render other programs useless and. Because leaving shared files intact does no harm, I suggest clicking the No or No to All button in the Remove Shared File? message box.

Removing Unwanted Software Programs

When you no longer need a program, you might as well remove it, especially if you are running low on disk space. Programs that you or someone else installed with an installation program can be removed cleanly and safely by Windows Me. But if you can't get Windows' help to remove a program, you have to remove it yourself by deleting its files. Read on to learn how to remove programs with Windows' help and remove them on your own.

Using Windows to Uninstall a Program

Figure 4.2 explains how to find out if Windows can uninstall a program and then how to proceed to uninstall it. When you are finished uninstalling, the Remove Programs From Your Computer dialog box appears and tells you what was uninstalled.

Scorched-Earth Policy: Removing a Program on Your Own

In Chapter 3 "Deleting Files and Folders" explains how to delete files.

If the program you want to remove can't be found in the Add/Remove Programs dialog box (see Figure 4.2), you have to remove it yourself. Be sure to consult the program's manual before doing so. If the program is a big or important one, your system might suffer when you uproot its files and remove it. You might leave behind accessory files. You might delete files that other programs need.

After you decide to take the plunge, identify the folders and files that belong to the program and delete them. Go ahead—strike them dead and hope for the best. Removing small programs this way has never done any harm to my computer, but I might be lucky.

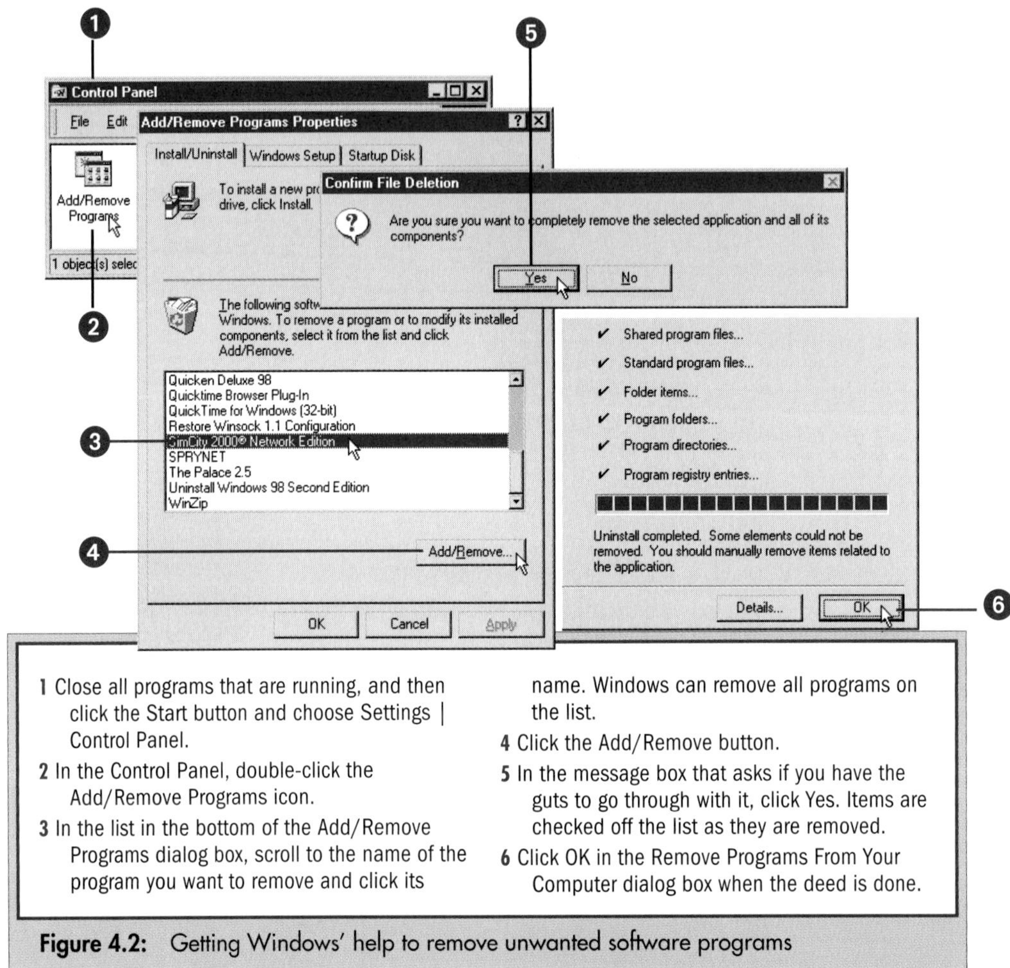

1 Close all programs that are running, and then click the Start button and choose Settings | Control Panel.
2 In the Control Panel, double-click the Add/Remove Programs icon.
3 In the list in the bottom of the Add/Remove Programs dialog box, scroll to the name of the program you want to remove and click its name. Windows can remove all programs on the list.
4 Click the Add/Remove button.
5 In the message box that asks if you have the guts to go through with it, click Yes. Items are checked off the list as they are removed.
6 Click OK in the Remove Programs From Your Computer dialog box when the deed is done.

Figure 4.2: Getting Windows' help to remove unwanted software programs

Installing a New Piece of Hardware

See "Installing a New Printer" later in this chapter if the hardware device you want to install happens to be a printer.

For the purposes of this book, "hardware" does not refer to screws, winches, hammers, or nails. In computer terminology, *hardware* is anything having to do with computers that has a hard surface—a monitor, mouse, or keyboard, for example. Software, if you could touch it, would crumble to dust.

EXPERT ADVICE

My advice for shopping for computers is to shop in local stores—and I don't mean chain stores, either. In cities and midsized towns, you can almost always find a computer shop that will put together the components for you. These made-to-order computers cost a little bit more, but they can be made precisely to your specifications, so you don't pay for extra software and hardware that you don't need and that can slow down your system. As for buying on the Internet or from mail-order catalogues, returning a hardware device you bought that way is much, much harder than bringing it back to the store yourself. No, I think the small shops that are springing up are really the way to go when it comes to buying computers.

The following few pages explain how to install a new piece of hardware and what to do if the installation doesn't work. If the hardware you want to install falls in the *plug-and-play* category, you've got it made. Plug-and-play devices can be installed in a matter of minutes (well, usually) because you don't have to dive into the Windows Me operating system and describe the device after you have plugged it into your system. To install a device that is not plug and play, you have to run the Hardware Wizard. Keep reading.

Installing a Plug-and-Play Hardware Device

To install a plug-and-play device, turn off your computer, carefully follow the instructions in the box to see how to plug the device into the computer, and turn the computer on. You're done. When you turn on the computer, Windows notices the new hardware device and installs a driver to make it run. If the device doesn't run, try installing it with the directions in the section that follows, and see "If the Hardware Device Doesn't Work…" later in this chapter.

Installing a Hardware Device That Isn't Plug and Play

To install a device that is not the plug-and-play variety, you have to attach it to your computer and then tell Windows what it is.

Windows can search for the device on your system for you. If it finds the device, all is well. Windows installs the correct drivers to run the device and that's the end of it. However, if Windows can't find the device, you state what it is, who manufactured it, and its model name yourself so that Windows knows which drivers to install. Follow these steps to run the Hardware Wizard and tell Windows about a new hardware device that isn't plug and play:

1. Close all programs, if any are running.
2. Click the Start button and choose Settings | Control Panel.
3. Double-click the Add New Hardware icon in the Control Panel.

4. Click Next in the first Add New Hardware Wizard dialog box.
5. Click Next again. Then wait as Windows searches for new plug-and-play devices on your system and fails to find any.
6. In the next dialog box, click Yes (Recommended) and click Next to have Windows search your system for new hardware devices that aren't plug and play.
7. The next dialog box warns you that the search can take several minutes (how true!). Click Next and be patient.
8. When the search is complete, either click the Finish button because it was successful, or click Next in the message box that tells you that Windows couldn't find any new devices (and keep reading). If you click Next, you see the Add New Hardware Wizard box shown on the top of Figure 4.3.
9. Click the kind of hardware you installed and click Next. The following wizard dialog box appears.
10. Select the name of the manufacturer on the left side of the dialog box and the model name on the right side (see Figure 4.3), and click Next.
11. Click the Next button when Windows tells you that it will install new drivers to support the new hardware device. If the right drivers are not available, you are asked to insert either a disk from the manufacturer, the Windows CD, or a Windows installation disk.

12. Click the Finish button when the ordeal is over.
13. Shut down and restart the computer.

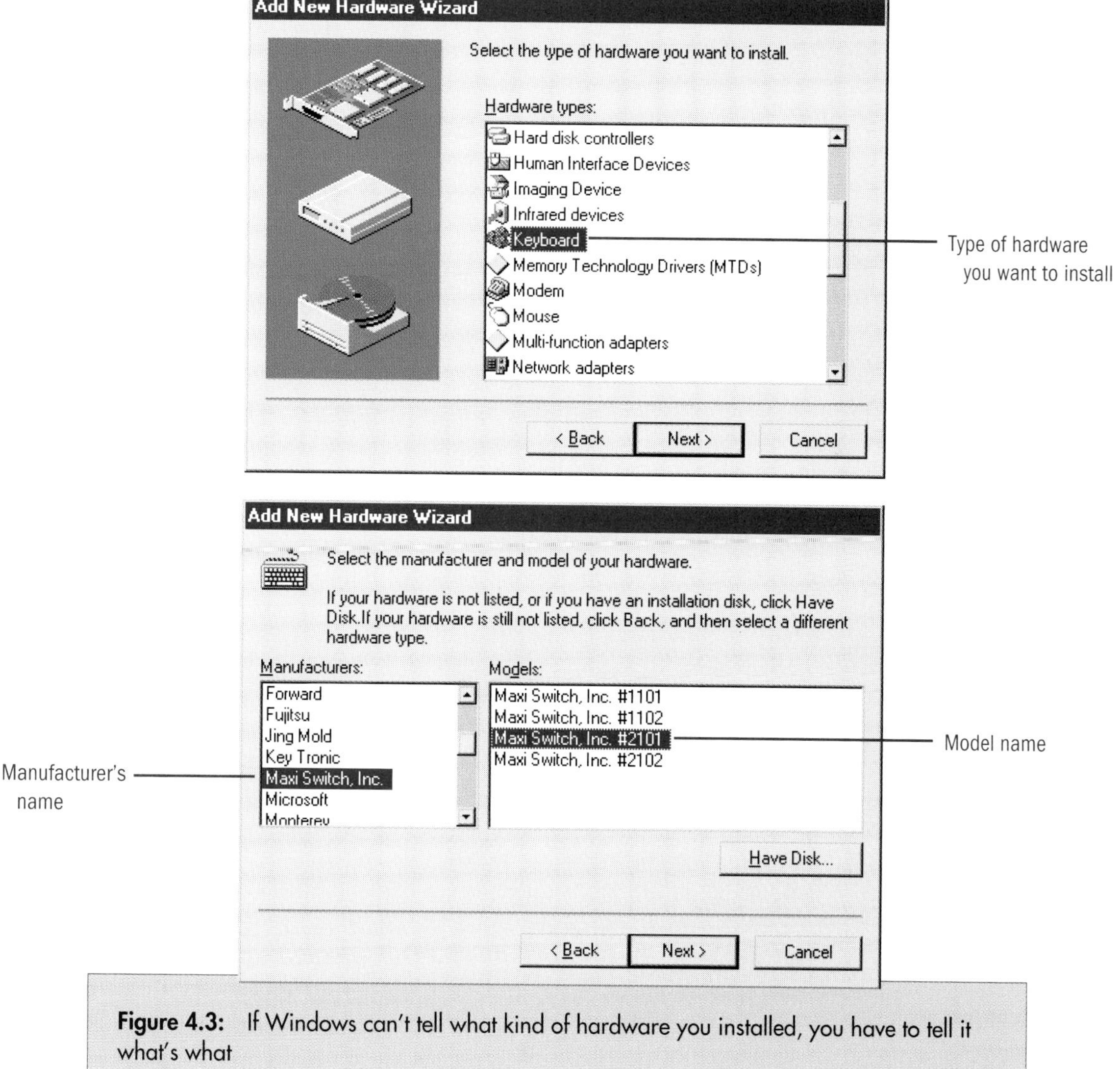

Figure 4.3: If Windows can't tell what kind of hardware you installed, you have to tell it what's what

All computer parts are designed to fit snugly. Whatever you do, don't use a lot of force to make cables and wires fit together.

If the Hardware Device Doesn't Work...

Nothing is more infuriating than installing a new piece of hardware and finding out that it doesn't work. You almost got electrocuted when you plugged in the power cord. You scraped your knee while snaking wires and cables around desk legs. And now the thing doesn't work!

Before you angrily take your new purchase back to the shop, try these tactics:

- See if the cables are fitted properly.
- Find out if the device is turned on and plugged in a wall socket.
- Re-read the manufacturer's installation instructions to see if you followed them correctly.
- Run the Hardware Wizard again. Dunno why, but sometimes the second or third time is the charm.
- Turn to "Getting Information About Your System" in Chapter 9 and follow the instructions for going to the Device Manager tab of the System Properties dialog box. On this tab, you can find out whether a device is really working. Look on the bottom of the Resources tab to see if the device conflicts with another device. If your new device doesn't appear in the System Properties dialog box, Windows doesn't know it's there. Probably it's not plugged in correctly.
- Write down error messages if you see any. Usually, a technician can interpret them for you, if speaking to a technician proves necessary.
- Try the Hardware Conflict Troubleshooter.

A *hardware conflict* occurs when two hardware devices attempt to use the same resources. When that happens, one device wins and one loses, and the losing device doesn't function correctly. The Hardware Conflict Troubleshooter can help find out if a hardware conflict has occurred. To use it, follow these steps:

1. Click the Start button and choose Help.
2. Click the Index link in the Help program, type **hardware conflict** in the Type in the Keyword text box, and click the Display button.
3. On the left side of the Help window, click the Hardware Troubleshooter option to start the Hardware Conflict Troubleshooter.
4. Select the option button called I Need to Resolve a Hardware Conflict on My Computer and click the Next button.
5. Keep answering questions, clicking Next, and hoping for the best.

Installing a New Printer

Before you can print anything, you have to tell Windows Me what kind of printer you use. All printers are not created equal. Some can print on envelopes and on paper of various sizes. Some can print in color. In order to print anything, Windows needs to know precisely which printer will do the work so that it can send the correct instructions to the printer.

In Chapter 7, "All about Printing" explains how to print a file and change a printer's default settings.

If your printer is plug and play, all you likely have to do to install it is turn off the computer, plug in the printer, and turn the computer on. Maybe you don't have to fool with printer settings, but if you purchase a new printer, you have to alert Windows Me.

By the way, installing a printer simply means to tell Windows Me about a printer you intend to use. More than one printer can be installed on a computer. Before you install a new printer, you don't have to uninstall another. Follow these steps to introduce Windows Me to a new printer:

1. Following the manufacturer's instructions, plug the printer into your computer.
2. Click the Start button and choose Settings | Printers. The Printers folder opens. In the folder are icons for each printer that has been installed and an icon called Add Printer:

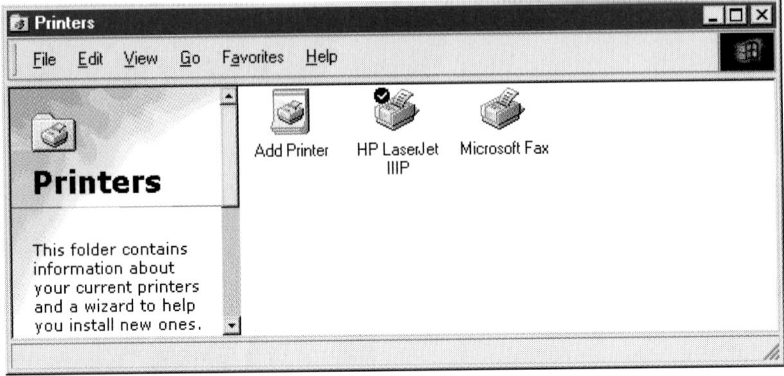

3. Double-click the Add Printer icon to see the Add Printer Wizard dialog box.
4. Click Next (or, if your computer is connected to a network, choose whether to install a local or network printer and then click Next). As shown in Figure 4.4, the Add Printer Wizard dialog box asks who manufactured your printer and which model it is. Windows has drivers for all printers listed in this dialog box.

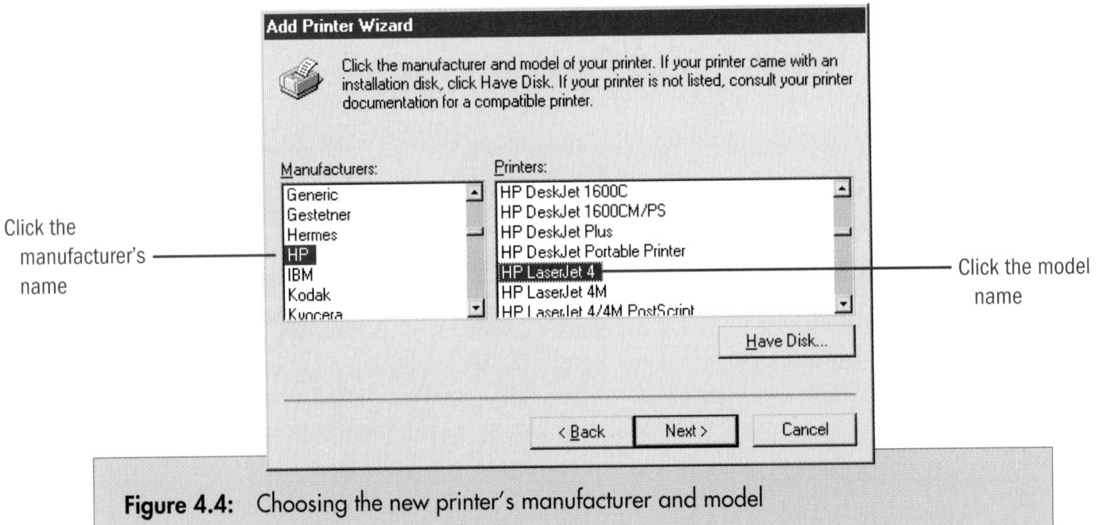

Figure 4.4: Choosing the new printer's manufacturer and model

5. Click the manufacturer's name.
6. Click the model name.
7. From the Manufacturers list, find and click on the name of the company that made your computer.
8. From the Printers list, find and click the model name of your printer. You can find this name on the printer itself. (If your printer isn't on the Manufacturers list, perhaps you can put it there by updating your copy of Windows Me. See Chapter 9.)
9. Click the Next button.
10. Choose the port through which you connected the printer to your computer (probably LPT1) and click Next. If you intend to connect two printers to your computer, consult the printer manual to find out which port to plug the second computer into.
11. In the next dialog box, click the Yes option button if you want your new printer to be the default printer. The *default printer* is the one that appears automatically in the Print dialog box when you give the command to print. You can still print with your new printer if it is not the default, but you will have to select it first in the Print dialog box.
12. Click Next.
13. Click Yes (recommended) to test drive the new printer.
14. Click the Finish button. If all the driver files for your new printer are already on the computer's hard disk, you are done, but Windows probably needs to copy the files from the Windows Me CD or a Windows Me floppy disk.
15. Insert the CD or the floppy disk (be sure to insert the right floppy) and click OK.

An icon for your new printer lands in the Printers folder. If your new printer is the default printer, a black check mark appears beside the icon.

TIP

If you can't find your printer on the Manufacturer's list, insert the disk that came with your printer in the floppy drive, click the Have Disk button, and click the Browse button in the Install from Disk dialog box. Your printer didn't come with a disk? Go to the manufacturer's Web site and see if you can download the driver file. Then click the Browse button in the Install from Disk dialog box, locate the file you downloaded, and select it.

TIP

If you change your mind about which printer is the default printer, click the Start button and choose Settings | Printers to open the Printers folder. Then right-click the printer that should be the default and choose Set as Default from the shortcut menu.

All About Fonts

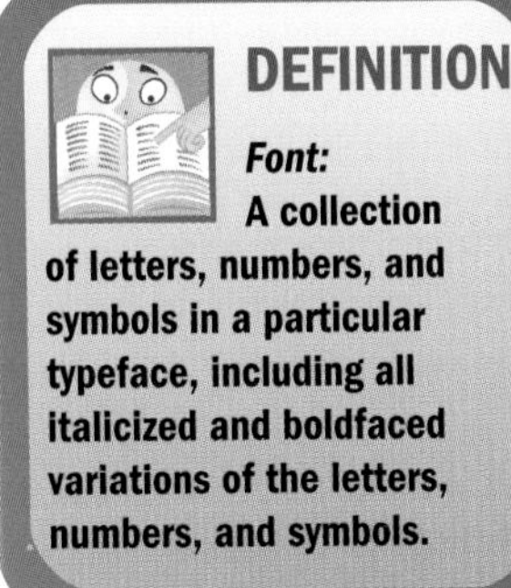

People who create fancy documents, signs, or certificates owe it to themselves to load many different fonts on their computers. That way, you get to choose from different fonts in your work. If it helps you understand what fonts are, *font* is a synonym for *typeface*. Fonts have lovely names—Garamond, Mistral, Verdana. As a connoisseur of Windows Me, you have the opportunity to use many fonts. Don't be shy about experimenting with fonts to find one that sets the right tone or calls attention to the right part of a page. But don't go overboard, either. A page with too many fonts looks like a ransom note.

Besides the fonts that come with Windows Me, other programs load fonts on your computer, so it's likely you can choose from a number of fonts. Generally speaking, fonts fall in two categories:

- **TrueType Fonts** These fonts look the same onscreen as they do when printed on paper. When in doubt, choose a TrueType font because you can be sure what it will look like on the printed page. The letters *TT* precede TrueType font names in dialog boxes and the Fonts folder.
- **Printer Fonts** These fonts are less reliable than TrueType fonts. They are designed for use by printers and sometimes look different onscreen and on the printed page. Next to the names of printer fonts in dialog boxes is a tiny image of a printer.

The next few pages explain how to find out which fonts are on your system and print samples of your fonts, load more fonts or remove fonts, and insert symbols and special characters in files.

Viewing Fonts and Printing Font Samples

So you want to get a clear look at the fonts you have, perhaps to find out which ones to use in a desktop publishing file or to find out which are expendable and can be deleted. Figure 4.5 shows how to examine the fonts on your system. By the way, do you know why, in Figure 4.5 and in typing class, "the quick brown fox jumps over the lazy dog?"

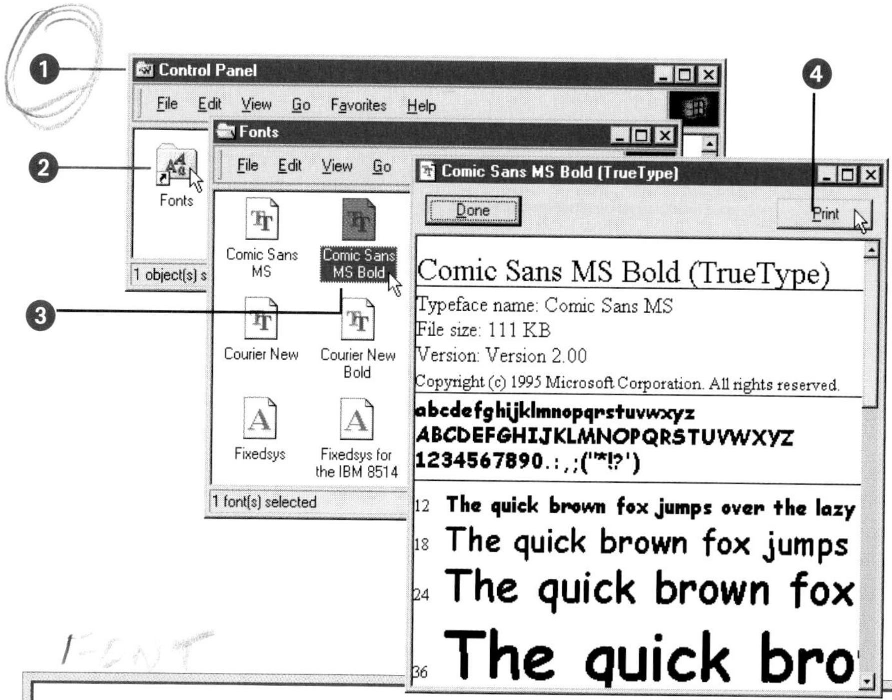

1 Click the Start button and choose Settings | Control Panel.

2 In the Control Panel window, double-click the Fonts shortcut icon to travel quickly to the Fonts folder. The Fonts folder lists all the fonts on the computer.

3 Double-click the name of a font that you want to examine. An eye chart appears so you can see examples of the font in various type sizes.

4 To print a sample page, click the Print button; otherwise, click Done.

Figure 4.5: Seeing which fonts are on your system

Because that sentence requires every letter of the alphabet, including *X* and *Z*.

Loading More Fonts on Your System

Follow these steps to load more fonts on your computer:

1. Click the Start button, choose Settings | Control Panel, and double-click the Fonts shortcut icon to open the Fonts folder (see Figure 4.5).
2. In the Fonts folder window, choose File | Install New Font.

3. In the Add Fonts dialog box, show Windows the way to the fonts you want to load by clicking choices in the Drives and possibly in the Folders list.

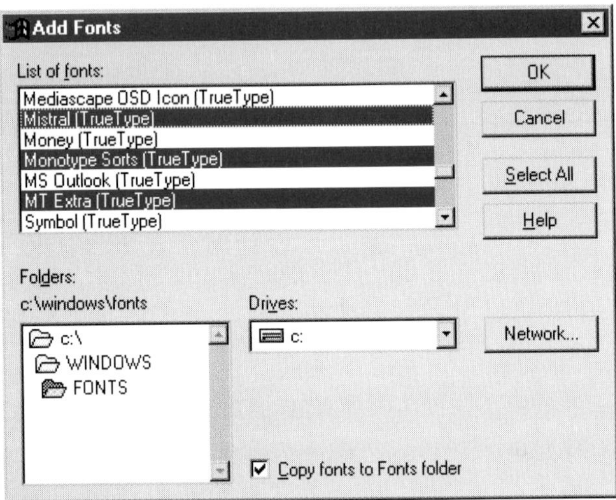

4. Click the name of the font you want to load. To load several fonts, CTRL-click them. Click the Select All button to select all the fonts.
5. Click OK. The new font is placed in the C:\Windows\Fonts folder. When you select a font in a Fonts dialog box, the name of your new font will appear on the list beside the other fonts.

Fonts can eat up valuable disk space. To remove a font, open the Fonts folder, click the name of the font (or CTRL-click to select several names), and choose File | Delete. Don't delete Windows Me fonts because Windows needs them for its menus. Only delete fonts that you installed yourself.

Character Map: Inserting Symbols and Special Characters

On the subject of fonts and characters, you can enter a foreign character or strange symbol in sophisticated programs like WordPerfect and Word merely by choosing a menu command. That isn't so in most programs. In most programs you can't enter an unusual character directly, so you have to seek the help of the Character Map by following these steps:

> **SHORTCUT**
> **Double-click a symbol to copy it directly to the Characters to Copy box.**

1. Click the Start button and choose Programs | Accessories | System Tools | Character Map. You see the Character Map shown in Figure 4.6. The symbol or character you select here will be copied to the Clipboard. From the Clipboard, you will paste the symbol or character into a file.
2. Choose a font from the Font menu.
3. Click to select a symbol or character. To get a good look, click and hold down the mouse button.
4. Click the Select button. The symbol or character you selected lands in the Characters to Copy box. You can select more than one character.
5. Click the Close button.
6. Back in your file, place the cursor where you want the symbol or character to go and press CTRL-V, choose Edit | Paste, or click the Paste button.

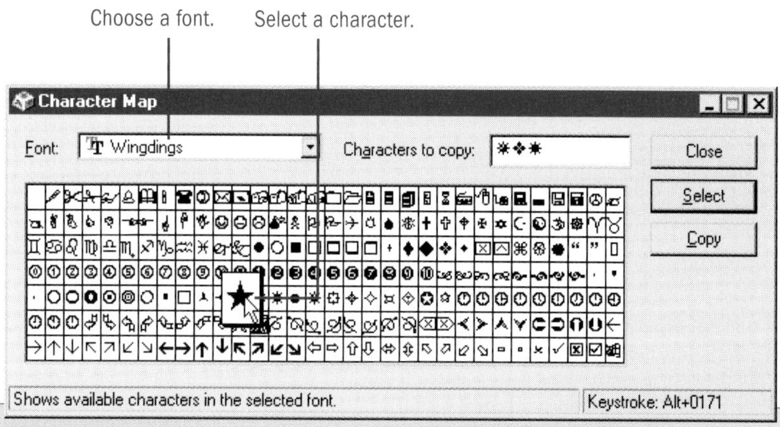

Figure 4.6: Enter foreign characters and symbols with the Character Map

Resetting the Clock, Calendar Date, and Time Zone

> **TIP**
>
> **If you don't care to see the clock on the Taskbar, click the Start button and choose Settings | Taskbar and Start Menu. Then, on the General tab of the dialog box that appears, uncheck the Show Clock check box.**

On the right side of the Taskbar, the clock tells the time. And if you gently slide the mouse pointer over the clock, you can learn today's date and the day of the week. Now and then, make sure the clock is accurate and reset the clock, if necessary. And if you cart your computer or laptop to a new time zone, reset the clock and tell Windows Me which time zone you crossed into. Windows uses the clock to time-stamp and date-stamp files when you save them. Unless the clock is accurate, you can't tell precisely when files were saved and which files are most up-to-date.

Figure 4.7 explains how to reset the time and date in the Date/Time Properties dialog box. As for the Automatically Adjust Clock for Daylight Savings Changes check box, Windows automatically sets the clock forward or backward at the appropriate hour if the check box is selected. Unless you live in one of those enlightened Midwestern towns where daylight savings time is not honored, leave the check mark in the check box.

Deciding How Numbers, Times, Dates, and Currency Are Displayed

When you installed Windows Me, you declared which language you speak and which region you live in. On the basis of that choice, Windows Me displays numbers, times, and dates in a certain way. Windows Me also chose a currency symbol for you. For example, if you chose English (United States) as your language and region, numbers are displayed to two decimal points, the dollar symbol ($) is the currency symbol, and time is displayed in AM/PM format. Many programs get their display formats from the choices you make in Windows.

Suppose you move to a different region of the world or you want to change number, time, date, or currency formats. In that case, visit the Regional Settings Properties dialog box by following these steps:

1. Click the Start button and choose Settings | Control Panel.

Regional Settings

2. In the Control Panel, double-click the Regional Settings icon. You see the Regional Settings Properties dialog box.
3. Either go to the Regional Settings Properties tab and choose a new region from the drop-down menu, or visit the Number, Currency, Time, and Date tabs and change the settings there.
4. Click OK.
5. Click Yes when Windows informs you that you have to restart the computer to make the settings take effect.
6. Twiddle your thumbs while the computer restarts.

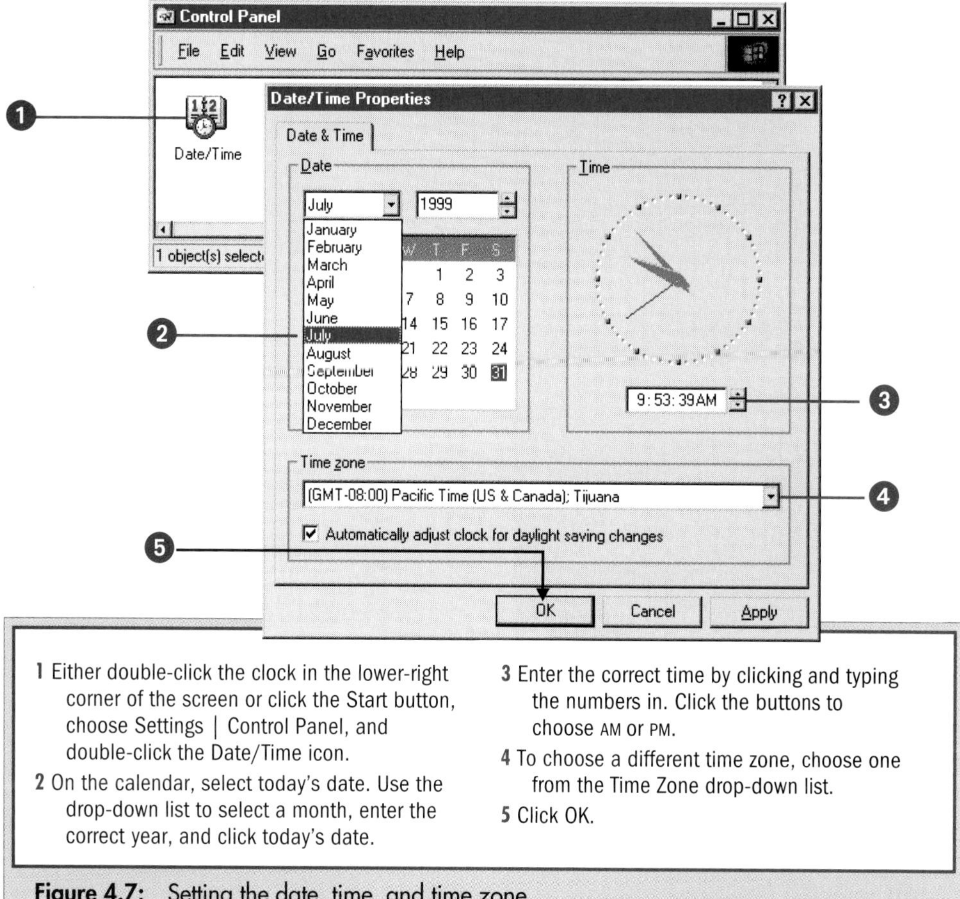

1 Either double-click the clock in the lower-right corner of the screen or click the Start button, choose Settings | Control Panel, and double-click the Date/Time icon.

2 On the calendar, select today's date. Use the drop-down list to select a month, enter the correct year, and click today's date.

3 Enter the correct time by clicking and typing the numbers in. Click the buttons to choose AM or PM.

4 To choose a different time zone, choose one from the Time Zone drop-down list.

5 Click OK.

Figure 4.7: Setting the date, time, and time zone

Did you know that writers don't have to pay income tax in Ireland? I should promptly change my computer's regional settings to English (Ireland) and emigrate to that most civilized of countries.

Connecting Your Computer to the Internet

DEFINITION

Internet service provider (ISP): **A telecommunications service that provides Internet access to subscribers for a fee.**

The last part of this chapter takes on a thorny subject: how to set up your computer so it can connect smoothly with the Internet. The bad news is that software standards haven't been devised to make setting up the connection easy. The good news is that all ISPs that are worth anything whatsoever will gladly help their customers connect to the Internet. All you have to do is call your ISP and ask for instructions.

Read on to find out how to connect your computer to an ISP and how to change the connection settings if that proves necessary. If you use a DSL line or cable modem to connect to the Internet, you need to call your ISP to get instructions for connecting. If your computer is connected to a network, it is probably connected to the Internet already. See your network administrator if the connection between your computer and the network isn't working correctly or you can't get on the Internet.

Making a Modem Connection to an ISP

Every Internet service provider is different, so you have to choose a bunch of different options and make a number of different settings to establish the connection between your computer and your ISP. Before you try to make the connection, collect all the information you need (I will explain what information you need shortly).

EXPERT ADVICE

These days, many ISPs provide an on-disk setup program that you can use to establish a connection between a computer and the Internet. The following instructions are for doing the setup work yourself, but if your ISP provides a program for doing it, by all means see if the setup program can do the job before you attempt to establish the connection on your own.

How to shop for an ISP is not a topic for this book, but when you choose an ISP (if you haven't chosen one already), be sure to find a local ISP. Users of the Internet are billed by their ISPs and the phone company when they cruise the Internet. If your ISP is not in the same area code as your computer, you will be billed for a long distance call each time you surf the Net.

Getting Information from Your ISP

Call your Internet service provider on the phone and read the following little speech: "Hello, I'm setting up my computer and modem to connect to your ISP and I need some information. To connect to you, Windows Me says I need all or some of this information." Then read the questions in Table 4.1 and scribble the answers in the margin of this book. The italicized step numbers in Table 4.1 refer to numbered steps in "Internet Connection Wizard: Setting Up Your ISP Connection," the next section in this chapter. Of course, you can get all this information from a manual instead of calling your ISP if you feel like slogging through the pages of a manual. Or maybe your ISP is ahead of the game and can send you all this information on a printout called "Setting Up Your ISP for Windows Me."

Internet Connection Wizard: Setting Up Your ISP Connection

With the answers to the questions in Table 4.1 in hand, and knowing what your password and user name are, follow these steps to start the Internet Connection Wizard and tell Windows how to make the connection between your computer and your Internet service provider:

1. Click the Start button and choose Settings | Control Panel, then double-click the Internet Options icon.

2. In the Internet Properties dialog box, click the Connections tab, and then click the Setup button to start the Connection Wizard.
3. In the first wizard dialog box, click the last option button, I Want to Set Up My Internet Connection Manually, or

Topic	What to Ask Your ISP
ISP Phone Number	
1. Phone Number	What's the dial-in phone number of the Internet service provider (ISP)? (*step 5*)
Dial-Up Connection: Advanced Connection Settings*	
2. Connection Type	Do you use a PPP (Point to Point Protocol) or SLIP (Serial Line Internet Protocol) connection? (*step 5*)
3. Logon Procedure	Do I need to type commands when I log on? If I do need to type commands in a terminal window, what commands do I type? Can I use a logon script? If I can use a script, tell me exactly how to type the commands in the script? (A *script* is a series of commands that are always the same.) (*step 5*)
4. IP Address	What Internet Protocol (IP) address do I use? Do you automatically assign one to me? If not, what is the IP address I should always use when I dial in? (*step 5*)
5. DNS Server Address	When I sign in, do you automatically assign me a DNS (Domain Name Server) address? If not, what is the address of the DNS server? Can you give me an alternate DNS server address in case the main DNS is not available? (*step 5*)
Internet Mail Account: E-Mail Server Types and Addresses	
6. Incoming Mail Server (POP3 or IMAP)	What type of server (POP3 or IMAP) do you use to process incoming mail? (*step 10*)
7. Incoming Mail Server Address	What is the address of the incoming mail server? (*step 10*)
8. Outgoing Mail (SMTP) Server	What is the address of the outgoing mail server? Is it the same as the address of the incoming mail server? (*step 10*)
9. Secure Password Authentication (SPA)	Do you provide Secure Password Authentication (SPA), or do I have to enter my e-mail account name and a password each time I log on? (*step 10*)

* In most instances, you don't need to know the advanced connection settings. If your ISP says you needn't concern yourself with this stuff, your ISP is probably right.

Table 4.1: ISP Information That the Internet Connection Wizard Needs

I Want to Connect Through a Local Area Network (LAN). Then click Next.

4. In the Setting Up Your Internet Connection dialog box, make sure I Connect Through a Phone Line and a Modem is chosen, and click Next. (If you are on a network, by all means let the

network administrator do the work of connecting your computer to the Internet. That's what they are being paid for.)

5. In the Internet Account Connection Information dialog box, enter the phone number of your ISP (the answer to question 1 in Table 4.1). Make sure the area code and country code are correct. If the call to your ISP is not a long-distance call, uncheck the Dial Using the Area Code and Country Code check box. Click Next to go to the next dialog box. If you made no marks next to questions 2 through 5 because your ISP doesn't require this information, you can click Next. However, if necessary, click the Advanced button and fill in the Advanced Connection Properties dialog box. You can fill in the dialog box (both the Connection and Addresses tabs) by referring to the answers you scribbled next to Table 4.1. 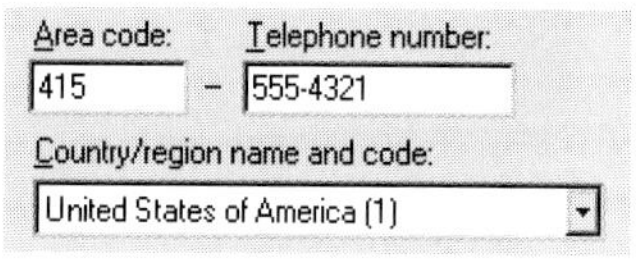
6. In the Internet Account Logon Information dialog box, enter your user name and password. Be sure to type upper- and lowercase letters correctly if that is necessary. Asterisks appear when you enter your password. The ISP should have provided you a password when you signed on. The user name is the part of your e-mail address that appears before the at symbol (@). For example, if your e-mail address is John_Doe@remain.com, John_Doe is your user name. Click Next. 
7. In the Configuring Your Computer dialog box, enter a descriptive name for the connection settings you just entered and then click Next. You can enter your ISP's name if you want. If you need to go back and change these connection settings at a later date, you will refer to them by the name you enter here. For example, if you name your dial-up connection settings Peter's Direct Connection, and you need to change the settings later on, perhaps to change the phone number, you will select Peter's Direct Connection in a dialog box and then revisit the Dial-Up Connection dialog boxes to change the settings. 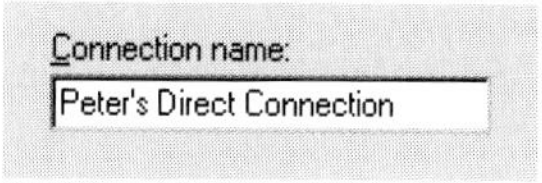
8. In the Set Up Your Internet Mail Account dialog box, click Yes if you intend to send and receive e-mail messages with this account. In the unlikely event that you don't want to send or

receive e-mail, click No and then click the Finished button. (If you already have one Internet account, you see the Internet Mail Account dialog box after you click Next. Click the Create a New Internet Mail Account option button and then click Next if you maintain accounts with two ISPs and you want to configure your computer to connect to the second one.)

Display name: Peter Weverka
For example: John Smith

9. In the Your Name dialog box, type your name as you want it to appear in the From line of outgoing messages. When others get messages from you, this is the name they will see along with the message. Then click Next.

E-mail address: peter_weverka@email.msn.com
For example: someone@microsoft.com

10. In the Internet E-mail Address dialog box, type the e-mail address that others need in order to send you e-mail messages. Be sure to enter your e-mail address correctly. Then click Next.

11. In the E-mail Server Names dialog box, refer to the answers you scribbled next to questions 6 through 8 in Table 4.1 and fill in the boxes. Then click Next.

12. In the Internet Mail Logon dialog box, click the second check box if your ISP uses Secure Password Authentication. (Refer to question 9 in Table 4.1 for the answer.) Otherwise, enter your password again, as I have done in the following illustration. Then click Next.

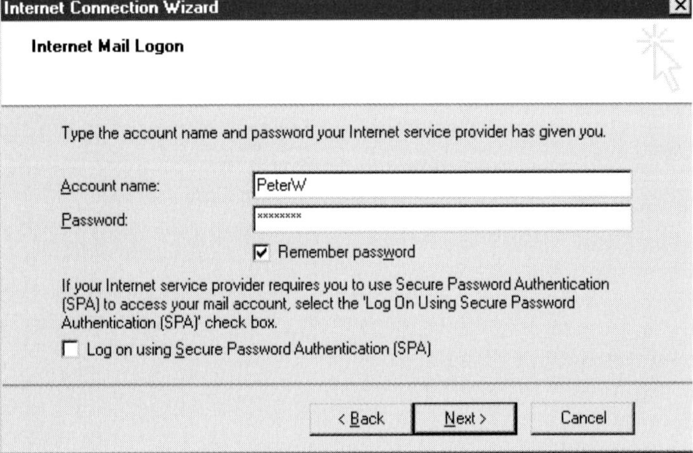

13. In the last dialog box, click Finish to see if your connection to the Internet works. If it doesn't work, keep reading.

Changing the ISP Connection Settings

Suppose your ISP changes phone numbers. Or you change your password. Or you did something wrong in the setup procedure and you have to change a connection setting. To fix the problem, click the Start button, choose Settings | Control Panel, and double-click the Internet Options icon. In the Internet Properties dialog box, click the Connections tab, as shown in Figure 4.8. The Dial-Up Settings box lists the connection between your computer and your ISP (or ISPs).

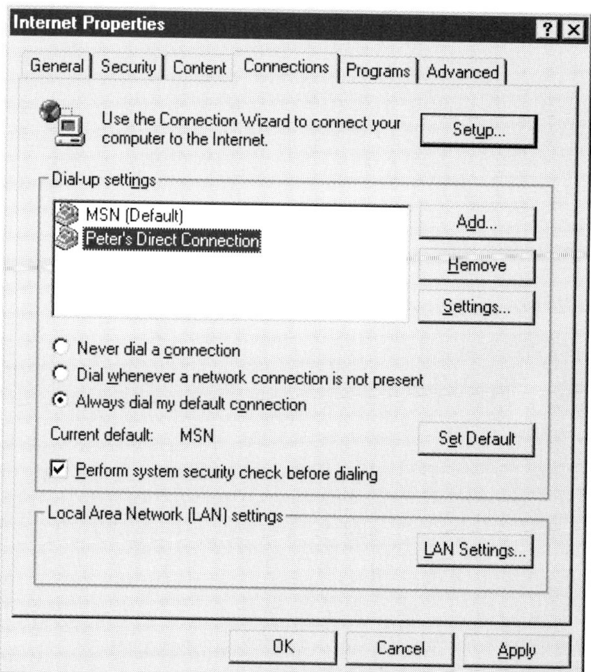

Figure 4.8: Go to the Connections tab of the Internet Properties dialog box to fine-tune an Internet connection

Follow these instructions to fine-tune your Internet connection:

- **Change the connection settings** Click a connection, if necessary, and then click the Settings button. You see the Settings dialog box. From here, you can change the settings you entered when you set up the connection. Click the Properties button to change phone numbers.
- **Choose a default connection** If your computer is connected to more than one ISP, select the ISP you want to connect to automatically when you start Internet Explorer. To do so, select a connection name and then click the Set Default button.
- **Remove a Connection** If you end your relationship with an ISP, sever the connection between your computer and the ISP as well. To do so, click a connection name and then click the Remove button.

CHAPTER 5

Working Faster in Windows Me

INCLUDES

- Creating and switching to different user profiles
- Changing the speed of the mouse and the look of the mouse pointers
- Making the keyboard work better
- Launching a program automatically when the computer starts
- Telling Windows which program is to open a file
- Moving names in, adding names to, and removing names from the Windows Me menus
- Changing the appearance of the screen
- Ten ways to reduce eyestrain

FAST FORWARD

Switch to Another User Profile or Use the Communal Settings ➥ pp. 117–121

1. Click the Start button, choose Log Off, and click Yes in the confirmation box.
2. In the Welcome to Windows dialog box, click Cancel to use the communal settings or else enter a user name and enter a password, if necessary, to work under a user profile.

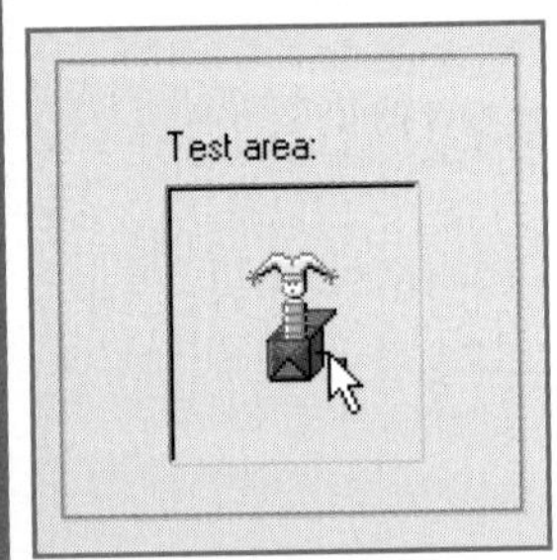

Change the Speed of the Mouse and the Size of Mouse Pointers ➥ pp. 122–125

1. Click the Start button, choose Settings | Control Panel, and double-click the Mouse icon.
2. On the Buttons tab of the Mouse Properties dialog box, adjust the double-click speed.
3. On the Pointers tab, change the look of the mouse pointers.
4. On the Pointer Options tab, change the speed at which the pointer moves.

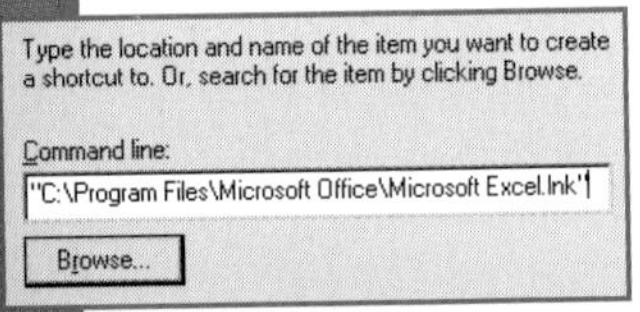

Start a Computer Program Automatically When Windows Starts ➥ pp. 126–128

- Create a shortcut icon for the program and place it in the C:\Windows\Start Menu\Programs\StartUp folder.
- Right-click the Taskbar and choose Properties. In the dialog box, click the Advanced tab, click the Add button, and click Browse. Locate and select the .exe file of the program, click the Open button, click Next, and select the StartUp folder. Click Next again, enter a name for the shortcut icon, click Finish, and click OK.

Tell Windows Which Program Opens a Certain Kind of File ➥ pp. 129–130

1. Click the Start button, choose Settings | Control Panel, and double-click the Folder Options icon.
2. On the File Types tab of the Folder Options dialog box, select the type of file you want to reassign and click the Change button.
3. In Open With dialog box, select the program with which you want to open the file and click OK.

Remove a Program Name from a Windows Menu ➥ p. 133

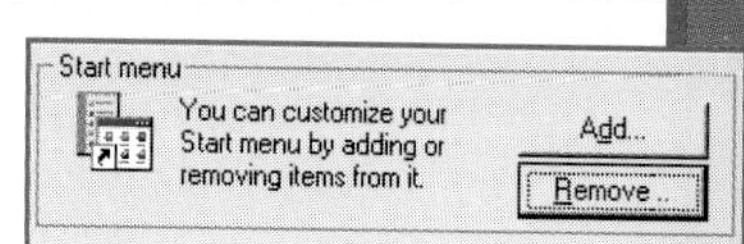

1. Right-click the Taskbar, choose Properties, and click the Advanced tab.
2. Click the Remove button, locate and select the name of the program you want to remove, click the Remove button, and click Close.

Move a Program Name Up or Down a Menu ➥ pp. 134–136

1. Move the pointer over the program name and click and drag the mouse pointer up or down on the menu. A black line shows where the menu name will appear when you release the mouse button.
2. Release the mouse button.

Make the Screen Easier to Read and Understand ➥ pp. 137–138

1. Right-click the desktop and choose Properties.
2. Click the Appearance tab in the Display Properties dialog box.
3. From the Scheme drop-down menu, choose a design for the screen and click OK.

Choose a Wallpaper Design for the Desktop ➥ p. 138

1. Right-click a photo or image you like and choose Set As Wallpaper.
2. Right-click on the desktop, choose Properties, and go to the Background tab of the Display Properties dialog box.
3. On the Display menu, choose Center, Tile, or Stretch.

This chapter picks up where Chapter 2 left off. Chapter 2 explains the handful of things you can do to make working with Windows Me easier. In this chapter, you learn the handful of things you can do to work faster. Study this chapter carefully and you will spend less time in front of your computer. Not that you'll become a member of the leisure class, but you will get the time for those tap dancing lessons you've always wanted.

This chapter shows how to make the mouse and keyboard function better. You learn how to make your favorite program appear instantly each time you start the computer and how to put the names of your favorite programs on the Start and Programs menus where you can find them in a hurry. You also learn how to tell Windows Me to always open a particular kind of file with a particular computer program. Oh, and this chapter also describes how to make the screen easier to look at and offers ten ways to reduce eyestrain.

By the way, if you share a computer with others and you start tinkering with the computer settings, they might get mad at you. To keep that from happening, you can save your supercharged settings as a "user profile." This means that when others sit at the computer, they see and use their own settings or the communal settings, but you get your own personalized settings. How to keep settings to yourself is the subject of the first part of this chapter.

When People Share a Computer: Using User Profiles

Suppose you want to redecorate your computer screen with a tie-dyed background and remove the names of programs you never use from the Programs menu. If you share your computer with others, you owe it to them to save your modifications as a user profile. That way, others who use your computer do not have to be unpleasantly surprised by the strange settings you made.

Keeping your settings to yourself requires doing two things:

- Creating a *user profile*—a user name and perhaps a password—for the new settings you want to make. After you create the user profile, changes you make to settings are made to your profile. They do not affect what others see when they use the computer.
- Teaching others who use your computer how to log on so that they see the settings they want to see, not the settings that are part of your user profile or a third party's user profile.

CAUTION

Be sure to tell the others who use your computer that you intend to create a user profile. After you create one, users see the Enter Password dialog box each time they start the computer. Tell others that they can simply click Cancel or press ESC in this dialog box to start the computer in the normal way.

The next few pages explain how to create, erase, and change a profile. You also learn how to log on to the computer in order to work with the communal settings or work with the settings that belong to a particular user profile.

Creating a New User Profile

When you work under a user profile, all customized settings are kept in that profile. They have no effect whatsoever on other profiles or the communal settings that all users of your computer share. Do the following to create a new user profile under which to keep the new settings you or others make to a computer:

1. Click the Start button and choose Settings | Control Panel.
2. In the Control Panel, double-click the Users icon (if you don't see it, click the View All Control Panel Options hyperlink). If this is the first time you've created a user profile, you see the Enable Multi-User Settings dialog box. Otherwise, you see the User Settings dialog box.

3. Either click the Next button or, if you've already created a user profile, click the New User button and then click Next.
4. In the Add User dialog box, enter a descriptive name for the user profile. Type your name, the name of another person who uses your computer, or the name of a certain kind of task you

want to do. Be sure to remember the name you enter—you will be asked to submit it whenever you change user profiles. Click Next.

5. In the Enter New Password dialog box, enter the same password in the Password and Confirm Password text boxes. Passwords are not case-sensitive. You don't have to enter a password. Leave the Enter a New Password dialog box empty and simply click Next if you think a password for protecting computer settings is unnecessary.
6. Click the Next button.
7. In the Personalized Items Settings dialog box, check each part of Windows Me that you want to customize. In the list, Desktop Folder refers to everything on the desktop—its background, shortcut icons, and so on. Items that you do not check cannot be customized. They retain all the settings that are also found in the communal settings.

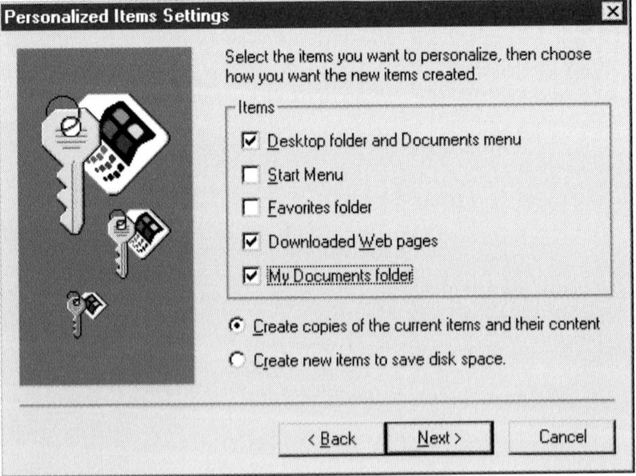

8. On the bottom of the dialog box, choose how you want to start changing the computer's settings:
   - **Create Copies of the Current Items and Their Content** Choose this option to use the settings that are in place and onscreen as the starting point for your new settings.

- **Create New Items to Save Disk Space** Choose this option to start from scratch with bare-bones settings for the items you chose in step 7. For example, if you checked Start Menu and Desktop Folder in step 7, almost all items are removed from the Programs menu and only a few icons remain on the desktop.

9. Click the Next button.
10. Click the Finish button and wait while Windows takes note of your personal settings.

You go back to the User Settings dialog box if you've created user profiles already. Click Close in the dialog box. If this is the first user profile you've created, take these additional steps:

11. Click Yes to restart Windows Me. When Windows restarts, you see the Welcome to Windows dialog box.
12. Enter your password and click OK (or simply click OK if you didn't enter a password for your user profile).

Start changing the settings. All changes you make become a part of your new user profile.

TIP

You can create as many user profiles as you want. If you use your computer for very different tasks—working on spreadsheets, desktop publishing, creating Web pages—create a user profile for each type of work you do. You'll save time that way. As this chapter demonstrates, Windows Me offers many different settings. Some are more suitable than others for working in different types of programs.

Switching to the Communal Settings or Another User Profile

When you work under the auspices of a user profile, all changes you make to settings are made to that profile, not to other profiles or the communal settings. Suppose you want to switch to a different profile or use the communal settings that all users of your computer share. Windows Me offers a special Log Off command for switching profiles. Where is the Log Off command? It's right under your nose, on the Start menu.

Follow these steps to switch to a new user profile or the standard settings that all users share:

1. Click the Start button and choose Log Off. If you are working under a user profile, the name of the profile appears after the words Log Off.
2. Click Yes when Windows asks if you are sure about logging off. You see the Welcome to Windows dialog box.

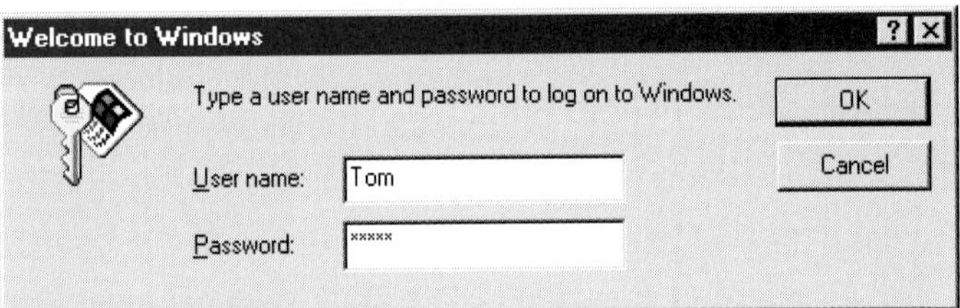

3. Either switch user profiles or use the communal settings:
   - **Different User Profile** Enter the profile's name, enter its correct password (or don't bother with the password if you never assigned one), and click OK.
   - **Communal Settings** Click the Cancel button or press ESC.

Users also see the Welcome to Windows dialog box when they start the computer. Be sure that everyone who uses your computer knows exactly what to do when they confront this forbidding dialog box.

Deleting and Altering User Profiles

The following steps explain how to delete a profile, alter a profile, or change its password. You can't delete a profile if you are logged on to the computer under the name of the profile you want to delete.

1. Click the Start button and choose Settings | Control Panel.
2. In the Control Panel, double-click the Users icon. You see the User Settings dialog box shown in Figure 5.1.

Users

3. Under Users, click the name of the profile that needs changing.
4. Click a button to delete the profile, change its password, or change its settings:

- **Delete** Click the Delete button to erase a profile. Then click Yes when Windows asks if you really want to do it.
- **Set Password** To change or remove a password, click the Set Password button. In the Change Windows Password dialog box, enter the old password and the new password twice to assign a new password to a profile. To remove a password, simply enter the old password in the Old Password text box. Then click OK twice in the message box.
- **Change Settings** Click this button to change which settings the profile has in common with the communal settings. When you click the Change Settings button, you see the Personalized Items Settings dialog box that you saw when you created the profile in the first place. Check items that you want to customize and uncheck items whose settings are to come from the communal settings. Then click OK.

5. Click Close in the User Settings dialog box.

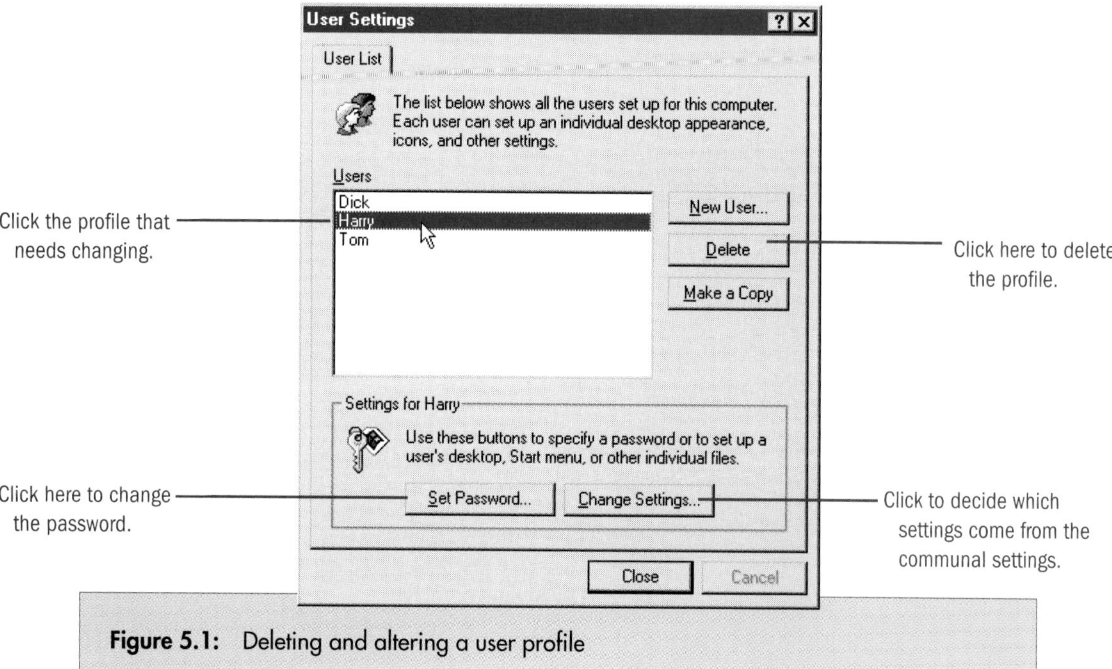

Figure 5.1: Deleting and altering a user profile

A Sleeker, Faster Mouse

Speed demons who prefer pointing and clicking with the mouse to giving commands with the keyboard can fine-tune the mouse and make it work just right. Windows Me offers many ways to adjust the mouse. You can change the double-click speed and pointer speed, change the look of mouse pointers, and even swap the left mouse button and right mouse button, a courtesy to left-handers. Read on.

Changing the Double-Click Speed and Pointer Speed

No matter what you want to do to the mouse, start by opening the Mouse Properties dialog box. Follow these steps to open it and change the double-click speed and the speed at which the pointer travels across the screen when you roll the mouse across the mousepad on your desk:

1. Click the Start button and choose Settings | Control Panel.

2. In the Control Panel, double-click the Mouse icon. You see the Buttons tab of the Mouse Properties dialog box.

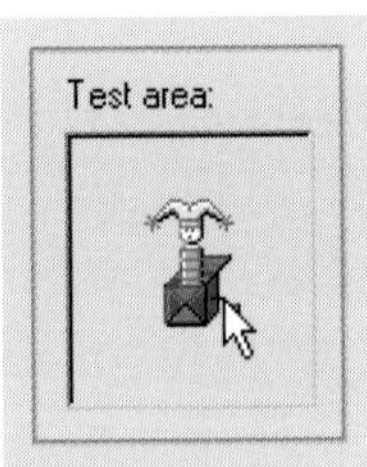

3. Under Double-click Speed, drag the slider toward Slow or Fast, and then try double-clicking the Jack-in-the-Box in the Test area.

   If Jack doesn't spring out of or go back in his box right away, you didn't double-click fast enough. Instead of double-clicking, you clicked twice in a row. The Fast setting on the extreme right is so fast, you might need to change your medication to accomplish a successful double-click.
4. Experiment with double-click speeds until you find one that is comfortable.
5. Click the Pointer Options tab in the Mouse Properties dialog box. On this tab you can adjust the speed at which the mouse pointer moves onscreen and see if pointer trails are for you.

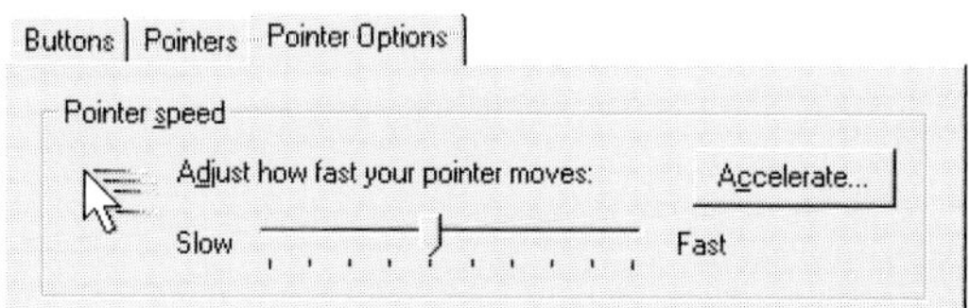

DEFINITION

Pointer trail: **A series of ghostly pointer images that describe in which direction the pointer is traveling onscreen. Pointer trails are a big help to laptop users because finding the pointer on a laptop screen can be difficult.**

6. To experiment with pointer speeds, drag the Pointer Speed slider toward Slow or Fast, click the Apply button, and roll the mouse gingerly across the top of your desk. Repeat this experiment until you find the right pointer speed. While you're at it, try clicking the Accelerate button and choosing an acceleration speed in the Advanced Settings dialog box.
7. To see whether pointer trails are for you and how thick a trail the pointer should leave, click the Show Pointer Trails check box, drag the slider toward Short or Long, and roll the mouse across the top of your desk. What do you think? Keep experimenting.
8. Click OK to close the Mouse Properties dialog box.

Changing the Pointer's Size and Shape

As you must have noticed by now, Windows Me throws different pointers on the screen, depending on what you want to do or what the computer says you must wait to do. When the computer is busy, you see an hourglass. When you move the pointer over text in a word processing file, you see the text select pointer, a vertical stripe that looks like a large letter "I." You can change the size and look of pointers by following these steps:

1. Click the Start button and choose Settings | Control Panel.
2. Double-click the Mouse icon in the Control Panel.
3. In the Mouse Properties dialog box, click the Pointers tab.

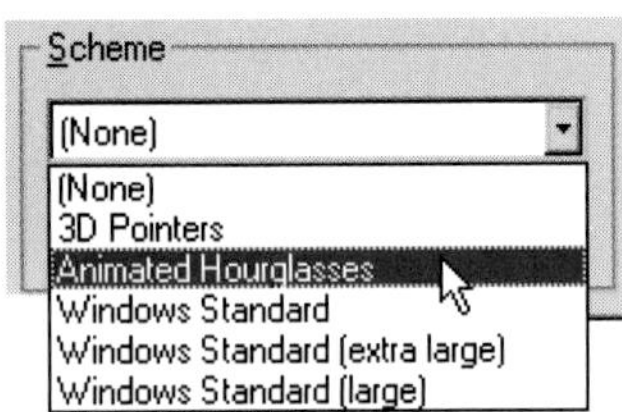

4. Open the Scheme drop-down menu and choose an option. The pointer to the right of the Scheme menu and the other pointers in the Pointers tab change shape so you can see what your choice means in real terms.
5. Experiment until you find a suitable pointer scheme and then click OK or Cancel.

For Lefties: Swapping the Mouse Buttons

In our democratic society dedicated to total equality, where every man and woman is the same before the law, not being able to swap the functions of the left and right mouse buttons would be criminal. Lefties, like their right-handed brethren, must be able to click and drag with the index finger and display a shortcut menu by clicking with the middle finger. To strengthen our democracy, the Buttons tab of the Mouse Properties dialog box offers an option button called Left-Handed that left-handers may click to achieve equality with their right-handed confrères. To afford yourself of this democratic luxury, visit the Buttons tab of the Mouse Properties dialog box and click the Left-Handed option button.

***Cursor*: The vertical line that marks the place onscreen where text appears when you start typing.**

Supercharging the Keyboard

Fast typists and people with sensitive fingertips can supercharge their keyboards. Well, "supercharge" is an exaggeration, but you can decide for yourself how sticky to make the keys and even tell Windows Me how fast to make the cursor blink. Figure 5.2 shows how to tell your keyboard exactly how to behave and the cursor how often to blink.

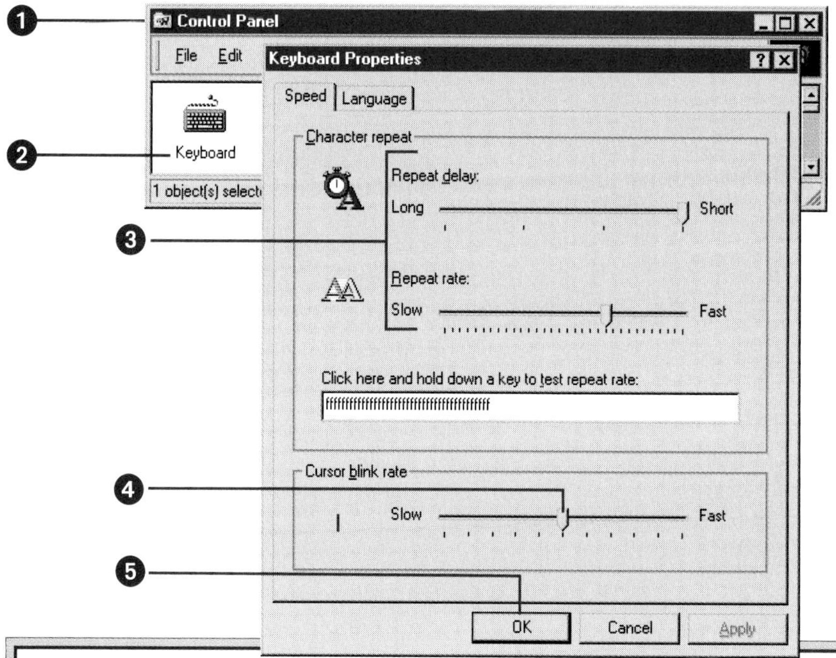

1 Click the Start button and choose Settings | Control Panel.
2 Double-click the Keyboard icon in the Control Panel. You see the Keyboard Properties dialog box.
3 Play with the Repeat Delay and Repeat Rate settings until you find a character repeat rate that is comfortable. You can test your settings by typing in the text box.
4 Under Cursor Blink Rate, watch the sample cursor and drag the slider between Slow and Fast until you find a comfortable rate. Eight out of ten doctors recommend a cursor blink rate that matches your heartbeat.
5 Click OK to close the dialog box.

Figure 5.2: Telling Windows how sticky to make the keys and how often to make the cursor blink

Starting Your Favorite Program When You Start Windows

SHORTCUT

The fastest way to tell Windows to start a program automatically is to simply create a shortcut icon for the program and place it in the C:\Windows\Start Menu\Programs\StartUp folder.

Everybody has a favorite program that they use time and time again. Instead of going to the trouble of starting your favorite program, you can kill two birds with one stone and make your favorite program start automatically when you turn on the computer. To accomplish this little magic trick, you have to know where on your computer the program file (the .exe file) of the program you want to start automatically is located. (Most .exe files are located in the C:\Program Files folder and its subfolders.)

Follow these steps to put a shortcut to your favorite program in the C:\Windows\Start Menu\Programs\StartUp folder so that Windows opens your favorite program when you start the computer:

1. Either click the Start button and choose Settings | Taskbar and Start Menu or right-click the Taskbar and choose Properties.
2. Click the Advanced tab in the Taskbar and Start Menu dialog box.
3. Click the Add button. You see the Create Shortcut dialog box. In this dialog box, you create a shortcut to the .exe file of the program you want to start automatically.
4. As shown in Figure 5.3, click the Browse button and, in the Browse dialog box, find and select the .exe file. Click the View button in the Browse dialog box, choose Details on the drop-down menu, and look in the Type column for the word "Application" to locate .exe files.
5. Click the Open button after you have selected the .exe file. Back in the Create Shortcut dialog box, the path to the .exe file appears in the Command line box.

In Chapter 2, "Decide How to List Files in Folders and Dialog Boxes" explains what file extensions such as .exe are and how to list them in dialog boxes and My Computer.

6. Click the Next button.

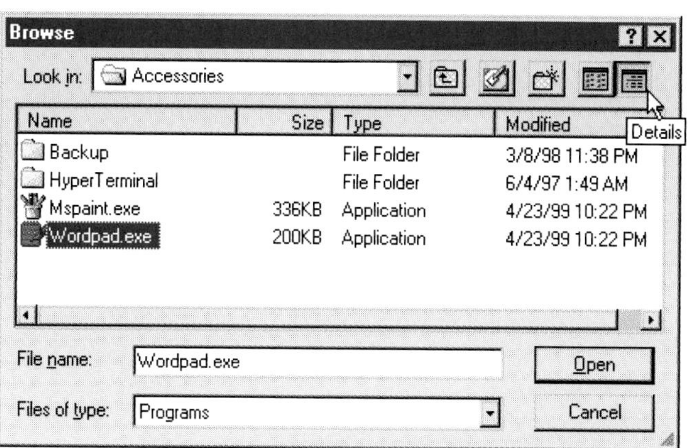

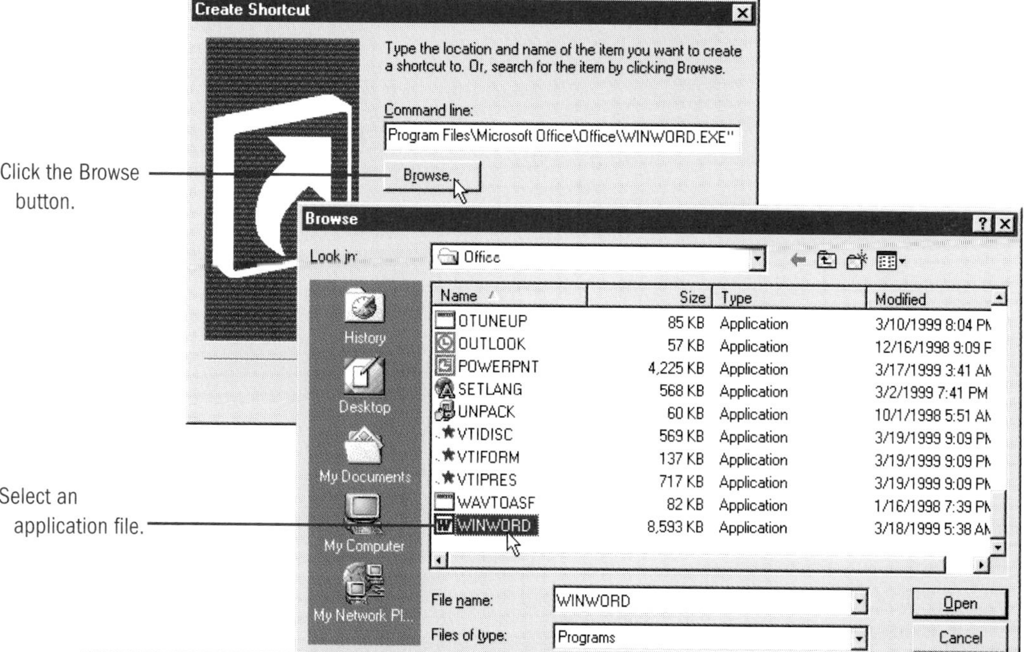

Figure 5.3: Choosing a program to start automatically when you start your computer

7. In the Select Program Folder dialog box, scroll to the bottom of the folder list and select StartUp. In this step, you are putting the shortcut you created in the StartUp folder.
8. Click the Next button. You see the misnamed Select a Title for the Program dialog box.
9. Enter a name for your shortcut icon—probably the program's name. If you decide later on to remove this shortcut icon from the StartUp folder so the program doesn't open automatically, you will do so by deleting the shortcut icon you name in this step.
10. Click the Finish button.
11. Click OK in the Taskbar and Start Menu dialog box.

Suppose you change your mind and decide not to start the program automatically each time you start your computer. To keep that from happening, do either of the following:

- Open the C:\Windows\Start Menu\Programs\StartUp folder in My Computer and delete the shortcut icon you created (right-click the icon and choose Delete from the shortcut menu).
- Revisit the Advanced tab in the Taskbar and Start Menu dialog box, click the Remove button, open the StartUp folder in the dialog box that appears (do so by clicking the plus sign beside its name), select the shortcut icon you created, and click the Remove button.

EXPERT ADVICE

To tell Windows Me *not* to start programs automatically when you start your computer, hold down the SHIFT key while Windows starts. With too many program shortcuts in the StartUp folder, a computer can take a long time to get going, but holding down the SHIFT key is a good way to get going in a hurry.

Telling Windows Which Program Opens a File

Suppose you double-click a file in My Computer to open it but it opens in the wrong program. Perhaps the wrong graphics program appears when you try to open a file and you want the file to open in a better, newer graphics program. You can tell Windows Me which program you want a certain kind of file to open in by default.

DEFINITION

Registry: **An all-important file in which Windows keeps information about computer programs and their settings, including which programs open which files automatically.**

Windows keeps track of which file types work with which programs in a thing called the *Registry.* When you install a new program, information about the file types that the program works with is added to the Registry. The Registry tells Windows Me which program opens which file type automatically. In the instructions that follow, you alter the Registry by giving new program-file assignments, but that doesn't mean you can't try to open any file whatsoever with the program of your choice. All you are dealing with here is the default mechanism for opening files.

Follow these steps to tell Windows Me which program to use to automatically open files of a certain type:

1. Click the Start button and choose Settings | Control Panel.
2. Double-click the Folder Options icon.
3. In the Folder Options dialog box, click the File Types tab. You see a list of registered file types, as shown in Figure 5.4. Windows recognizes all the files on the list. Windows has preconceived ideas about which program to automatically open these files in.
4. Scroll down the list and select the type of file you want to reassign. In the bottom half of the dialog box, next to the words Opens With, you can see which program automatically opens the file you chose. When you have finished reassigning the file, a new program name will appear beside the words Opens With.

TIP

To find the file type you are looking for, try clicking the Extensions button or File Types button at the top of the list of files. Clicking these buttons arranges the files, respectively, in extension order and file type order.

5. Click the Change button. You see the Open With dialog box. It lists the names of all programs installed on your computer.
6. Scroll to and select the name of the program with which you want to open files of the type in question. If you can't find the program on the list, click the Other button, locate the program file in the Open With dialog box, and click the Open button.
7. Click the Close button.

If I were you, I would then open My Computer, find a file of the type you expect to open automatically with your new program, and double-click it to make sure Windows Me opens the file with the right program.

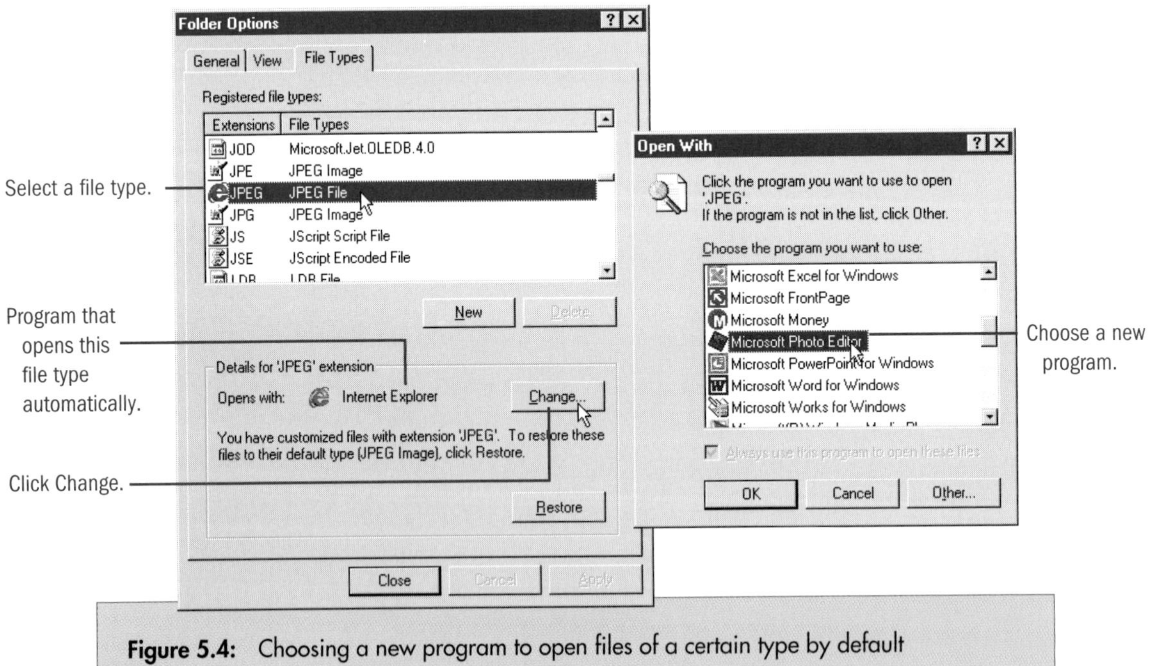

Figure 5.4: Choosing a new program to open files of a certain type by default

Customizing the Windows Me Menu System

The Windows menus—the Start menu, Programs menu, and the submenus on the Programs menu—can get awfully crowded. Sometimes finding the name of a program you want to open is difficult. And sometimes the name of a program you want to open doesn't appear on any menu.

To make it easier for you to select programs on the Windows menus, this section explains how to remove a program name from a menu, add a program name to a menu, create your own submenu, and move a program name or submenu from one menu to another. Windows offers special commands for doing these chores, and you can also move and remove program names in Windows Explorer if you are adept with that program. Read on.

The Fast Way to Move and Remove Program Names and Submenus

Most names on the Windows menus are really shortcut icons. When you click a program name on a menu, you activate a shortcut to the program that you want to open. Windows maintains the shortcuts in special folders in the C:\Windows\Start Menu folder and its subfolders. By moving a program's shortcut icon to a different folder or subfolder, you can also move its name to a different menu. By deleting a program's shortcut icon in a folder, you can remove its name from a menu.

In Chapter 2, "Create the Shortcut Icons You Need" explains how shortcuts work

Figure 5.5 shows the Programs menu and the contents of the C:\Windows\Start Menu\Programs folder (in My Computer). Do you notice the similarities between the names on the Programs menu and the names of the shortcut icons in the Programs folder? If you look closely at the figure, you can see that the Programs menu selections are identical to the shortcut icons in the folder.

As long as you know your way around the C:\Windows\Start Menu subfolders and you are comfortable moving and deleting

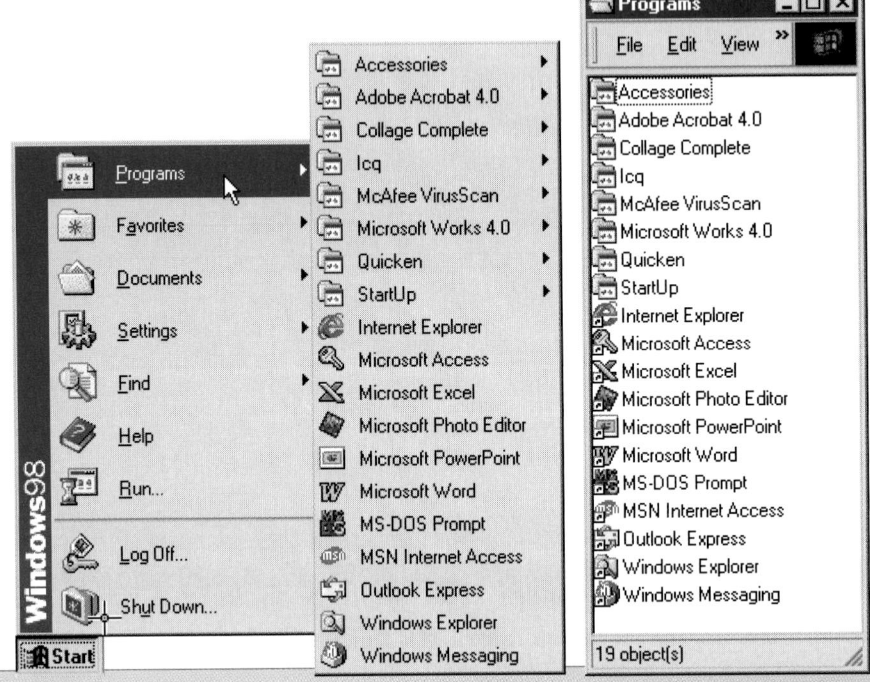

Figure 5.5: You can decide where or whether program names appear on the Windows menus (left) by moving and removing program shortcut icons in C:\Windows\Start Menu and its subfolders (right)

> **TIP**
>
> **As you fool with the menus and program names, leave My Computer open on the right side of the screen. After you move a program's name, click the Start button and see if you can find it on the menus. If you can't find it or you moved it to the wrong location, choose Edit | Undo Move in My Computer and start all over.**

shortcut icons in My Computer, you've got it made. You can simply open My Computer to C:\Windows\Start Menu or one of its subfolders and do the following:

- **Move or copy a program's name to a different menu** Drag the program's shortcut icon to a different folder. For example, to move the Windows Media Player from the Programs | Accessories | Entertainment menu to the Programs menu, move its shortcut icon from the C:\Windows\Start Menu\Programs\Accessories\Entertainment folder to the C:\Windows\Start Menu\Programs folder.
- **Move a submenu to a new location** Drag a folder into another folder. For example, to move the Accessories submenu

from the Programs menu to the Start menu, drag the Accessories folder into the Start Menu folder.

- **Remove a program's name from a menu** Right-click the program's shortcut icon and choose Delete.

TIP

The fastest way to remove a program name from a menu is to right-click it on the menu and choose Delete on the shortcut menu.

Removing a Program Name from a Menu

Removing a program name from a menu in no way removes the program from your computer. The program is removed in name only. Figure 5.6 shows how to remove a program name from a menu, either

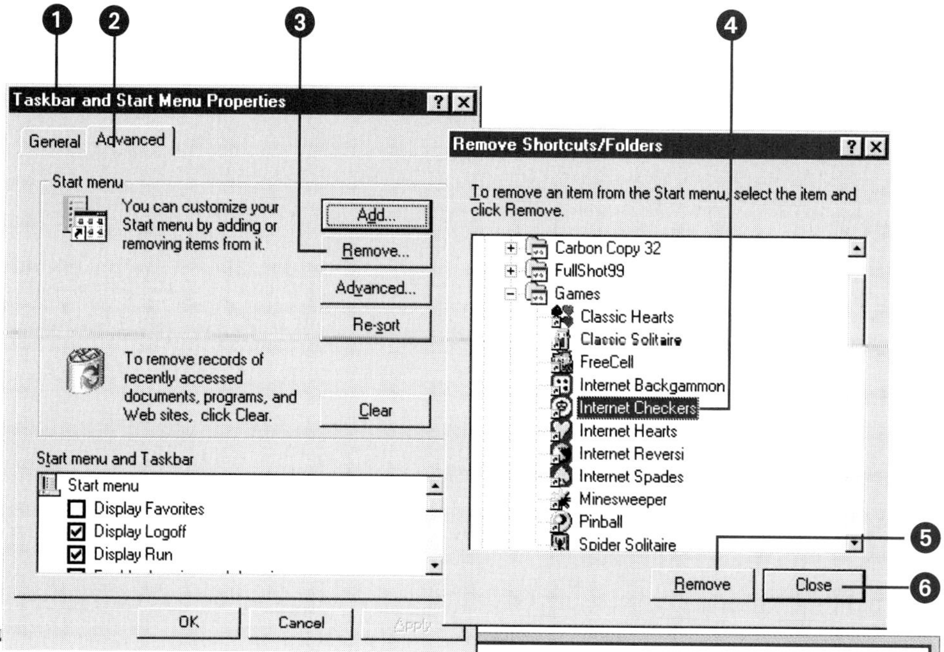

1 Right-click the Taskbar and choose Properties or click the Start button and choose Settings | Taskbar and Start Menu.

2 Click the Advanced tab in the Taskbar and Start Menu dialog box.

3 Click the Remove button. You see the Remove Shortcuts/Folders dialog box.

4 Click the plus signs next to menu names to find and select the name of the program you want to remove from the menus.

5 Click the Remove button.

6 Click the Close button.

Figure 5.6: To remove a program's name from a menu, select it in the Taskbar Properties dialog box and click Remove

because you removed the program itself or you intend to open the program with a shortcut icon.

Moving a Program Name or Submenu to a Different Menu

When you attempt to move a program name or submenu to a different menu, Windows Me opens My Computer to help you along. Guess what? Moving a program name or submenu requires the same techniques described earlier in "The Fast Way to Move and Remove Program Names and Submenus." Follow these steps:

1. Click the Start button and choose Settings | Taskbar and Start Menu or right-click the Taskbar and choose Properties.
2. Click the Advanced tab in the Taskbar and Start Menu dialog box.
3. Click the Advanced button. There it is—My Computer opens to the Start Menu folder.

Turn back a few pages to learn how to move program names and submenus in Windows Explorer. Be sure to click the Start button and make sure that you moved the program name or submenu to the right place. If you didn't, choose Edit | Undo Move in My Computer and try again.

TIP

To quickly put a program name at the top of the Start menu, find the program's .exe file in My Computer and drag the file onto the Start menu.

Adding a Program Name to a Menu

Sometimes you install a new program and shortly thereafter find out that the program's name isn't on a menu. You can fix that problem as long as you know where on the hard disk to find the program file (the .exe file) of the program whose name you want to add to a menu. Follow these steps to add a program name to one of the Windows Me menus:

1. Right-click the Taskbar and choose Properties from the shortcut menu.
2. Click the Advanced tab in the Taskbar and Start Menu dialog box.

3. Click the Add button. You see the Create Shortcut dialog box. In this dialog box, you will create a shortcut to the program whose name you want to put on a menu.
4. Click the Browse button.
5. In the Browse dialog box, find and select the .exe file of the program whose name you want to add, and then click the Open button. You return to the Create Shortcut dialog box. The path to the program appears in the Command Line text box.

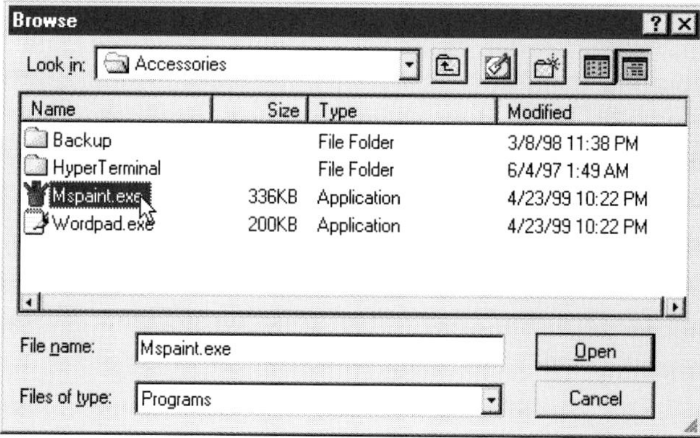

6. Click the Next button. You see the Select Program Folder dialog box. This is where you tell Windows Me which menu or submenu to put the program name on. Each folder represents a menu or submenu.

7. Click the folder whose name corresponds to the menu or submenu that you want to put the program name on, and then click Next.
8. Enter a program name. The name you enter will appear on the menu or submenu you chose in step 6.
9. Click the Finish button and click OK in the Taskbar and Start Menu Properties dialog box.

Adding a Folder Name to the File | Send To Menu

My Computer offers the File | Send To command for quickly sending files to different folders on your computer, to a floppy disk, or to

In Chapter 2 "Create the Shortcut Icons You Need" explains shortcut icons. In Chapter 3, "Making Backup Copies to a Floppy Disk" explains how to use the File | Send To menu to quickly back up files.

different places on the network to which your computer is connected. To begin with, only a few folder names appear on the File | Send To menu, but you can add a folder or two by following these steps:

1. Create a shortcut to the folder in question and give it a descriptive name.
2. In My Computer, open the SendTo folder located at C:\Windows\SendTo.
3. Copy or move the shortcut icon into the SendTo folder.

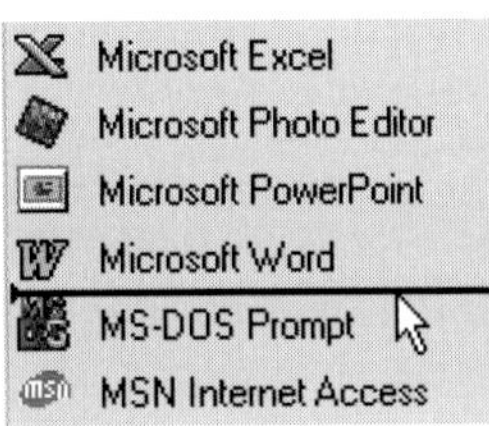

Rearranging Names on Menus

New program names land at the bottom of menus. Suppose you want to move a program name to the top, middle, or bottom of a menu. To move a name up or down the ladder, click and drag it upward or downward. When the black line is where you want the program name to be, release the mouse button. You can't rearrange menu names on the Start menu, by the way.

Creating Your Own Submenu

So you want to create a new submenu and put all your favorite programs on it. To do that, follow these steps:

1. Open My Computer and go to the C:\Windows\Start Menu\Programs folder.
2. Click the Folders button, if necessary, and, on the left side of the window, select the Start Menu folder to put your new submenu on the Start menu, or select Programs to put your new submenu on the Programs menu.
3. Choose File | New Folder, enter a name for your new submenu, and press ENTER.

Now all you have to do is put program names on your new submenu. Happy hunting!

Making the Screen Easier to Look At

Eyes were not meant to stare at computer screens all day, which makes being able to change the screen appearance all the more valuable. Experiment with different screen designs freely and often to find one that suits you. These pages explain how to choose one of the prefabricated Windows schemes for the desktop, choose a wallpaper image for the desktop, and prevent eyestrain.

In Chapter 2 "Make the Desktop Look Just-So" presents other ways to make the screen easier to look at.

Choosing a Screen Design

Figure 5.7 explains how to change the look of the Windows desktop. Since this book is for busy people, I neglect to explain the Item and

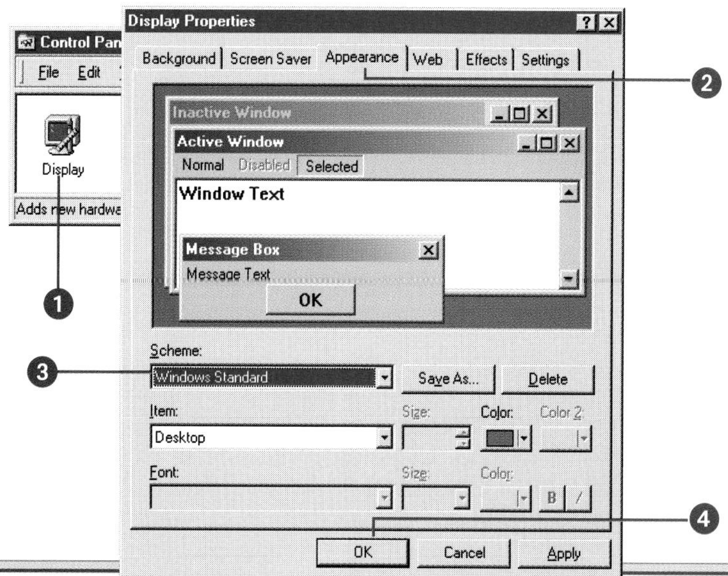

1 Either right-click the desktop and choose Properties or click the Start button, choose Settings | Control Panel, and double-click the Display icon.

2 Click the Appearance tab in the Display Properties dialog box.

3 From the Scheme drop-down menu, choose a screen design that tickles your fancy or is easy on your eyes. At the bottom of the menu are schemes that make text larger and easier to read.

4 Click OK to close the Display Properties dialog box.

Figure 5.7: For a design scheme that is easy on the eyes, visit the Appearance tab

Font choices on the Appearance tab (refer to Figure 5.7). One of these days, if you're desperate for anything to do, revisit the Appearance tab and choose a part of the screen from the Item menu, then choose a size and color for the part of the screen you chose. If the part of the screen is a title bar, menu, or other component with writing on it, you can choose a font size and color for the letters from the Font menu. In the end, you will click Cancel to destroy the monster you created or else choose Windows Standard from the Scheme drop-down menu.

Choosing Wallpaper for the Desktop

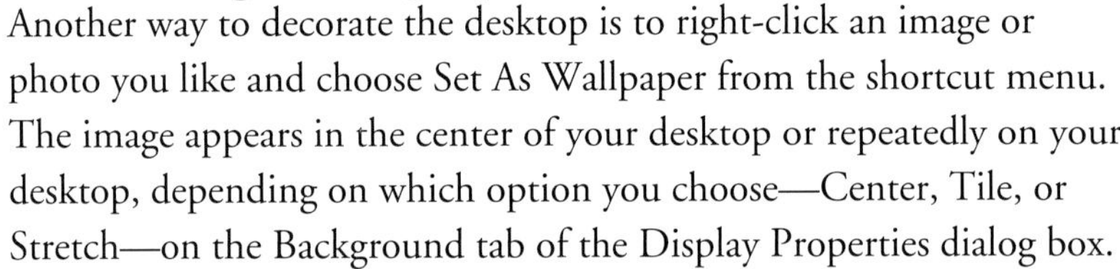

Another way to decorate the desktop is to right-click an image or photo you like and choose Set As Wallpaper from the shortcut menu. The image appears in the center of your desktop or repeatedly on your desktop, depending on which option you choose—Center, Tile, or Stretch—on the Background tab of the Display Properties dialog box.

To get to the Background tab, right-click a blank space on the Windows desktop, choose Properties, and click the Background tab. Then open the Picture Display drop-down menu and choose Center, Tile, or Stretch. The sample screen in the dialog box shows you what your choice looks like in real terms. To remove the so-called wallpaper from the desktop, choose None from the Wallpaper menu on the Background tab.

Ten Ways to Prevent Eyestrain

People who spend many working hours in front of a computer screen owe it to themselves to look after their health. Computers are dangerous to the lower back, the wrists, and the eyes. In Windows Me, you can do a number of things to reduce eyestrain—ten things, in fact. Several of the techniques for reducing eyestrain listed here are described elsewhere in this book, but all are mentioned here so you can pick and choose the techniques that help you.

As nature made you, you were not meant to stare at a computer screen all day. Nature wants you to scour the horizon for edible plants, high-protein animals, and ferocious predators. Fortunately,

Windows Me offers many techniques for reducing eyestrain. Herewith are some of them.

1. Keep the Monitor in the Proper Light. Glare on a monitor screen causes eyestrain. Keep the monitor out of direct light to reduce glare and use an adjustable light to illuminate whatever it is you are working with besides your computer and monitor. If you are using a laptop, however, do put the monitor in direct light. Laptops are sidelit or backlit, and they work better in full lighting.

2. Play with the Knobs on the Monitor. Those funny knobs on the monitor can be useful indeed. Twist them, turn them, and experiment until you find a look that is comfortable for your eyes.

3. Opt for a Smaller Screen Resolution. With a smaller screen resolution or area, everything looks bigger, although things can get cramped, too. To get a smaller resolution, right-click on the desktop and choose Properties. In the Display Properties dialog box, click the Settings tab. Then drag the Screen area slider to the left, so the setting reads 640 by 480 pixels, and click OK. Try this setting on for size.

4. Put Large Icons on the Desktop and in Folders. To make the icons on the desktop and in folders larger, right-click on the desktop and choose Properties. In the Display Properties dialog box, click the Effects tab, check the Use Large Icons check box, and click OK.

5. Make the Icons on the Start Menu Larger. To make the icons on the Start menu larger, right-click the Taskbar and choose Properties. Then, in the Taskbar Properties dialog box, uncheck the Show Small Icons in Start menu check box, and click OK.

6. Use Large Display Fonts. Large display fonts make menu choices and icon names easier to read. To see if you like them, right-click the desktop and choose Properties to open the Display Properties dialog box, and click the Settings tab. Then click the Advanced button. On the Font Size drop-down menu, choose Large Fonts. Windows says that the large fonts can only take effect after you restart the computer. Restart the computer and see how you like large fonts.

7. Make the Mouse Pointers Larger. Another way to make your eyes last longer is to make the mouse pointers larger. Click the Start button and choose Settings | Control Panel. Then double-click the Mouse icon, click the Pointers tab in the Mouse Properties dialog box, and choose Windows Standard (extra large) or Windows Standard (large) from the Scheme drop-down menu.

8. For Laptop Users: Use Mouse Pointer Trails. Pointer trails can help laptop users find the mouse pointer onscreen. To tell Windows to display pointer trails, click the Start button and choose Settings | Control Panel. Then double-click the Mouse icon, click the Pointer Options tab, and check the Show Pointer Trails check box in the Mouse Properties dialog box.

9. Choose a High-Contrast Screen Appearance. As a drastic measure, choose a high-contrast screen appearance. Right-click the desktop and choose Properties. In the Display Properties dialog box, click the Appearance tab, open the Scheme drop-down menu, and choose one of the High Contrast options.

10. Gaze at the Horizon. Every so often, leave your desk, step to the window, part the curtains, and stare. Stare at the most faraway point you can see. Stare and dream. Then blink a few times and marvel at how good the world looks when you're not staring at a computer screen.

CHAPTER 6

Traveling the Internet with Internet Explorer

INCLUDES

- Connecting to and disconnecting from the Internet
- Surfing the Internet quickly and productively
- Finding people's phone numbers and addresses on the Internet
- Subscribing to Web sites
- Copying photos, video, pictures, and text from the Web
- Choosing which Web site you go to first when you connect to the Internet

FAST FORWARD

Start Internet Explorer in a Bunch of Different Ways ➥ pp. 144–145

- Double-click the Internet Explorer icon on the desktop or Quick Launch toolbar.
- Double-click a URL shortcut icon on the desktop.
- Enter or choose a Web address on the Address toolbar and press ENTER.

Disconnect from the Internet ➥ p. 146

- Double-click the Internet icon and choose Disconnect in the Connected To dialog box.
- Right-click the Internet icon and choose Disconnect.

Search for Data on the Internet ➥ pp. 147–150

1. Click the Search button.
2. Enter keywords for the search in the text box in the Search bar, and then click the Search button.

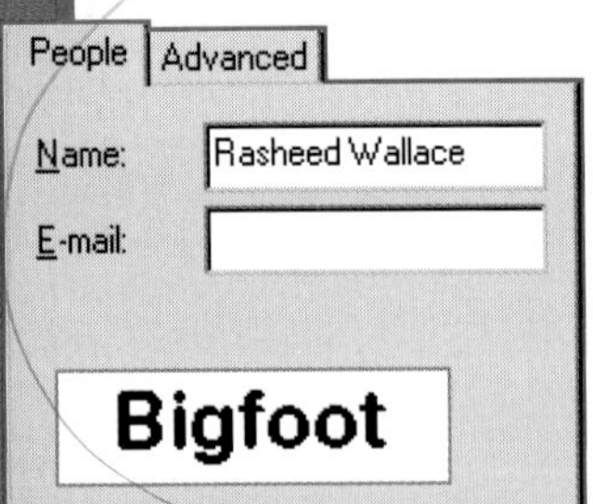

Find Someone's Address or Phone Number on the Internet ➥ pp. 150–151

1. Click the Start button and choose Find | People.
2. Choose a search service from the Look In list, enter a name, and click the Find Now button.
3. You can also click the Web Site button and search for addresses at a service's Web site.

Go Back to Web Pages You Visited Before ➥ pp. 152–153

- Click the Back or Forward button—or open the drop-down Back or Forward menu and choose a Web page.
- Click the History button, click a day or week on the Explorer bar, click a Web site name, and then click a page to display it onscreen.

Choose a Home Page— the Page You Go to First ➥ p. 157

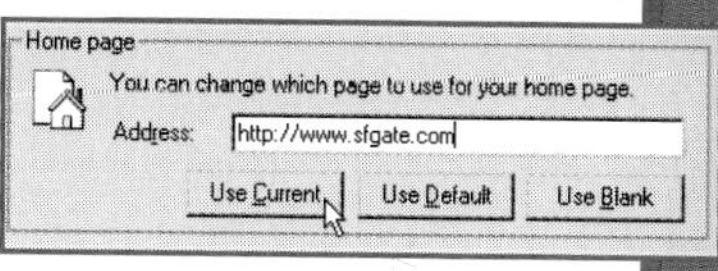

1. Go to the page you want to be your home page and choose Tools | Internet Options.
2. Click the Use Current button.

Download Web Pages Automatically So You Can View Them Offline ➥ pp. 159–160

1. Choose Favorites | Organize Favorites and double-click the Links folder icon.
2. Click the Web page you want to download automatically and then click the Make Available Offline check box.

Copy a Picture, Web Page, or Text from a Web Site ➥ pp. 161–162

- **Pictures and photos** Right-click the picture and choose Save Picture As. Then locate the folder in which to save the picture and click the Save button in the Save Picture dialog box.
- **Video** Right-click the video link and choose Save Target As. In the Save As dialog box, choose a folder in which to download the movie file, and click the Save button.
- **Text** Drag over the text and choose Edit | Copy or press CTRL C.
- **Web pages** Choose File | Save As, find a folder for storing the page in the Save Web Page dialog box, and click the Save button.

Windows Me comes with a *browser* for traveling the Internet called Internet Explorer. In this chapter, you learn how to explore cyberspace with Internet Explorer. Here you will find instructions for searching the Internet, finding the addresses and phone numbers of people on the Internet, subscribing to Web sites, and scavenging pictures and text from the Web. You also learn how to choose which Web site you visit first when you go on the Internet.

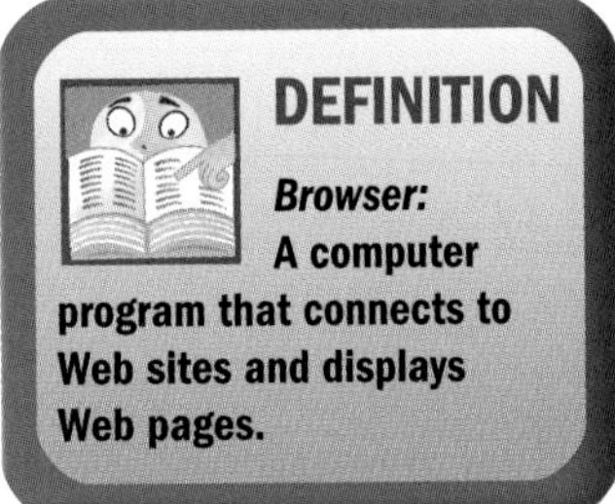

DEFINITION

Browser: **A computer program that connects to Web sites and displays Web pages.**

The Basics: Connecting and Disconnecting

Near the end of Chapter 4 "Connecting Your Computer to the Internet" explains how to set up a connection between your computer and the ISP or online service that you use.

After you have established the connection between your computer and an Internet service provider (ISP), you are ready to blast off. The next few pages explain how to start Internet Explorer, what to do if the connection doesn't work, and how to shut down Internet Explorer. Better fasten your safety belts.

TIP

You can decide for yourself how large the toolbar buttons in Internet Explorer are and whether they are labeled. Choose View | Toolbars | Customize. In the Customize Toolbar dialog box, experiment with the options on the Text Options and Icon Options drop-down menus.

The Six Ways to Start Internet Explorer

Figure 6.1 demonstrates the six different ways to start Internet Explorer and begin traveling the Internet. Don't worry, you won't be quizzed about these six ways. Some are better than others. It's hard to beat double-clicking the Internet Explorer icon on the desktop, but typing an address into the Address bar is convenient as well if you are a good typist and you know exactly where you want to go. Cruise the Internet a few times and you will quickly discover your favorite techniques.

What happens after you give the command to start Internet Explorer depends on how your computer is connected to the Internet. If you have a modem connection, you see a password dialog box. Fill it in, if necessary, and click OK. If you connect to the Internet by way

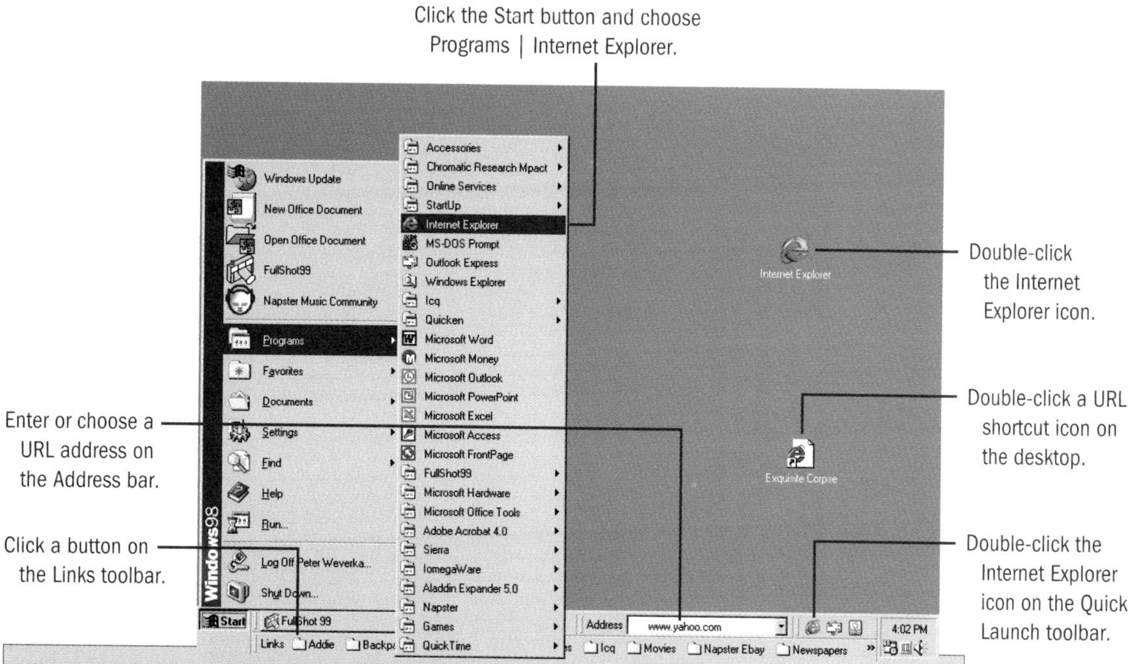

Click the Start button and choose Programs | Internet Explorer.

Double-click the Internet Explorer icon.

Double-click a URL shortcut icon on the desktop.

Double-click the Internet Explorer icon on the Quick Launch toolbar.

Enter or choose a URL address on the Address bar.

Click a button on the Links toolbar.

Figure 6.1: The six ways to open Internet Explorer

of a DSL line, cable modem, ISDN, or T1 line, you are connected as of the moment you turn on your computer and enter a password. In other words, you are permanently connected to the Internet.

Soon Internet Explorer opens your home page (refer to "Eight Ways to Search the Internet Faster" later in this chapter if you don't like the home page you see). If you use a modem connection, you can tell when you are truly online because the Internet icon—a pair of blinking computer monitors—appears in the tray in the lower-right corner of the screen next to the clock.

If You Can't Connect to the Internet...

A failed connection can occur for many reasons. The fault might lie not with you but elsewhere. There might be too much static on the phone line or a busy signal at the other end. To fix a missed connection from your side, try these techniques:

- See if the modem is connected correctly. Is the phone line plugged into the right place on both the computer and the modem?
- Make sure the address of your home page was entered correctly. Internet Explorer goes straight to the home page when you go online, but if the address is wrong it can't do that. If worse comes to worst, choose Tools | Internet Options and click the Use Default button on the General tab in the Internet Properties dialog box. Your default home page is likely to work.
- While the Internet Properties dialog box is open, click the Connections tab and make sure the Always Dial My Default Connection button is selected (if you aren't working on a network).
- I hate to say it, and it would certainly be tragic to have to do the setup work again, but see if you set up the connection between your computer and your Internet service provider or online service incorrectly. (See "Connecting Your Computer to the Internet" in Chapter 4.) If necessary, reestablish the connection.

Disconnecting from the Internet

Disconnecting from the Internet is certainly easier than getting on it. Follow these instructions to disconnect from the Internet:

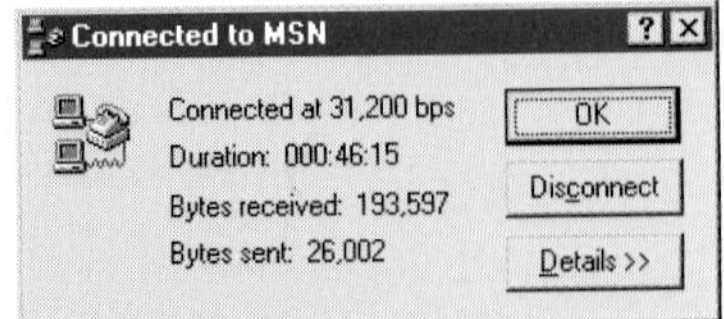

- Double-click the Internet icon and click the Disconnect button in the Connected To dialog box. Notice that the dialog box also shows how long you've been online and how fast your modem is.
- Right-click the Internet icon in the lower-right corner of the screen and choose Disconnect.
- Choose File | Work Offline.

Surfing the Internet

Surfing the Internet is a skill, and entire books have been written on the subject. To keep you from having to slog through one of those long, tedious, boring computer books, the following pages tell it in a hurry. These pages explain how to visit a Web site whose address you know, search the Internet, revisit sites you've been to, and bookmark a site so you can return to it. Also in this section are eight tried-and-true techniques for surfing the Internet quickly.

Visiting a Web Site Whose Address You Know

Every Web site and Web page has an address, also known as a URL, or *uniform resource locator*. While you are online, you can read the addresses of Web pages by glancing at the Address bar in Internet Explorer (if you don't see the Address bar, right-click a toolbar or the menu bar and choose Address Bar). To go to a Web site whose address you know, carefully type the address in the Address bar and press ENTER.

Later in this chapter, "Bookmarking a Site So You Can Go to It Quickly" explains how to bookmark sites so you can visit them later merely by making a menu selection.

If you've entered the address before, you're in luck. Internet Explorer may recognize the address, in which case it appears on the drop-down menu and you can select it. Or, if you entered the address recently, you can click the down arrow on the Address bar and, on the drop-down menu, click the address of the Web page you want to visit.

DEFINITION

Hyperlink: **An electronic shortcut between two Web pages or Web sites. By clicking a hyperlink, you can go directly to another location on the Web.**

Clicking Hyperlinks to Go Here and There

After you arrive at a Web site, you are sure to find many hyperlinks. Hyperlinks come in the form of text, pictures, and images. You can tell when your pointer is over a hyperlink because the pointer turns into a gloved hand. What's more, a brief description of where the link will take you appears onscreen as well.

Probably the most adventurous way to surf the Internet is to click hyperlinks and see where your search takes you. Fans of the World Wide Web are fond of saying that the Web is a three-dimensional world that brings together like-minded people from different places and different times. Click a few hyperlinks, see where your search leads, and decide for yourself whether the Web is a three-dimensional world or a mishmash of infomercials and unsound opinions. You can always backtrack by clicking the Back button, as "Revisiting Sites You've Been to Before" explains later in this chapter.

Later in this chapter, "Eight Ways to Search the Internet Faster" presents what is probably the fastest way to search—by starting from a search service's home page.

Searching for Information on the Internet

To look for information on the Internet, you choose a search service, enter criteria for the search, click the Search button, note how many Web pages your search yielded, look through the list of Web pages, click a page that you want to visit, and see the page onscreen. Sounds simple enough, but searching the Internet can be frustrating because the Internet is crowded with all sorts of junk. Follow these steps to search the Web with Internet Explorer's search commands:

1. Click the Search button. The Explorer bar appears on the left side of the screen, as shown in Figure 6.2. At the top of the Explorer bar are five option buttons for telling Internet Explorer what to search for. Make sure Find a Web Page is selected. You can click and drag the border between the Explorer bar and the Internet Explorer window to make the Explorer bar wider or narrower.

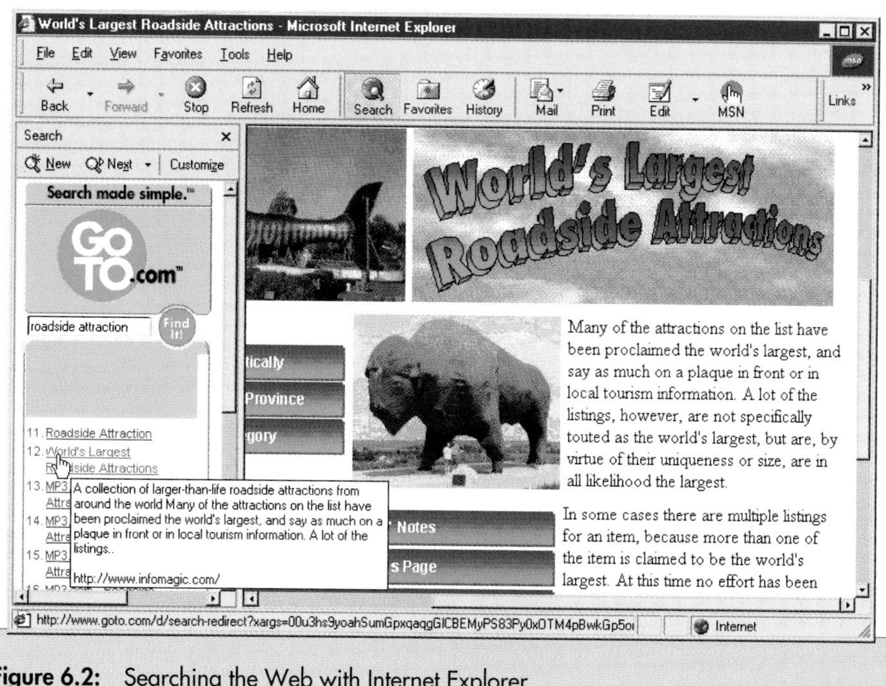

Figure 6.2: Searching the Web with Internet Explorer

2. In the Find a Page Containing text box, enter a keyword or keywords for the search.
3. Click the Search button (or the Find It button or whatever its called) on the Explorer bar. In a moment or two, a list of Web site names appears below the button. The order in which sites are listed depends on "keyword density," the number of times a keyword appears on the site and the keywords' proximity to the start of the page.

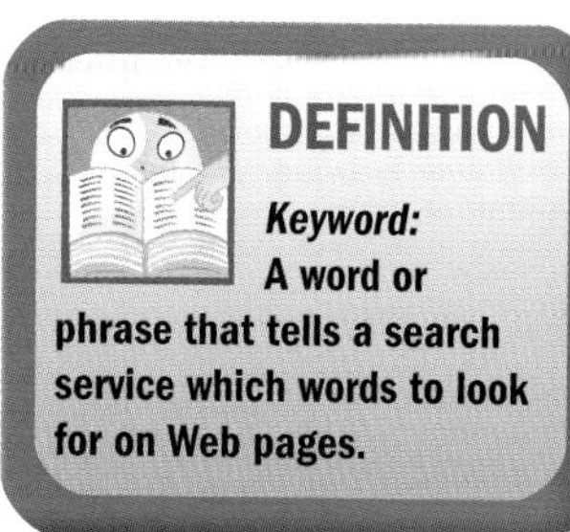

DEFINITION

Keyword: **A word or phrase that tells a search service which words to look for on Web pages.**

EXPERT ADVICE

The secret to finding what you are looking for on the Internet is to enter the right keyword or combination of keywords for the search. The more carefully you choose keywords, the more fruitful your search will be. Choose keywords that pinpoint what you are looking for. For example, entering *giants* finds all Web pages with that word on it—a lot of Web pages, no doubt. But entering *giants san francisco baseball schedule* yields only Web pages with all five of those keywords—considerably fewer Web pages than a search for *giants* yields.

TIP

To find what you are looking for on a long Web page, choose Edit | Find (on This Page) or press CTRL-F, enter a word or two in the Find dialog box, and click Find Next. The page scrolls to the word or words you entered.

4. Scroll down the list and click on a Web page that interests you (at the bottom of the list is a button you can click to see the next set of Web pages). By placing the pointer over a Web site name, you can read a brief description of the Web site. In a moment, the page you clicked appears on the right side of the screen, if indeed it is there, and Internet Explorer can find and display it.
5. Click the Search button to hide the Explorer bar and be able to read the Web page better. To see the Explorer bar again, click the Search button one more time.
6. To visit a different Web page, click its name on the list in the Explorer bar.

You can go back to the Explorer bar and click another Web page to visit it. Here's another bit of advice: Try pressing F11 to shrink the Internet Explorer buttons and get a better look at the Web page. Press F11 a second time to get the buttons back.

Finding People's E-Mail Addresses and Phone Numbers on the Internet

Data isn't the only thing you can search for on the Internet. You can also look for lost loves, long-lost friends, schoolyard bullies from days gone by, and bass players and drummers from obscure rock and roll bands. Figure 6.3 shows how to search for others' e-mail addresses, street addresses, and phone numbers.

EXPERT ADVICE

You can search with your favorite search service from the Explorer bar. To do so, click the Customize button in the Explorer bar, and, in the Customize Search Settings dialog box, select your favorite service and click the Use One Search Service for All Searches option button. The service you choose will appear automatically in the Explorer bar next time you click the Search button.

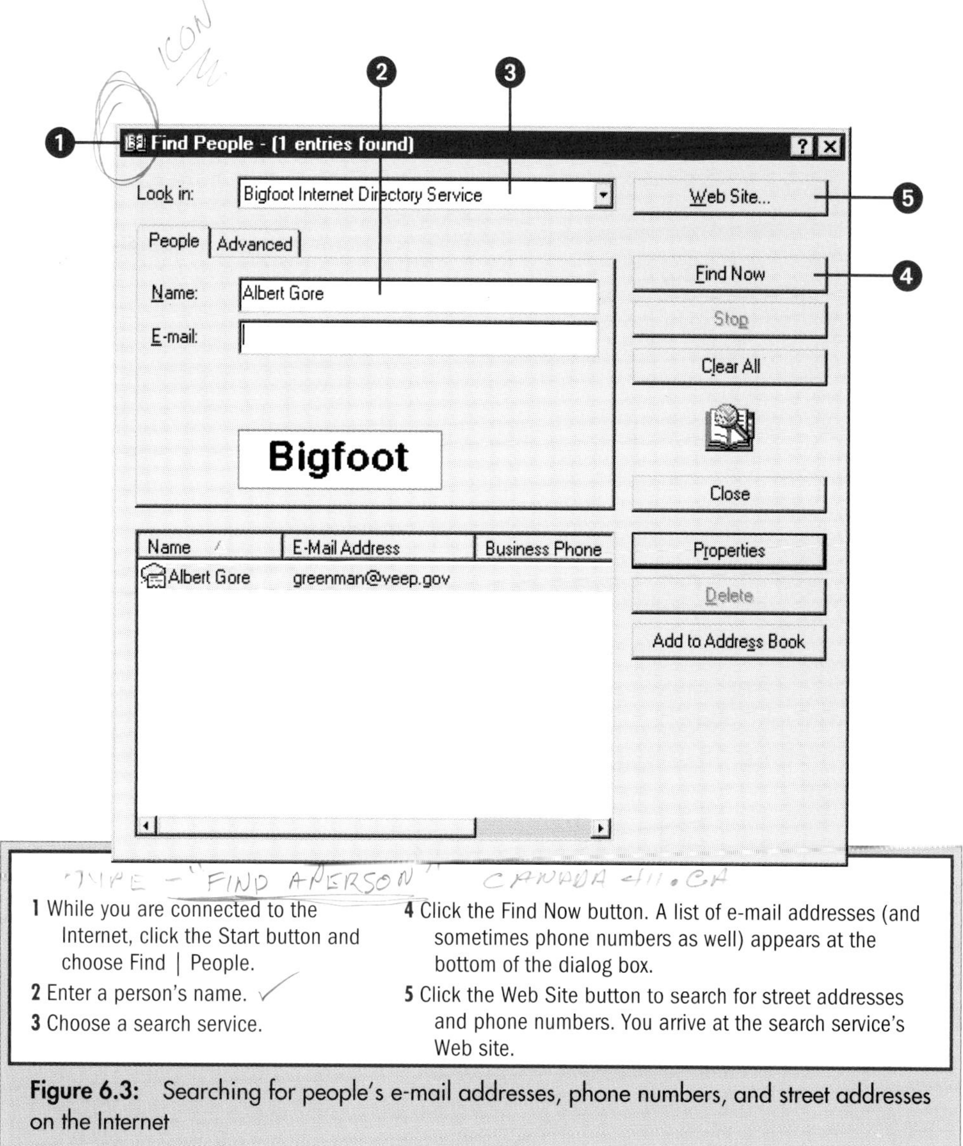

1 While you are connected to the Internet, click the Start button and choose Find | People.

2 Enter a person's name.

3 Choose a search service.

4 Click the Find Now button. A list of e-mail addresses (and sometimes phone numbers as well) appears at the bottom of the dialog box.

5 Click the Web Site button to search for street addresses and phone numbers. You arrive at the search service's Web site.

Figure 6.3: Searching for people's e-mail addresses, phone numbers, and street addresses on the Internet

Revisiting Web Sites You've Been to Before

Surfing the Internet is an adventure. Many a Web surfer ventures too far and wishes to return to a page that they visited before. Fortunately, backtracking is pretty easy. By clicking the Back button or its drop-down menu, you can visit the pages you viewed since you started

Internet Explorer. You can even view a Web page you visited in the past 20 days by clicking the History button. Following are the numerous ways to revisit sites with Internet Explorer.

Back and Forward Buttons Click the Back button (or press BACKSPACE) to see the page you last saw; click the Forward button to move ahead to the page from which you just retreated. Next to the Back and Forward buttons are drop-down menus that you can click to leap backward or forward by several Web pages. Don't be shy about using these drop-down menus. All you have to do to leap forward or backward is click the down-arrow and click a Web page name.

History Button Internet Explorer is watching you! The program keeps a record of the Web sites and Web pages you visited in the past 20 days. To return to one of those Web pages, you can click the History button and take it from there. Figure 6.4 demonstrates how to backtrack by clicking the History button.

Favorites Button The fastest way to revisit a site is to bookmark it (the subject of the next part of this chapter). To visit a site you bookmarked, do either of the following:

- Click the Favorites button. The Explorer bar opens and you see the contents of the C:\Windows\Favorites folder. Click the Links subfolder to see sites you bookmarked and then click a name.
- Choose Favorites | Links and click the name of the site you want to visit.

EXPERT ADVICE

Don't want your supervisor to know which Web sites you've been visiting? To remove a Web site from the History list in the Explorer bar, right-click the site and choose Delete. To remove all of the Web sites on the list, choose Tools | Internet Options and click the Clear History button on the General tab of the Internet Options dialog box. You can also tell Internet Explorer how many days' worth of Web sites to stockpile by entering a number in the Days to Keep Pages in History text box.

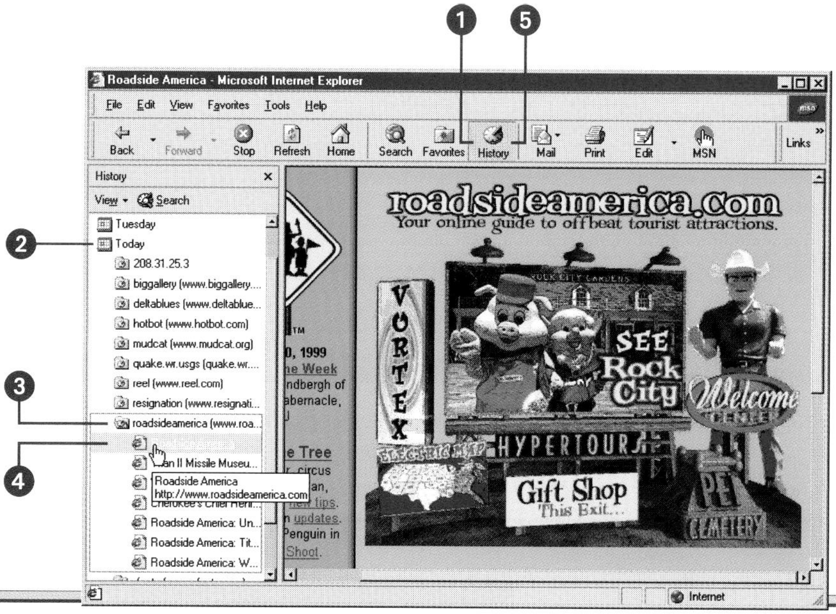

1 Click the History button. The Explorer bar opens.
2 Click a day of the week button or the Week Of button. You see an alphabetical list of the addresses of Web sites you visited that day or week.
3 Click a Web site. Web pages on the Web site appear below the site you clicked. You can click the View button and arrange the Web sites by date visited, in alphabetical order, and in other ways besides.
4 Click a Web page. The page appears in Internet Explorer.
5 Click the History button again to close the Explorer bar.

Figure 6.4: You can revisit any Web site you visited in the past 20 days

Bookmarking a Site So You Can Go to It Quickly

When you bookmark a site in Internet Explorer, you put a shortcut to it in the Favorites\Links folder. From there, opening it is easy (as the last paragraph in the previous section of this chapter makes plain). Don't be shy about bookmarking a site—you can always "unbookmark" it, as I explain shortly. These pages describe how to bookmark sites and manage your bookmarks.

Bookmarking Your Favorite Web Sites

Figure 6.5 shows how to bookmark a site and make visiting it very, very easy. You are hereby encouraged to bookmark a site if you feel the least bit desire to return to it later. Unless you bookmark a site, finding it again can be like finding the proverbial needle in a haystack.

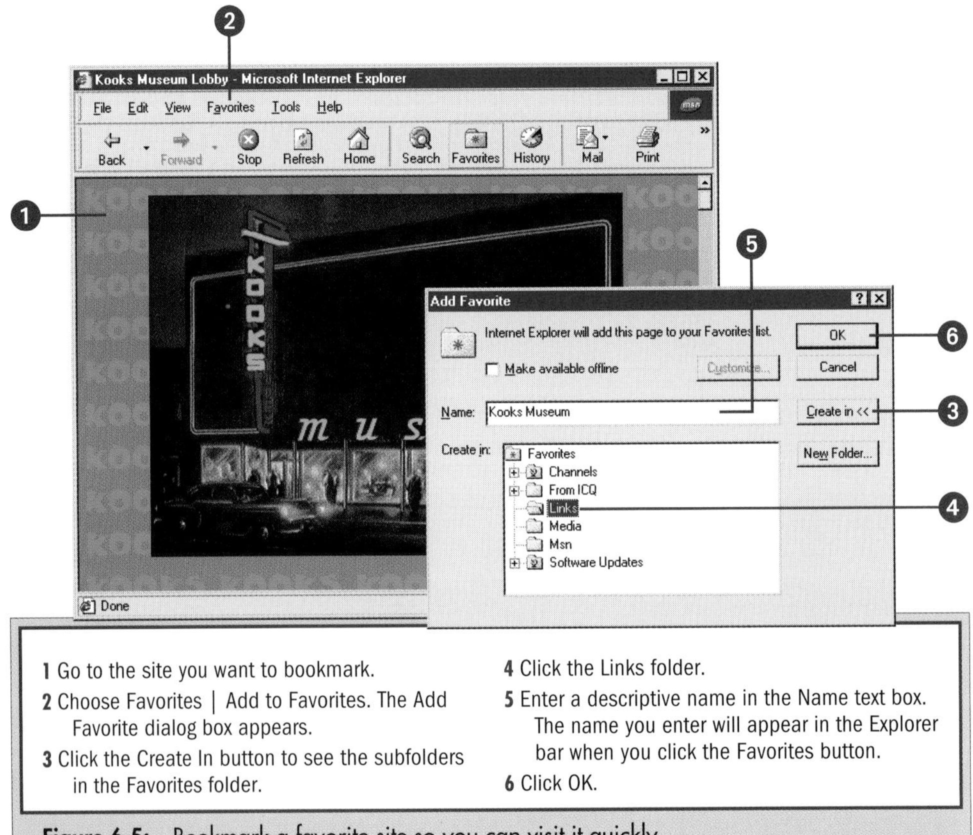

1 Go to the site you want to bookmark.

2 Choose Favorites | Add to Favorites. The Add Favorite dialog box appears.

3 Click the Create In button to see the subfolders in the Favorites folder.

4 Click the Links folder.

5 Enter a descriptive name in the Name text box. The name you enter will appear in the Explorer bar when you click the Favorites button.

6 Click OK.

Figure 6.5: Bookmark a favorite site so you can visit it quickly

EXPERT ADVICE

Be sure to click the Links folder and place the shortcut to your Web site there. If you forget to do so and put the shortcut in the Favorites folder, your Favorites folder will soon fill up with shortcuts to Web sites. Many computer programs make opening a file in the Favorites folder very easy, but if you crowd the Favorites folder with Web site shortcuts, you'll have trouble finding anything there.

Renaming, Deleting, and Managing Bookmarks

Follow these steps to rename a bookmarked site, "unbookmark" it, or change its position on the menu:

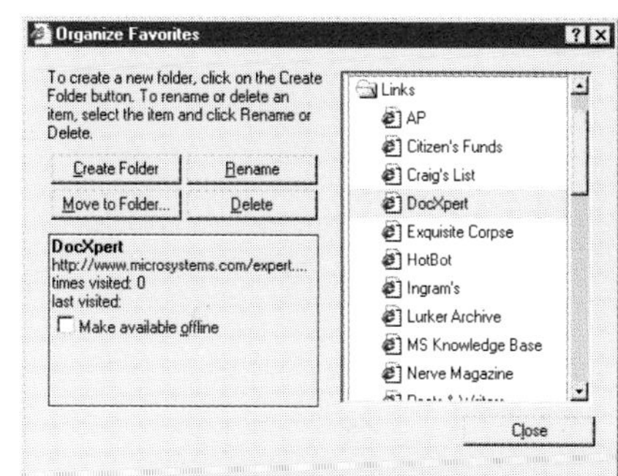

1. Choose Favorites | Organize Favorites. You see the Organize Favorites dialog box.
2. Click the Links folder to see the names of Web sites you have bookmarked.
3. Click a Web site name.
4. Delete, rename, or move the bookmark:
   - **Delete** Click the Delete button and then click Yes when you are asked if you really want to delete it.
   - **Rename** Click the Rename button and type a new name.
   - **Move to a different folder** Click the Move to Folder button and select another folder in the Browse for Folder dialog box.
   - **Move up or down in the list** Drag a Web site name up or down the dialog box to move it up or down on the Explorer bar and Favorites | Links menu.

EXPERT ADVICE

It would be a sad day if your computer crashed and you lost the shortcuts to all the sites you bookmarked. To make a backup copy of your bookmarks, open the C:\Windows\Favorites\Links folder and copy all of the shortcuts in the folder to a floppy disk. If your computer fails, copy the backup shortcuts on the floppy disk to the C:\Windows\Favorites\Links folder.

Eight Ways to Surf the Internet Faster

In some circles, the World Wide Web is known as the "World Wide Wait." If you get impatient when you surf the Internet, try one of these eight techniques for surfing the Internet faster. Some of the techniques are described elsewhere in the book, but all are gathered here because waiting for the Web is most frustrating indeed, and, busy person that you are, I want you to be able to pick and choose quickly among speed techniques.

1. Start the Search from a Service's Home Page. The easiest way to search the Internet is to take the time to go to the home page of a search service and use the search options that the service provides. Table 6.1 lists the Web addresses of different search services, or search engines, as they are sometimes called. The services in the table each provide special commands for searching the Internet. After you have experimented with a few services, you will find one you like—and you will learn to use its search commands well.

2. Learn to Use the Back Button and Forward Button Drop-Down Menus. Most people know that there is a Back button in Internet Explorer for revisiting pages and a Forward button for returning to pages you retreated from. But many people don't realize that you can click the down arrow beside the Back or Forward button and see a menu with all the pages you visited. Instead of going backward or forward one page at a time, use the Back or Forward drop-down menus to leap several pages ahead or behind.

Search Service	Address
Ask Jeeves	www.aj.com
AskMe	www.askme.com
Google	www.google.com
HotBot	www.hotbot.com
Infoseek	www.infoseek.com
InvisibleWeb	www.invisibleweb.com
Magellan	www.mckinley.com
Metacrawler	www.metacrawler.com
Open Directory Project	www.dmoz.org
Snap!	www.snap.com
Yahoo	www.yahoo.com

Table 6.1: Search Services and Their Home Page Addresses

3. Bookmark Pages You Intend to Revisit. By bookmarking pages and putting them in the Links folder in the Favorites folder, you can get to them quickly. All you have to do is click the Favorites button, click the Links folder icon, and click the page. You can also choose Favorites | Links and click the name of a page. See "Bookmarking a Site So You Can Go to It Quickly " earlier in this chapter.

4. Change Your Home Page. When you start Internet Explorer and connect to the Internet, by default you go to what Microsoft calls your "home page." You also go there when you click the Home button. Unfortunately, software manufacturers have a habit of commandeering the home page. When you install new software, you sometimes discover that your home page has mysteriously become that of a software manufacturer! Do you want to go there every time you visit the Internet? Do you want to go to a glittery corporate Web site that takes a long time to load?

Instead of a corporate home page, choose a home page that you are genuinely interested in and visit often. For that matter, choose a page that loads quickly so you don't have to wait before leaping onto the Internet. To choose a home page of your own, go to the page you want to make your home and choose Tools | Internet Options. You see the General tab of the Internet Options dialog box. Click the Use Current button. The address of the page you like appears in the Address box. Click OK.

5. Open a Second Window for Surfing. Here's a little trick that makes surfing the Internet a little faster: Open a second Internet Explorer window. With two windows open, you can surf the Internet in one window and leave the other open to a page you want to stick with. And if you get stuck on a Web page that is taking too long to download, you can simply click the Close button to close the window without closing Internet Explorer altogether.

To open a second window, press CTRL-N or choose File | New | Window.

6. Make Use of the Edit | Find Command on Long Web Pages. On a Web page with lots of text, finding what you are looking for can be difficult. Rather than strain your eyes, use the Find command. All you have to do is enter the text you're looking for and click the Find Next button. The page scrolls to the text you entered. Choose Edit | Find to activate the Find command.

7. Click the Stop Button Early and Often. Don't be afraid to click the Stop button. If you click a hyperlink and nothing happens for a moment or two, chances are nothing will happen. Click the Stop button to stop the search and turn it in another direction.

8. Don't Display Fancy Stuff on Web Pages. A lot of time on the Web is wasted waiting for fancy pictures and animations to arrive on your computer. To spare yourself the wait, you can tell Internet

Explorer not to download fancy stuff but instead only download it if you say so. Follow these steps:

1. Choose Tools | Internet Options.
2. Click the Advanced tab in the Internet Options dialog box.
3. Scroll to Multimedia in the list and uncheck Show Pictures, Play Animations, Play Videos, and/or Play Sounds.

You can still see pictures or play animations on Web pages after you have elected not to show them. To do so, right-click the picture or animation icon on the Web page and choose Show Picture on the shortcut menu.

Making Web Pages Available for Offline Viewing

To save a bit of time and keep the telephone lines from being tied up, you can download Web pages from the Internet and view them offline. Despite appearances, a Web page is nothing more than a computer file. After the Web page files have been downloaded to your computer, you can view them at your leisure as though you were viewing them on the Internet. Viewing pages offline is a fast way to surf the Internet because you don't have to wait for the pages to download from the Internet—the pages are already downloaded and on your computer. However, downloading the pages can take time, depending on how many graphics, animations, and other fancy gizmos they contain. Also, you can't click hyperlinks (because your computer isn't connected to the Internet), and the Web pages aren't updated.

In order to download a Web page automatically, you must have bookmarked it. Figure 6.6 shows how to tell Internet Explorer which Web pages you want to download automatically and read while you are not connected to the Internet.

Earlier in this chapter, "Bookmarking Your Favorite Web Sites" explains how to bookmark Web pages.

To download the pages you have earmarked for downloading, go online and choose Tools | Synchronize. You see the Items to Synchronize dialog box. Make sure a check mark appears beside each page you want to download, and then click the Synchronize button.

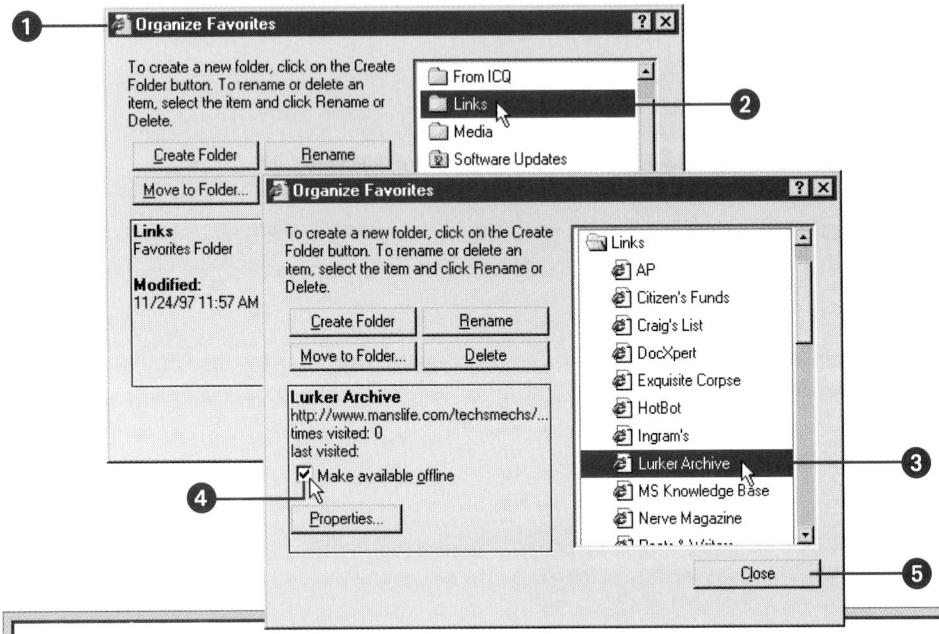

1 Choose Favorites | Organize Favorites to open the Organize Favorites dialog box.

2 Click the Links folder icon. You see a list of the Web sites you have bookmarked.

3 Click the Web page you want to download automatically.

4 Click the Make Available Offline check box.

5 Click the Close button.

Figure 6.6: Telling Internet Explorer which Web pages you want to download automatically

The Synchronizing dialog box appears as Web pages are copied to your computer.

After you disconnect from the Internet, choose Favorites | Links and then choose the name of the Web page you downloaded to your computer to view the Web page. Of course, you can also click the Favorites button, click the Links folder in the Explorer bar, and click the name of the Web page.

EXPERT ADVICE

If you prefer to view Web pages while you are offline, you likely need more room for storing downloaded pages. To get more room, choose Tools | Internet Options and then click the Settings button on the General tab of the Internet Options dialog box. In the Settings dialog box, drag the Amount of Disk Space to Use slider to the right to get more space for Web pages.

Copying Pictures, Photos, Videos, and Text from the Internet

To the delight of copyright lawyers and the displeasure of photographers and artists, you can copy any picture on the Internet. You can also copy text and entire Web pages. You can even copy videos. Follow these steps to copy an image, photograph, or picture:

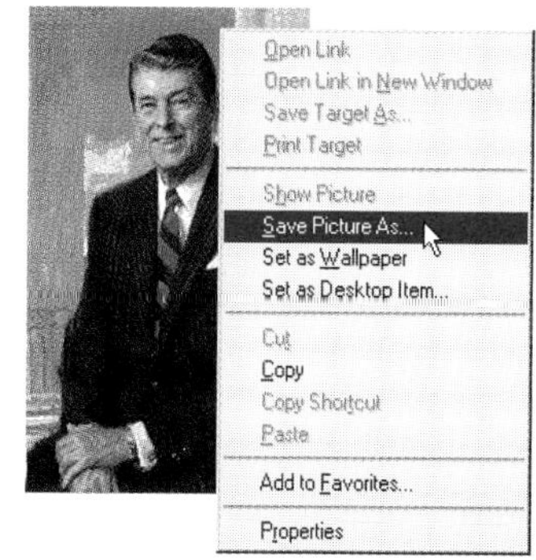

1. Wait until the image, picture, or photograph has downloaded to your computer.
2. Right-click the image and choose Save Picture As.
3. Use the tools in the Save Picture dialog box—the drop-down Save In menu and Up One Level button—to locate the folder in which you want to save the image.
4. Double-click the folder so its name appears in the Save In box.
5. Enter a descriptive name for the image in the File Name text box if you want to.
6. Click the Save button.

To copy a video, right-click its hyperlink and choose Save Target As. You see the File Download dialog box and then, shortly afterward, the Save As dialog box. Choose a folder for the video, enter a name in

WARNING

Copying text or art that you didn't write or create yourself is okay, but using the material in your own work without obtaining the permission of the creator or owner is considered a violation of the copyright laws.

the File Name text box if you want, and click the Save button. Slowly but surely, the video file is downloaded to your computer. To view the file, open My Computer, locate the file, and double-click it.

To copy text from a Web page, simply drag the mouse pointer over it (or press CTRL-A to copy the entire page). When the text is highlighted, right-click it and choose Copy from the shortcut menu. The text is copied to the Clipboard. Click where you want to paste it, and choose File | Paste or click the Paste button.

To copy an entire Web page, choose File | Save As. In the Save Web Page dialog box, locate the folder where you want to save the Web page, and click the Save button.

To print an entire Web page, click the Print button. That's all there is to it. If you want to be choosy about how the page is printed, choose File | Print and choose from the options in the Print dialog box. Go this route, for example, if you want to print more than one copy or print the pages that are linked to the page you want to print.

CHAPTER 7

Communicating with the Outside World

INCLUDES

- Storing the addresses of clients and friends in the Address Book
- Sending and receiving e-mail messages and files
- Visiting, posting messages to, and subscribing to newsgroups
- Printing files and canceling print jobs

FAST FORWARD

Look Up a Name and Address in the Address Book ➥ pp. 167–170

1. In Outlook Express, click the Addresses button.
2. Scroll to find a name on the list, and double-click the name to see a box with addressee information.

Send a File with an E-mail Message ➥ pp. 170–171

1. Click the Attach button.
2. In the Insert Attachment dialog box, locate and select the file or files you want to send. To select more than one file, hold down the CTRL key and click.

Send an E-mail Message ➥ pp. 170–172

1. Click the New Mail button.
2. Fill in the New Message window and click the Send button.

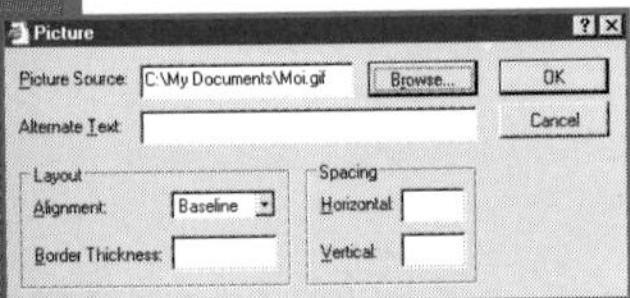

Send a Picture Inside of an E-mail Message ➥ p. 173

1. Place the cursor where you want the graphic to go and choose Insert | Picture.
2. Click the Browse button, locate and select the graphic in the Picture dialog box, and click Open.
3. Choose an Alignment option.
4. Click OK.

Read E-mail Messages That Were Sent to You ➥ pp. 174–176

1. Select the Inbox folder to open the Inbox window.
2. Click the message you want to read in the top of the window. The message text appears in the bottom of the Inbox window.

Explore the Newsgroups to Find One of Interest ➥ pp. 178–180

1. Click the folder icon of the news server you want to explore.
2. Click the Newsgroups button.
3. Type a search word in the Display Newsgroups Which Contain text box.
4. Click a newsgroup name and click the Go To button.

Subscribe to a Newsgroup ➥ p. `181

- Click a newsgroup in the Newsgroup Subscriptions dialog box and then click the Subscribe button.
- Right-click a newsgroup's name in the Outlook bar and choose Subscribe on the shortcut menu.

Post a Message on a Newsgroup ➥ pp. 181–183

- Click the message that needs a reply, if you want to reply to a message.
- Click the New Post button to submit a message on a new topic, the Reply Group button to reply to someone else's message, or the Reply button to reply directly to the author of a message.

Keep a File from Being Printed ➥ pp. 185–186

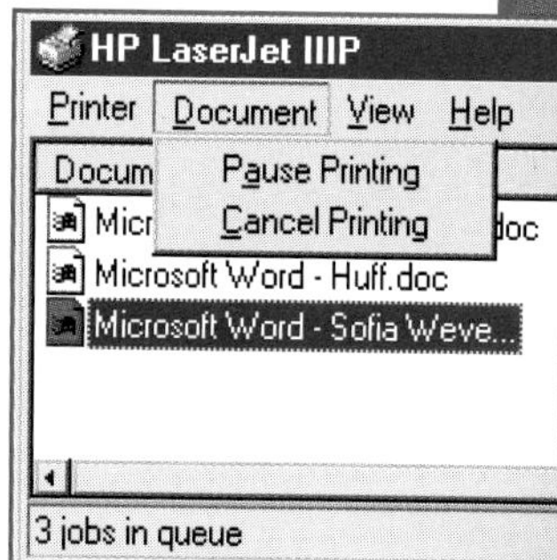

1. Double-click the Printer icon in the lower-right corner of the screen.
2. In the Printer window, either choose Printer | Purge Print Documents to keep all files from printing, or click a file on the list and choose Document | Cancel Printing to keep a single file from printing.

This chapter explains how to communicate with the rest of the world from your computer. You've been hibernating too long. Everyone is asking about you. The world wants to know where you've been, what your opinions are, and how long you propose to stay in hiding. In this chapter, you learn how to bust out of your cyber-cocoon and tell the world what's what.

Windows Me includes a program called Outlook Express for sending e-mail and for visiting newsgroups and posting messages to newsgroups on the Internet. This chapter explains Outlook Express. It also spells out how to print files. You will also learn how to keep the addresses of friends, coworkers, and clients in the Windows Address Book where you can get to them in a hurry.

Outlook Express: Sending and Receiving E-mail

In Chapter 4, "Connecting Your Computer to the Internet" explains how to establish a connection between your computer and the Internet.

As long as you have a modem and an Internet connection, you can send and receive e-mail messages. *E-mail,* or *electronic mail,* is the computer equivalent of letters sent through the post. It goes without saying, but e-mail messages reach their recipients faster than letters and postcards (people who prefer e-mail to conventional mail sometimes call conventional mail services "snail mail"). You can even attach files to e-mail messages, as the following pages demonstrate. Sorry, you can't send chocolate by e-mail. Nor can you put a drop of perfume on an e-mail message or enclose a lock of hair.

Read on to find out how to send and receive e-mail, send and receive computer files, and keep addresses in the Address Book. Oh, I almost forgot: To start Outlook Express, double-click the Outlook Express icon on the desktop or the Quick Launch toolbar, or else click the Start button and choose Programs | Outlook Express.

Entering Addresses in the Address Book

Rather than enter the e-mail addresses of clients and friends over and over again when you send them e-mail, you can keep addresses in the Address Book. After an address is in the book, all you have to do to address an e-mail message is select a name from a list. Besides e-mail addresses, you can keep street addresses, phone numbers, fax numbers, and other stuff in the Address Book. The Address Book is a good place to store information about clients, coworkers, and friends. Following are instructions for entering a name in the Address Book, looking up a name, and changing the particulars about a person whose name you entered.

SHORTCUT

To very quickly enter in the Address Book the e-mail address of someone who has sent you e-mail, right-click the sender's message in the Inbox and choose Add Sender to Address Book on the shortcut menu.

Entering a Name and Address in the Address Book

Figure 7.1 demonstrates how to enter a person's name, e-mail address, and other pertinent information in the Address Book. Entering a name is pretty simple, except where these tabs in the Properties dialog box are concerned:

- **Choosing how to display the entry in the Address Book** On the Name tab, open the Display drop-down menu and choose how you want the name or business to appear in the Address Book. Names appear last name first, unless you choose a different option from the Display drop-down menu.
- **Recording e-mail addresses** Enter the e-mail address in the E-Mail Addresses text box on the Name tab and click the Add button.

TIP

On the Other tab, describe the person and say why you entered him or her in the Address Book. Later, when you remove names from the book, you can go to the Other tab, and find out who the person is and whether he or she needs removing.

Looking Up Names and Perhaps Changing Addressee Information

Figure 7.2 shows how to look up a client or friend in the Address Book and perhaps change the particulars concerning his or her address, phone number, and whatnot. In an Address Book with many

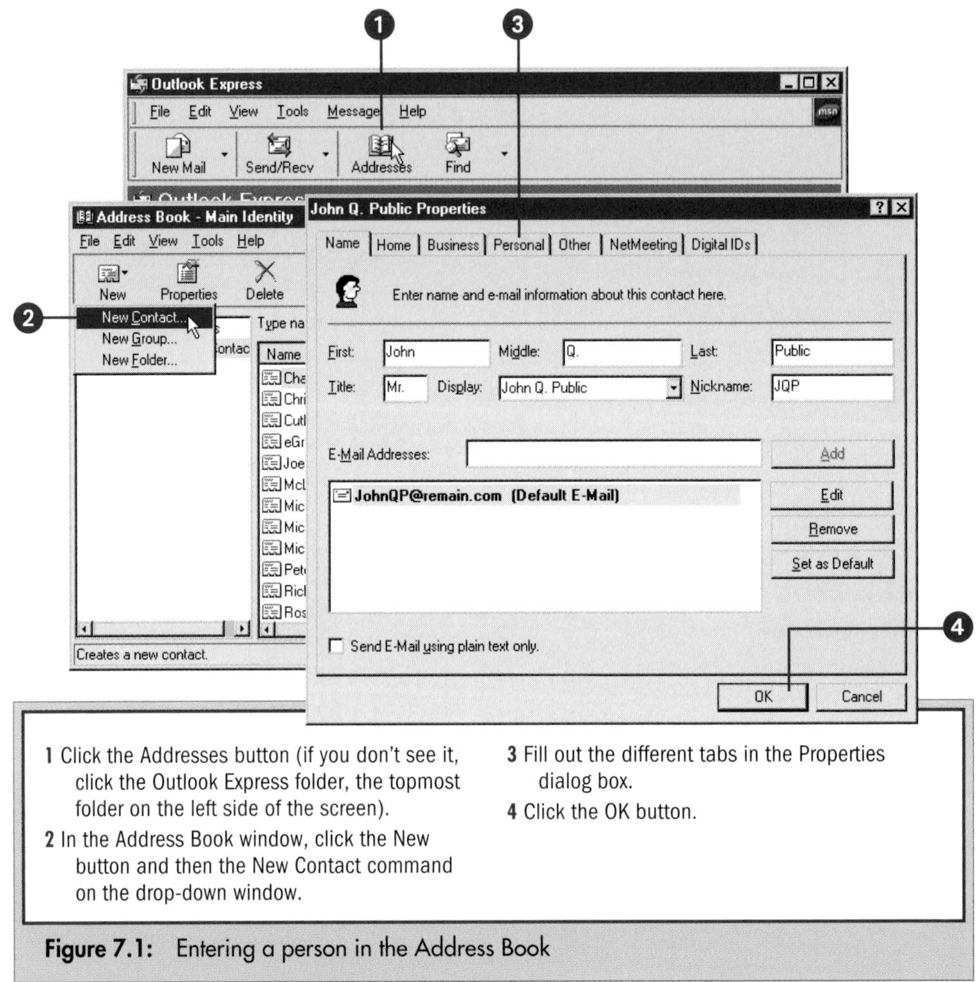

Figure 7.1: Entering a person in the Address Book

names, try these techniques for finding a name if scrolling doesn't do the job:

- Enter the first couple of letters in the Type Name or Select from List text box. The list scrolls to the name you entered.
- Click the Name button (it's located at the top of the Name column—choose View | Details if you don't see it). Click once to arrange names in alphabetical order from Z to A, click again

to arrange names by first name, and again to arrange names by first name from Z to A.

- If worse comes to worst, click the Find People button, enter a name, choose Address Book from the Look In drop-down menu, and click the Find Now button in the Find People dialog box.

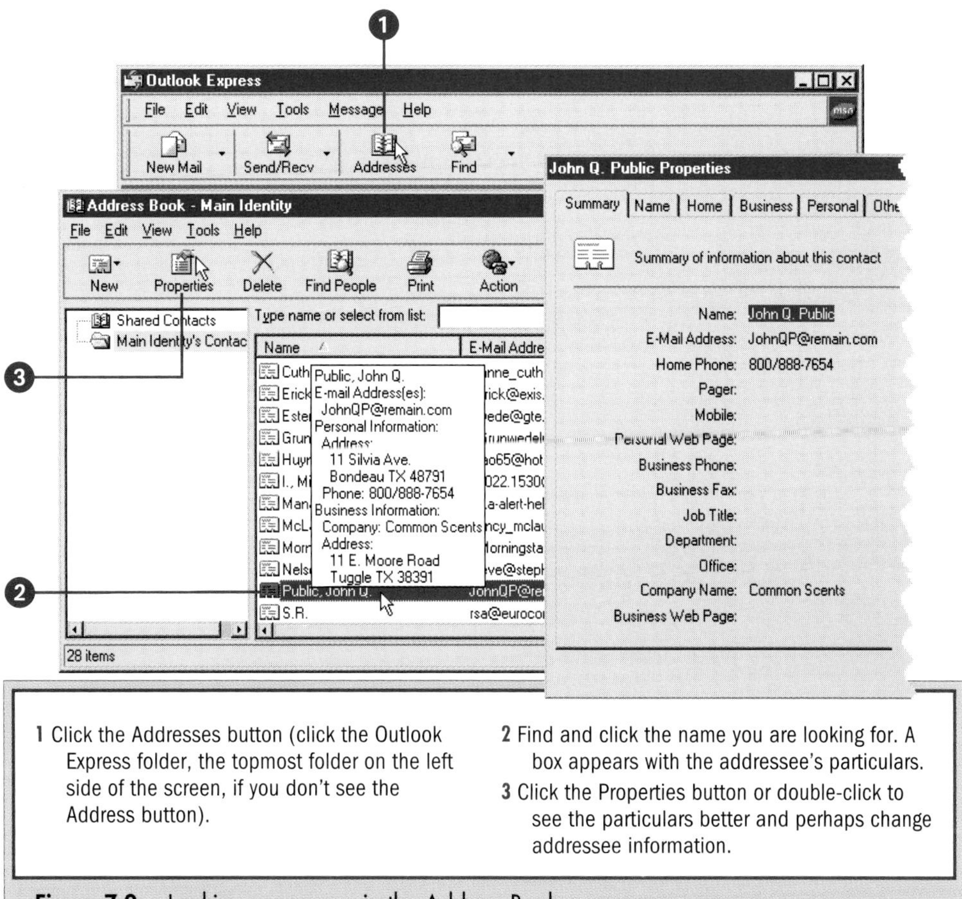

1 Click the Addresses button (click the Outlook Express folder, the topmost folder on the left side of the screen, if you don't see the Address button).

2 Find and click the name you are looking for. A box appears with the addressee's particulars.

3 Click the Properties button or double-click to see the particulars better and perhaps change addressee information.

Figure 7.2: Looking up a name in the Address Book

EXPERT ADVICE

Losing an Address Book with many important names and addresses would be tragic. To back up the Address Book, go to the C:\Windows\Application Data\Microsoft\Address Book folder and copy the Address Book file to a floppy disk. While you're visiting the Address Book folder, create a desktop shortcut for the Address Book if you often look up names there. "Create the Shortcut Icons You Need" in Chapter 2 explains how to create a shortcut.

Composing and Addressing an E-mail Message

As long as the address of the person to whom you want to send an e-mail message is on file in the Address Book, composing an e-mail message is pretty simple. Follow these steps to do so:

1. Click the New Mail button. You see the New Message window.

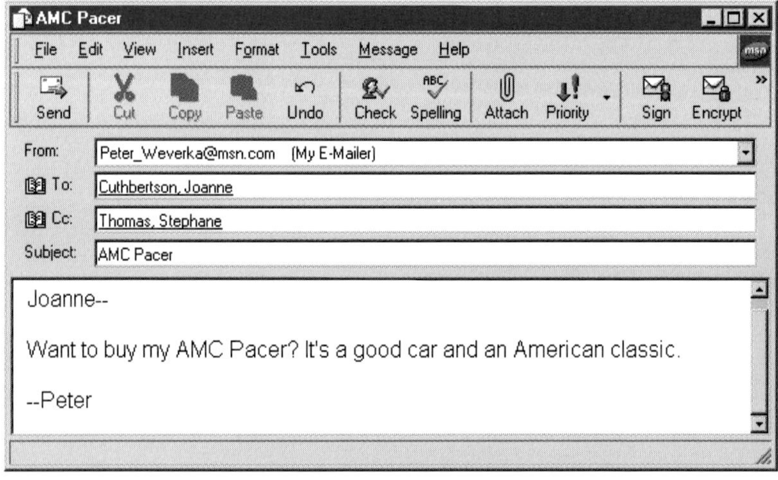

2. On the Subject line, briefly describe your message. When others receive the message, they will see what you type on the Subject line first. Notice how the New Message window changes names after you enter a subject.

SHORTCUT

With a little luck, you don't have to open the Select Recipients dialog box. Instead, type the first few letters of the recipient's name in the To box. If Outlook Express recognizes the name from the Address Book, the name appears.

3. Type your message in the bottom half of the New Message window. You can use the buttons in the New Message window to format the message in various ways. For example, you can boldface or italicize parts of the message. And don't forget to press F7 or choose Tools | Spelling to spell-check your message.
4. To tell Outlook Express who gets the message, click the tiny envelope next to the word "To." You see the Select Recipients dialog box with the names of people in the Address Book who have e-mail addresses.

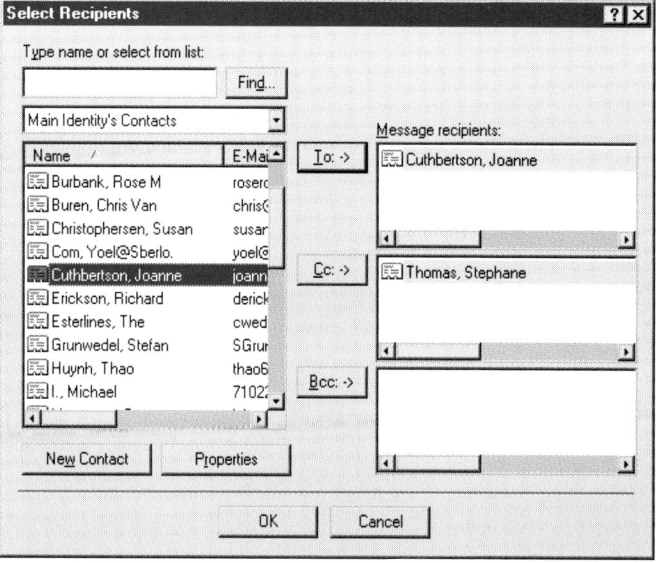

5. Click a name on the list and then click the To button. The name you chose appears in the Message recipients box. You can also send copies and blind copies of messages:
   - **Copy (Cc)** When you send a copy of the message, the person who receives it is told that a copy has been sent and is given the name of the people who received copies. To send a copy, click a Name on the list and then click the Cc button.

- **Blind copy (Bcc)** When you send a blind copy, the person who receives the message is *not* told that a copy was sent to a third party. To send a blind copy, click the name and then click the Bcc button.

6. Click OK to close the Select Recipients dialog box. The names of people who will receive the message now appear in the New Message window.
7. Click the Send button (or choose File | Send Later).

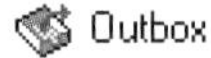

The message is sent right away if you happen to be connected to the Internet, but if you are not connected, the Connect To dialog box appears. Click Cancel if you want to hold off sending the message. Until you send a message, it is kept in the Outbox. To edit or perhaps delete a message that you haven't sent yet, click the Outbox folder in the Outlook bar on the left side of the screen, select the message, and click Delete to delete it or double-click to read and change it.

Sending a File Along with Your E-mail Message

Yes, it can be done. You can send files along with e-mail messages. Follow these steps to send a file and an e-mail message at the same time:

1. While the New Message window is open and you are composing a message, either click the Attach button or choose Insert | File Attachment. You see the Insert Attachment dialog box.
2. Locate and select the file or files you want to send. To select more than one file, hold down the CTRL key and click.
3. Click the Attach button. A new text box called Attach appears in the New Message window and you see the names of the file or files you want to send:

Attach: Fig7-02.pcx (74.1 KB) Fig7-01.pcx (57.8 KB)

Sending a Picture Inside of a Message

If it pleases you, you can put a graphic inside of an e-mail message you send as long as the file is a GIF or JPEG image. To view the graphic, the person to whom you send it must have an e-mail program like Outlook Express that is capable of displaying graphics. Take note of where on your computer the graphic file is and follow the instructions in Figure 7.3 to send your graphic inside of a message.

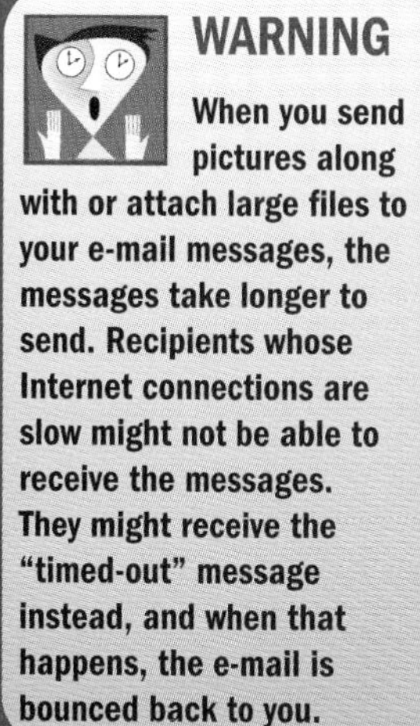

WARNING

When you send pictures along with or attach large files to your e-mail messages, the messages take longer to send. Recipients whose Internet connections are slow might not be able to receive the messages. They might receive the "timed-out" message instead, and when that happens, the e-mail is bounced back to you.

Sending and Receiving Your E-mail

Sending and collecting e-mail is kind of confusing, since how the mail is sent and received depends on whether your computer is

1 Place the cursor where you want the graphic to go.
2 Choose Insert | Picture.
3 Click the Browse button.
4 In the Picture dialog box, locate the graphic file, select it, and then click the Open button.
5 Choose an Alignment option.
6 Click OK.

Figure 7.3: Sending a picture inside of an e-mail message

TIP

To merely send or receive your mail, click the down arrow beside the Send/Recv button and choose Receive All or Send All.

connected to the Internet and how you give the command to send and receive e-mail:

- **Connected to the Internet** When you are connected to the Internet and you click the Send button to send an e-mail message or the Send/Recv button to receive and collect your mail, outgoing messages are sent from the Outbox and incoming messages arrive in the Inbox.
- **Not connected to the Internet** When you are not connected to the Internet and you click the Send or Send/Recv button, you see the Connect To dialog box so you can connect to the Internet and send your messages.

After you are connected, you see a message box like the one shown here. It shows how many messages are being received. You can click the Details button to see, on the Tasks tab at the bottom of the message box, whether e-mail is being successfully sent and received.

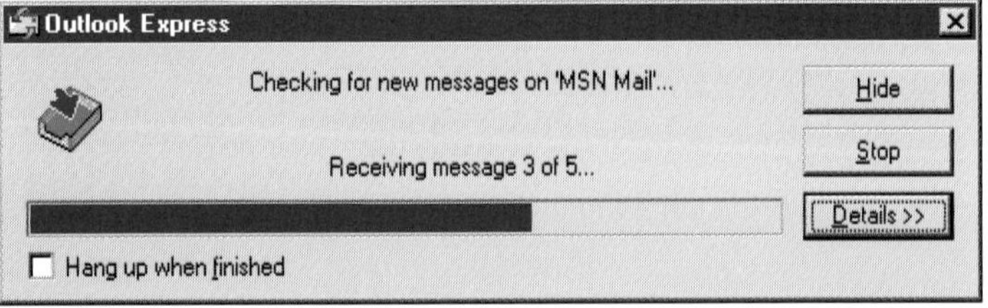

If you've received mail, the Inbox folder name appears in boldface, the number of messages you've received appears in parentheses beside the Inbox folder, and a tiny image of an envelope appears in the lower-right corner of the screen next to the clock.

Reading E-mail Messages and Files

Messages arrive in the Inbox folder. To see the Inbox and read messages there, click the Inbox folder icon in the Outlook bar. As shown in Figure 7.4, you can see senders' names, message subjects, and the date on which messages were received in the top half of the Inbox window. In the bottom half is the text of the message that has been selected.

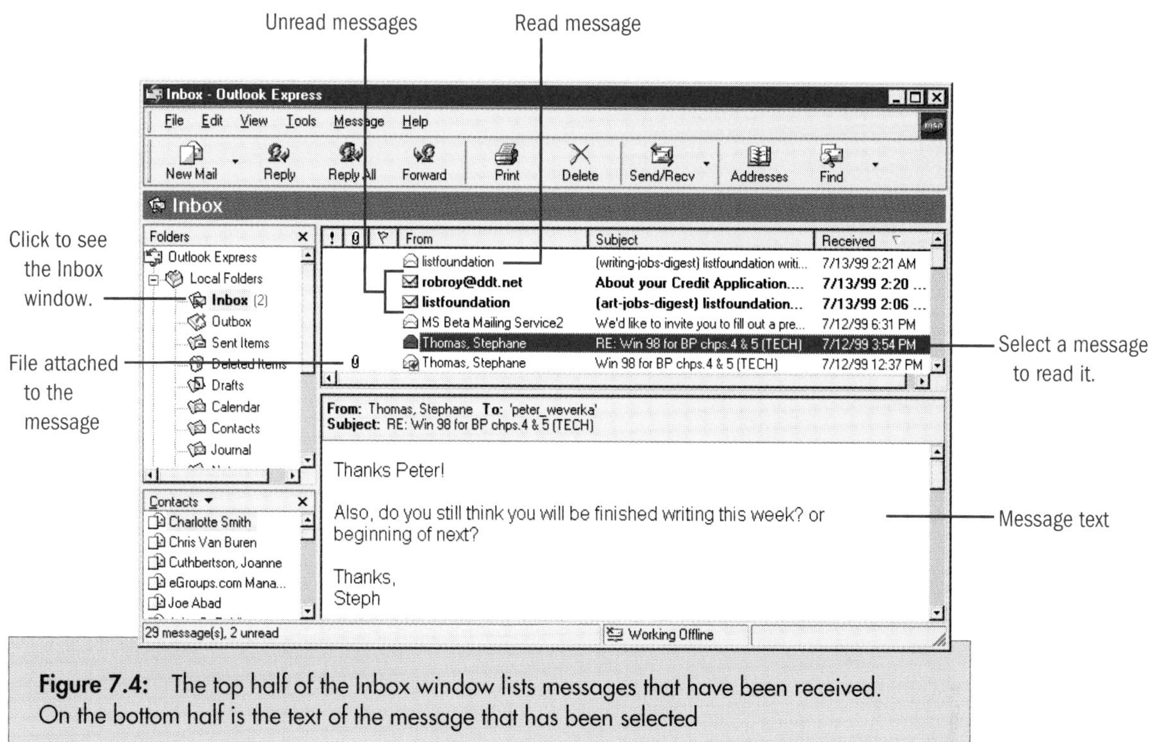

Figure 7.4: The top half of the Inbox window lists messages that have been received. On the bottom half is the text of the message that has been selected

To get a quick read of what is in the Inbox window, observe the following:

- An open envelope appears next to messages that have been read. Next to unread messages is a closed envelope.
- A paperclip appears next to a message if a file was sent along with it.
- Click the From button or the Received button (located at the top of the From and Received columns) to arrange messages by name or by date.
- Drag the border between the top and bottom half of the window to see more messages or to get more room for displaying the text of a message.

EXPERT ADVICE

To make text easier to read in the Outlook window, try this technique: Choose Tools | Options and click the Read tab in the Options dialog box. Then click the Fonts button, and, in the Fonts dialog box, choose a font you find easy to read. You can also choose a Font Size option to make text larger or smaller.

Reading an E-mail Message

To read an e-mail message, click it in the top half of the Inbox window (see Figure 7.4) and read it in the bottom half. Use the scroll bar to read a message in its entirety, or, if the message is especially large, double-click the sender's name in the top half of the window. The message appears in a window of its own. Click the Maximize button to make the window fill the screen so that you can read the message more comfortably.

Opening and Saving Files That Were Sent to You

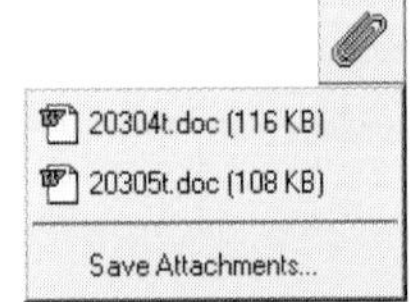

When a file has been sent along with an e-mail message, a paperclip appears next to the message in the Inbox window. If you click the message, a somewhat larger paperclip appears on the stripe between the top and bottom half of the Inbox window. Click the large paperclip and you can read the name of the files that were sent to you.

Follow these instructions to open or save files that were sent to you:

- **Opening a file** Click the paperclip and then click the name of the file. The file opens onscreen. Choose File | Save As to save the file in a folder of your choice.
- **Saving a file** Click the paperclip and then click the Save Attachments command. You see the Save Attachments dialog box. Click the Browse button, find and select the folder where you want to save the file, and click OK. Then click the Save button in the Save Attachments dialog box.

Replying to and Forwarding E-mail Messages

Suppose you receive a message that deserves a reply. Rather than go to the trouble of addressing a reply, you can click the Reply button and simply enter your message. Outlook Express also offers a Reply All button for addressing messages to all parties who received copies of the original message, and a Forward button for forwarding a message to a third party.

Follow these steps to reply to or forward a message:

1. Starting in the Inbox window, select the message you want to reply to or forward.
2. Click the Reply, Reply All, or Forward button:
   - **Reply** Opens the New Message window with the sender's name already entered in the To box and the original message in the text box below. Write a reply and click the Send button.

   - **Reply All** Opens the New Message window with the names of all parties who received the message in the To and Cc boxes. Type your reply and click the Send button.
   - **Forward** Opens the New Message window with the text of the original message. Click the small envelope next to the To button to open the Select Recipients dialog box and choose the names of the parties to whom the message will be forwarded. Click OK, and then add a word or two of commentary on the original message and click the Send button.

Storing and Managing E-mail Messages

When you click the Delete button to delete a message in the Inbox folder, the message doesn't disappear forever. It lands in the Deleted

Items folder. Likewise, copies of the messages you send are placed in the Sent Items folder. Being able to reread a message you sent or recover a message you deleted is nice, of course. To review a sent or deleted message, click the Sent Items or Deleted Items folder in the Outlook bar, and then find and select the message.

However, the Deleted Items and Sent Items folders soon get crowded with useless e-mail messages. To get rid of these messages, open the Sent Items or Deleted Items folder, and hold down the CTRL key as you click the messages you want to delete. Then click the Delete button and click Yes when Outlook Express asks if you really want to delete the messages.

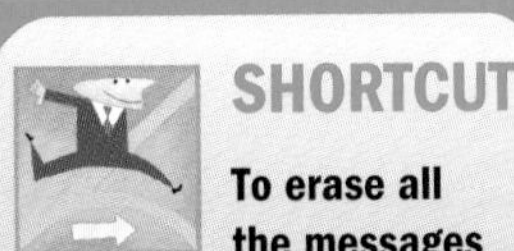

SHORTCUT

To erase all the messages in the Deleted Items folder, right-click the folder and choose Empty 'Deleted Items' Folder on the shortcut menu.

Outlook Express: Exploring Newsgroups

Besides being an e-mail program, Outlook Express doubles as a *newsreader,* a computer program for reading e-mail messages on and submitting e-mail messages to newsgroups. Newsgroups come and go, but they number in the tens of thousands. In theory, each newsgroup concerns one topic, but newsgroups are not regulated. No rules pertain. A crackpot can drop a message about any topic whatsoever in a newsgroup and no one can stop him.

DEFINITION

Newsgroup: **A collection of messages, or postings, about a certain topic.**

To visit a newsgroup, you connect to Usenet, a news server that tracks the names of all newsgroups. Then you visit a newsgroup that interests you and read a few messages. If the newsgroup is one that piques your interest, you can subscribe to it. Subscribing makes it easy to revisit a newsgroup later on. Of course, you can also add your two cent's worth and post a message of your own on a newsgroup. Better read on.

CAUTION

A lot of objectionable material is found on newsgroups. Newsgroups are not monitored or regulated. Cranks and crackpots like nothing better than posting their messages on newsgroups. If you are easily offended or have a low opinion of others' ability to argue intelligently, be careful which newsgroups you visit.

Finding a Newsgroup That Interests You

Before you can start exploring newsgroups, you have to connect to a news server. The most common news server is netnews, the one provided by Usenet, the primary source for newsgroups. Online services such as America Online offer their own news servers as well. You can tell which news servers are available on your computer by scrolling to the bottom of the Outlook bar and glancing at the news server folder names. You will find one folder for each news server that is accessible from your computer.

Follow these steps to connect to a news server and find newsgroups that interest you:

1. On the left side of the Outlook Express screen, click the folder icon of the news server whose newsgroups you want to explore.
2. What you do next depends on whether you have subscribed to any newsgroups on the server:

   - **Subscriber** The names of newsgroups you subscribe to appear in the window. Click the Newsgroups button to see the Newsgroup Subscriptions dialog box shown in Figure 7.5.
   - **Nonsubscriber** If you have not subscribed to any newsgroups or this is the first time you have attempted to connect to the news server, a dialog box asks if you would like to see a list of newsgroups. Click Yes. You see the Newsgroup Subscriptions dialog box shown in Figure 7.5. However, if you have never connected to the server before, you are invited to download the names of newsgroups to your computer. Downloading the names takes a while, but when the names have downloaded you see the Newsgroup Subscriptions dialog box shown in Figure 7.5.
3. In the Display Newsgroups Which Contain text box, type a word that describes a topic that interests you. Newsgroup names with the word you entered appear in the dialog box.
4. Scroll through the list and click a name that seems promising.

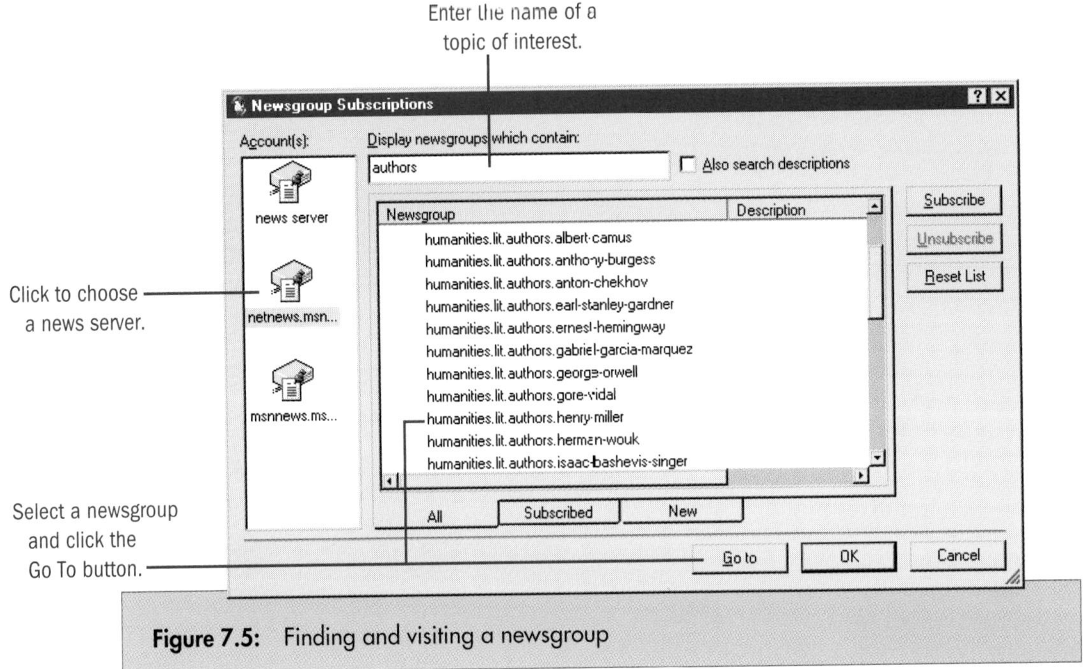

Figure 7.5: Finding and visiting a newsgroup

5. Click the Go To button. The name of the newsgroup appears in the Outlook bar on the left side of the Outlook Express window.
6. Do one of the following, depending on whether you are currently online:
   - **Not online** If you are not online, click the Connect button and, in the Connect To dialog box, click the Connect button there to visit the newsgroup.
   - **Online** You go straight to the newsgroup. A list of the last 300 messages posted to the newsgroup—messages on the list are called "headers"—is sent to your computer.
7. Click a message to read it (later in this chapter, "Reading and Posting Messages on Newsgroups" explains the details of reading messages).

Visiting, Subscribing to, and Unsubscribing from Newsgroups

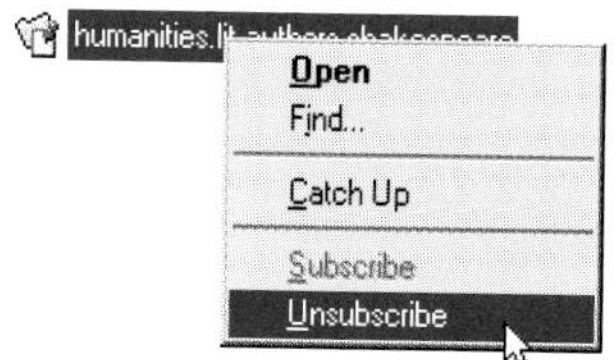

Subscribe to a newsgroup if there is even the slightest chance that you want to visit it again. Newsgroups are so numerous, and their names are so cryptic, finding one you've been to before is nearly impossible unless you subscribe. Besides, unsubscribing is easy. To unsubscribe, right-click the newsgroup's name in the Outlook bar and choose Unsubscribe from the shortcut menu.

Follow these instructions to subscribe to a newsgroup after you have found it:

- **In the Newsgroup Subscriptions dialog box** (See Figure 7.5) Click a newsgroup and then click the Subscribe button.
- **In the Outlook Express window** Right-click the newsgroup's name in the Outlook bar and choose Subscribe on the shortcut menu.

After you subscribe to a newsgroup, you can download messages that have been posted to the group to your computer. Then you can read the messages at your leisure. Figure 7.6 explains how to download messages from a newsgroup.

Reading and Posting Messages on Newsgroups

After you arrive at a newsgroup or download its messages to your computer, messages appear in the top of the window, as shown in Figure 7.7. To read a message, click it and read the text in the bottom of the window, or, to open the message in its own window and read it more comfortably, double-click the message. A plus sign appears beside messages to which others have responded. To read the responses, click the plus sign (+) next to a message and view the responses.

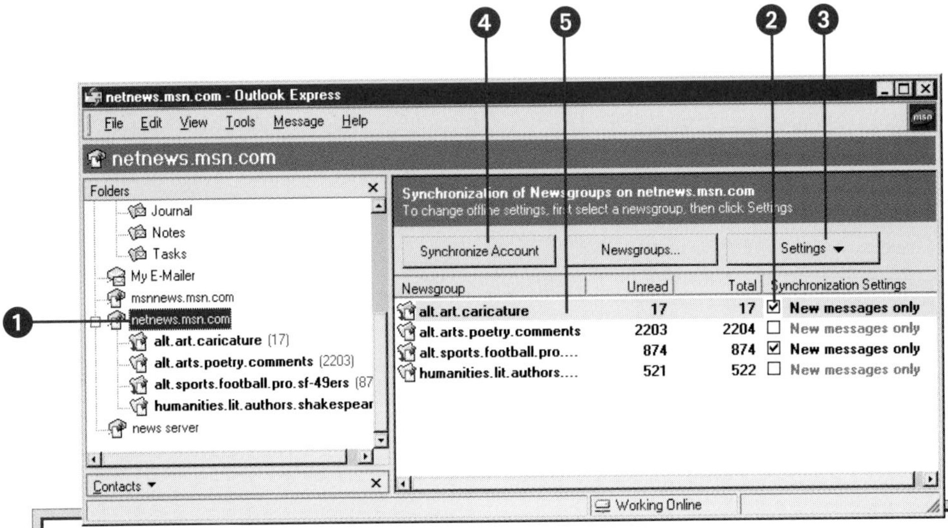

1 In the Outlook bar, click the news server folder with the newsgroup whose postings you want to read. The names of newsgroups you subscribe to appear in the Outlook Express window.

2 Click the check box next to each newsgroup whose postings you want to download.

3 For each newsgroup whose posting you want to read, click the Settings button and choose an option to tell Outlook Express which postings you want to download. The options are All Messages, New Messages Only, or Headers Only.

4 Click the Synchronize Account button. The messages are downloaded to your computer.

5 Click a newsgroup name and then click a message to read it.

Figure 7.6: Downloading messages from a newsgroup to which you subscribe

Outlook Express offers three ways to register your opinion in a newsgroup and either post a message or send a message directly to another author. Click the message that deserves a reply and follow these steps:

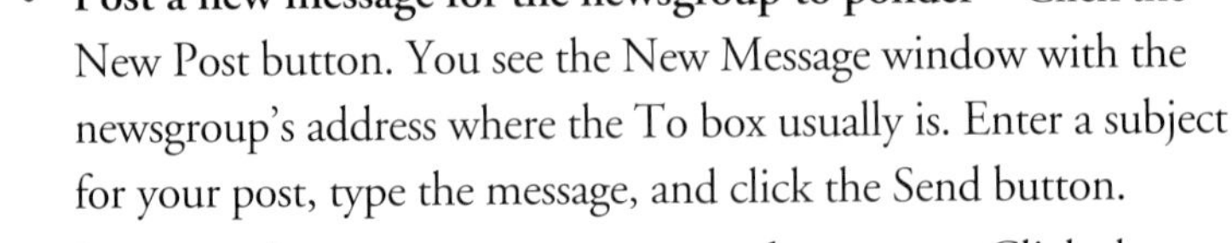

- **Post a new message for the newsgroup to ponder** Click the New Post button. You see the New Message window with the newsgroup's address where the To box usually is. Enter a subject for your post, type the message, and click the Send button.

- **Post a reply to a message someone else wrote** Click the message you want to reply to and then click the Reply Group button. The New Message window opens with the text of the message to which you are replying. A subject is already entered

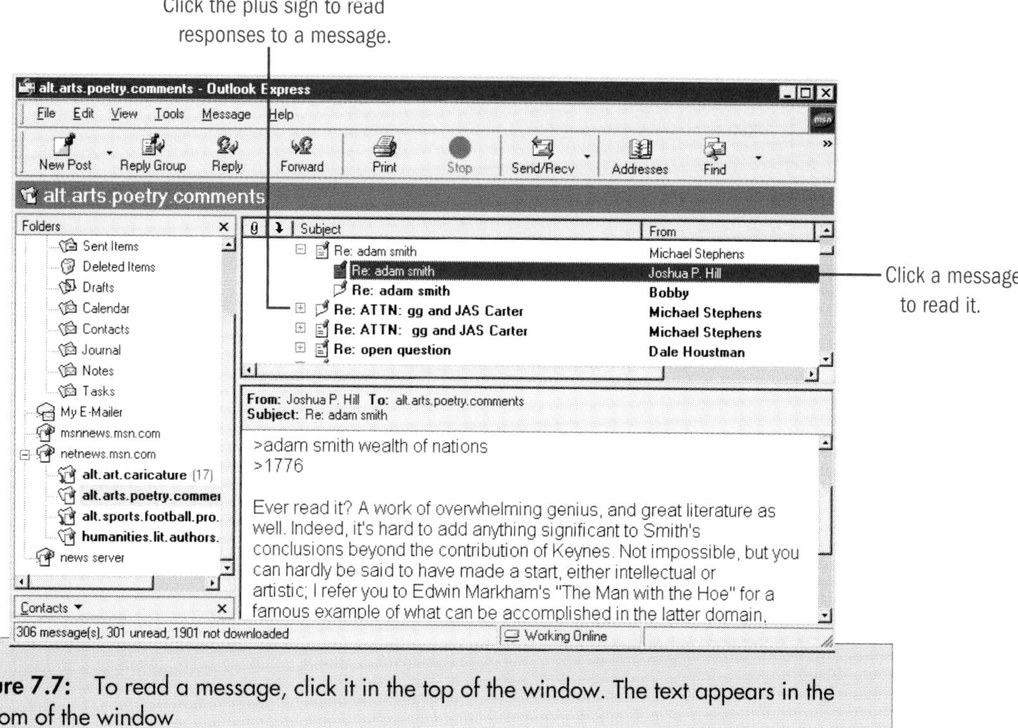

Figure 7.7: To read a message, click it in the top of the window. The text appears in the bottom of the window

in the Subject box. Type your reply and click the Send button. Be sure to erase the text in the message to which you are replying before you write your reply.

- **Reply personally to the author of a message** Click the Reply button. The New Message window opens with the author's e-mail address in the To box and the text of the original message. Enter your reply and click the Send button. Your message goes straight to the person named in the To box—it is not posted on the newsgroup.

All About Printing

Fifteen years ago, paper company executives were wringing their hands over the coming of the paperless office. Paper was supposed to become obsolete. The paperless office, however, is still a pipe dream. Despite the Internet and e-mail, most communication is done on

In Chapter 4 "Installing a Printer" explains how to install a printer.

paper. This section describes how to print a file, choose which printer to use if you have more than one, and cancel or change the order of print jobs. You also learn some tried-and-true techniques for handling a printer that doesn't do its job right.

Printing All or Part of a File

Most computer programs offer a Print button that you can click to print a file in its entirety. Printing an entire file is fine and dandy, but suppose you want to print part of a file, several copies, or print the file on your color printer instead of your black-and-white model? Figure 7.8 shows how to do just that.

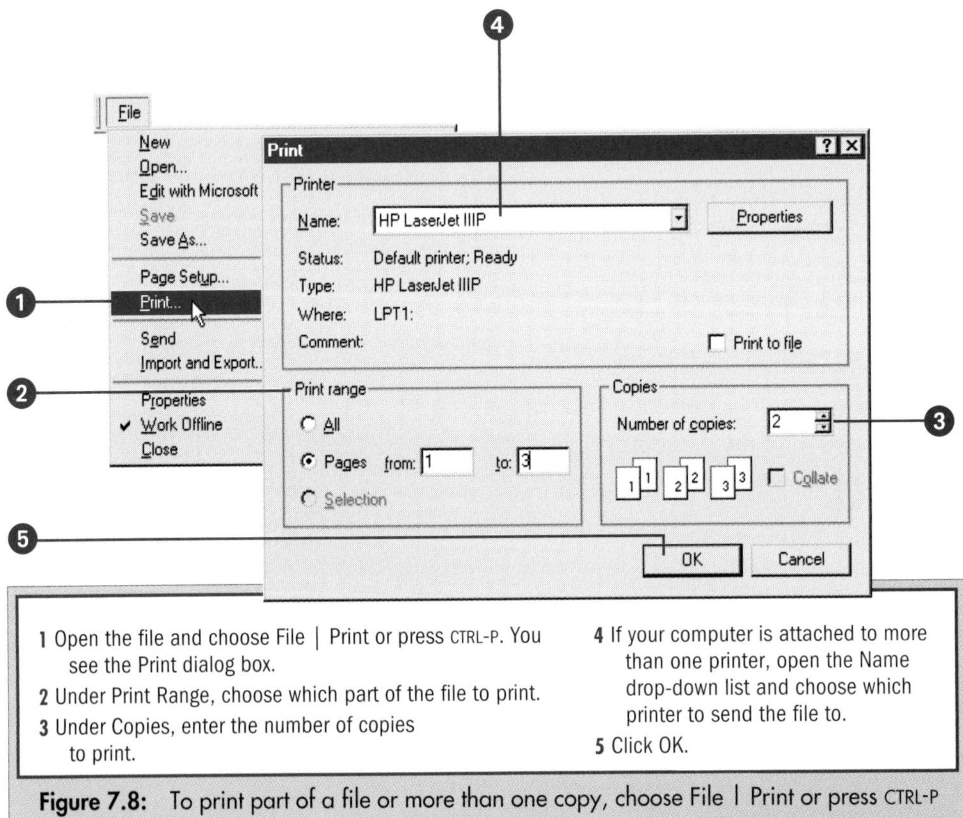

Figure 7.8: To print part of a file or more than one copy, choose File | Print or press CTRL-P to open the Print dialog box

The fastest way to print an entire file is to find it in My Computer and simply drag it to a printer shortcut icon on the desktop. Figure 7.9 demonstrates how to do that. "Create the Shortcut Icons You Need" in Chapter 2 describes how to create a shortcut. To get to the Printers folder and create a shortcut to a printer, click the Start button and choose Settings | Printers.

Canceling a Print Order or Changing the Order of Print Jobs

Suppose you give the order to print a file or a bunch of files but then you want to keep a file from being printed or change the order

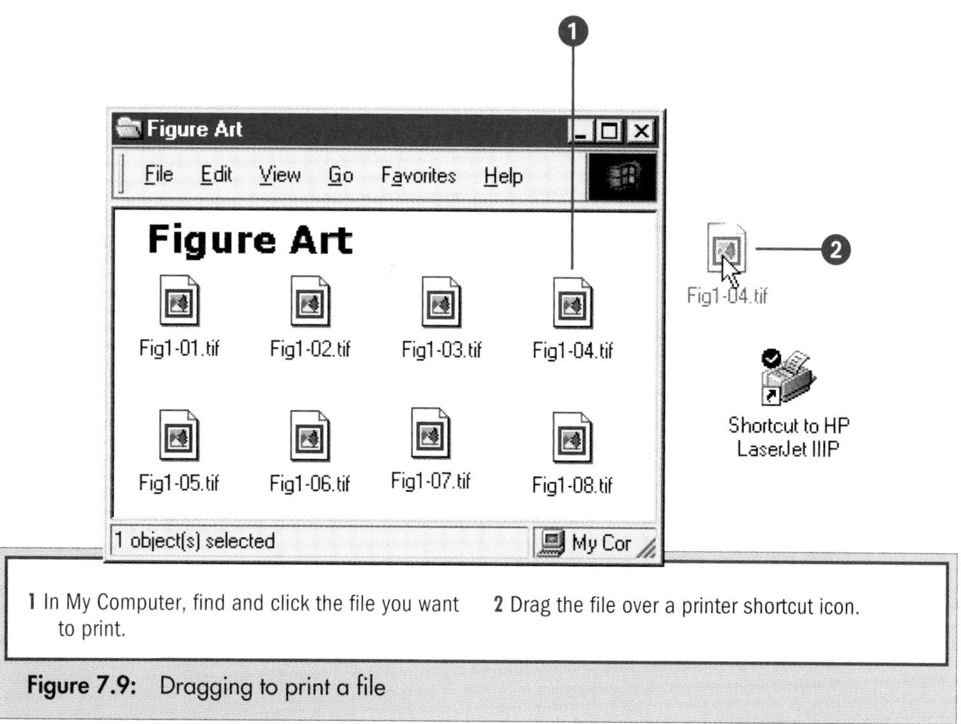

Figure 7.9: Dragging to print a file

EXPERT ADVICE

You can change a printer's default settings and save yourself the trouble of always having to choose options in the Print dialog box. Perhaps you work in a law office, for example, and you always print on legal-size paper. To change a printer's default settings, click the Start button and choose Settings | Printers. In the Printers folder, right-click a printer and choose Properties. On the six tabs of the Properties dialog box, select default settings and then click OK.

in which files are printed. Follow these steps to control how files are printed:

1. Double-click the Printer icon in the lower-right corner of the screen (next to the clock) or else click the Start button and choose Settings | Printers.
2. In the Printers folder, double-click the icon of the printer you are using. You see a Printer window similar to the one in Figure 7.10. Files are shown in the order in which they will be printed.
3. Do the following to change the order in which files are printed or stop printing a file:
   - **Change the print order** Click a file at the top or near the top of the list and choose Document | Pause Printing. As shown in Figure 7.10, the word "Paused" appears in the

SHORTCUT

To stop printing files without having to go to the Printer window, click the Start button and choose Settings | Printers. Then right-click the printer icon in the Printers folder and choose Purge Print Documents.

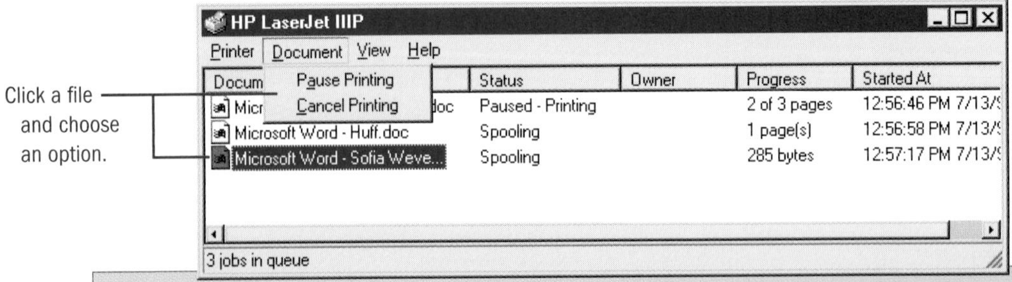

Figure 7.10: In the Printer window, you can stop printing documents or change the order in which they are printed

Status column. Files further down the list will now be printed before the one that has been "paused." To resume printing the file, click it and choose Document | Pause Printing again.

- **Stop Printing a File** Click the file and choose Document | Cancel Printing. The file is removed from the list.
- **Stop Printing All Files** Choose Printer | Purge Print Documents.

What to Do When You Can't Print Anything

Few things are more frustrating than not being able to get a printer to work correctly. When you get one of those "There was a problem sending your document to the printer" messages, try these techniques to solve the problem:

- See if the printer is turned on. Is paper in the paper tray? Is the right size paper in the paper tray?
- Find out if the power cord that connects your computer to the printer is plugged in correctly on both ends. For that matter, is the printer plugged in a wall socket?
- Make sure you are sending the file to the right printer if more than one printer is connected to your computer.

CHAPTER 8

Creating Bitmap Images with Paint

INCLUDES

- Understanding what bitmap graphics are
- Learning your way around the Paint screen
- Drawing lines and shapes
- Moving and copying shapes
- Applying color to graphics
- Entering text
- Creating a bitmap image for your Windows desktop

FAST FORWARD

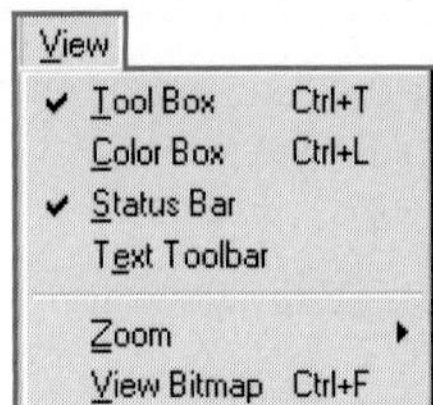

Choose which Tools and Toolbars Appear Onscreen ➡ pp. 192–195

- Select or unselect options on the View menu to decide whether to display or hide the Tool box, Color box, and Status bar.
- Click the Text button in the Tool box, draw a text box, and choose View | Text Toolbar to choose a font and font size for text.
- Different tools appear on the Tool box menu, depending on which button you click in the Tool box.

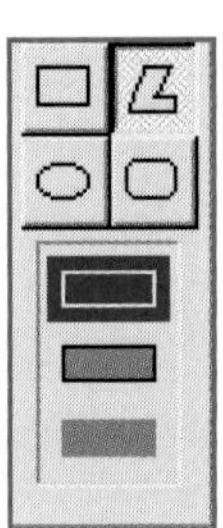

Draw Lines and Shapes ➡ pp. 196–199

- Click the Pencil, Brush, Airbrush, Line, or Curve button in the Tool box and start dragging to draw a line. After you click the Brush, Line, and Curve button, the Tool box menu offers commands for choosing the thickness of the line.
- Click the Rectangle, Polygon, Ellipse, or Rounded Rectangle button and start dragging to draw a shape. After you click, the Tool box menu offers commands for drawing a plain shape, an empty shape, or a filled-in shape.

Bring Color to a Part of Your Graphic ➡ p. 199

1. Select a color in the Color box or click the Pick Color button and then click a part of your graphic to choose a color there.
2. Click a button on the Tool box. To fill in a shape or the background, click the Fill with Color button and then click on the item that needs a color.

Move and Copy Lines and Shapes ➡ p. 200

1. Click the Free-Form Select or Select button and drag around the items to select them.
2. Move the pointer over the selection rectangle.
3. Either drag to move the item or hold the CTRL key and drag to copy it.
4. Click the top or bottom option in the Tool box menu to tell Paint how to place the item in regard to any item it overlaps.

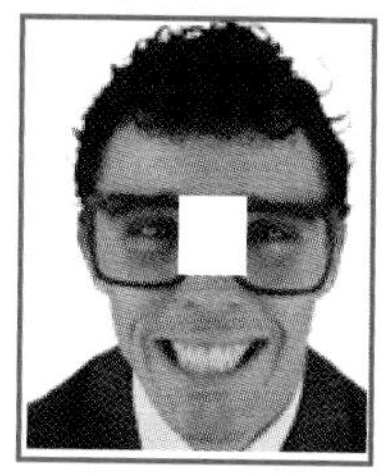

Erase Part of a Graphic ➥ p. 200

- Click the Eraser/Color Erase button and drag.
- Click the Free-Form Select or Select button, drag around what you want to erase, and press the DELETE key.
- Draw over what you want to erase.

Enter Text to Make It Part of Your Graphic ➥ p. 200

1. Click the Text button.
2. Drag to draw a rectangle onscreen.
3. Choose View | Text Toolbar, and, on the Text toolbar, choose a font and font size.
4. Type the text.

Create a New Image for Your Windows Desktop ➥ pp. 202–203

1. Create and save the image.
2. Choose File | Set As Wallpaper (Tiled). This command makes the bitmap image the background for the Windows Me desktop.
3. Click the Show Desktop button on the Quick Launch toolbar to examine your image.

A painter might take issue with the name "Paint" for the Paint computer program. As far as I can tell, the program has little in common with painting. Use Paint to view, create, and manipulate *bitmap graphics,* also known as *bit images.* A bitmap graphic is one that is composed of thousands of tiny squares. The squares correspond to *pixels* on your computer screen. Taken together, the squares form images, patterns, or letters. Only the French painter Georges Seurat, a pointillist whose work consisted of thousands of dots painted on the canvas, might take pleasure in using Paint.

This chapter explains how to construct bitmap graphics with Paint. You find out what bitmap images are, get acquainted with the Paint screen, and learn how to draw lines and shapes. You also find out how to move and copy items, handle color, erase parts of a graphic, and enter text. Finally, this chapter explains how to create a graphic of your own for the Windows desktop.

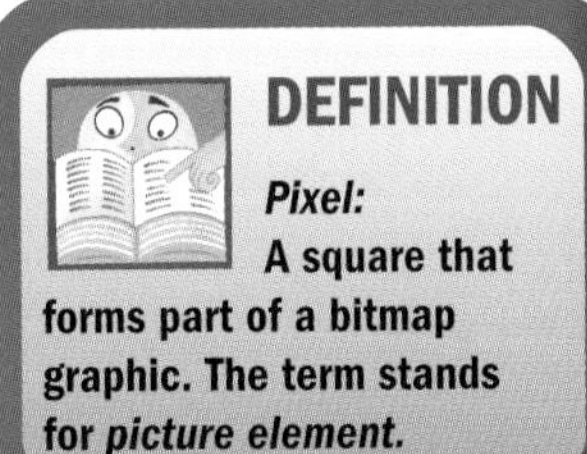

How Paint Works to Make Bitmap Graphics

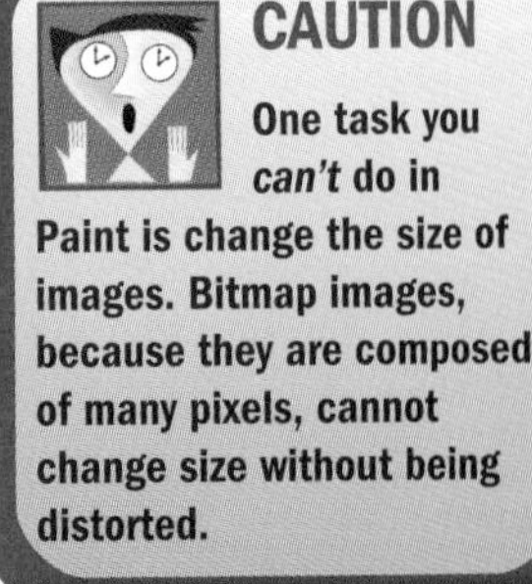

Most images you see on the Internet are bitmap images. The format has become very popular for Web pages. After you create a bitmap image in Paint, you can choose the File | Save As command to save it as a .jpeg or .gif image that can be used on a Web page. Paint is also great for manipulating images—for cropping them, rotating them, or changing around their colors.

Figure 8.1 demonstrates how bitmap graphics work. The left side of the figure shows the standard screen pointer at normal size. On the right side of the figure, however, the 8x Zoom command has been chosen, you see the pointer at eight times its normal size, and you see that the pointer is actually composed of 46 different squares. The artist who created the screen pointer did so by arranging black dots in such a way that they would look like an arrow when seen at normal size.

Try this little experiment to help you understand bitmap graphics:

1. Open your computer to a Web site or file with a graphic image.
2. Press the PRINT SCREEN key (sometimes labeled PRINT SCRN and located to the right of F12). As Chapter 3 explains, pressing PRINT SCREEN copies an image of the screen to the Clipboard.
3. If you haven't done so already, open the Paint program by clicking the Start button and choosing Programs | Accessories | Paint.
4. Choose Edit | Paste (click Yes if Paint asks whether to enlarge the bitmap image). The image, a bitmap image, appears in the Paint window.

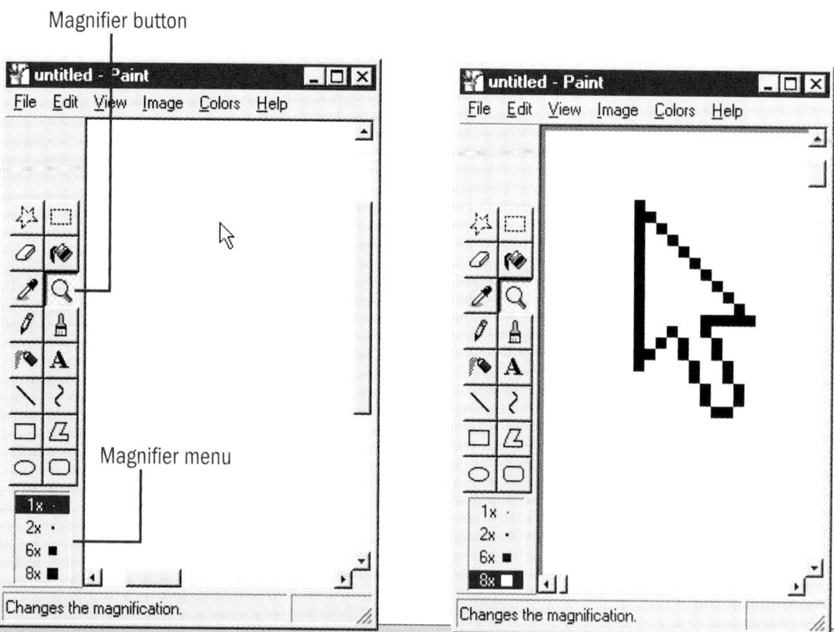

Figure 8.1: A bitmap image (left) and the same image enlarged eight times so you can see the pixels with which it was drawn (right)

EXPERT ADVICE

By default, files you create in Paint are saved as .bmp images, not .jpeg or .gif images. Unfortunately, however, .bmp images take up a lot of disk space, which is a disadvantage when you use them on Web pages, because they take a long time for visitors to Web pages to download. Before you use a Paint image on a Web page, save it as a .gif image: Choose File | Save As, open the Save As Type drop-down menu in the Save As dialog box, choose Graphics Interchange Format (*.gif), and click the Save button.

5. As shown in Figure 8.1, click the Magnifier button and then choose 8x from the Magnifier menu. You see the hundreds of squares from which the image, a bitmap graphic, is composed.
6. Choose View | Show Grid (or press CTRL-G). Now you can see precisely where each pixel is located.

No, you don't have to draw lines and shapes one pixel at a time. Paint offers many tools for drawing and splashing color on graphics. But no matter what you create in Paint, you create a bitmap image—an image composed of thousands of square pixels.

Finding Your Way Around the Paint Screen

TIP

Choose View | View Bitmap (or press CTRL-F) to enlarge the screen such that you see only the graphic you are working on, not the Paint toolbars or menu. Click anywhere onscreen to see the Paint screen again.

To start the Paint program, click the Start button and choose Programs | Accessories | Paint. As shown in Figure 8.2, Paint offers a bunch of different tools for creating and manipulating graphics. By selecting or unselecting options on the View menu, you can decide which tools appear onscreen. Sometimes you don't need all the tools. When working on a large graphic, removing some of the toolbars is often preferable because you get more room to work in the main screen.

Paint offers the following tools and toolbars for creating and manipulating graphics. Choose options on the View menu to decide which tools and toolbars appear onscreen:

- **Tool box** Offers buttons that you can click to draw lines and shapes, enter text, erase parts of a graphic, fill a graphic with color, and enlarge or shrink a graphic onscreen.

Figure 8.2: Choose options on the View menu to decide which tools are available onscreen

- **Tool box menu** Offers a set of tools. Which tools appear depends on which button you click in the Tool box. When you click the Line button, for example, five lines of varying widths appear in the Tool box menu. Click a line to determine how wide a line you draw.
- **Color box** Offers colors you can select when drawing lines, filling shapes with color, entering text, or filling an image with color.
- **Status bar** Shows the coordinates of the cursor location, and, when you draw shapes or lines, the size of shapes or lines in pixels. (To change the unit of measurement, choose Image | Attributes, and, in the Attributes dialog box, choose inches or centimeters as the unit of measurement.)
- **Text toolbar** Offers menus for changing fonts, choosing a font size, and boldfacing, italicizing, and underlining text. You must click the Text button in the Tool box and draw a text box onscreen before you can choose or display the Text toolbar.

EXPERT ADVICE

Constructing an image requires a lot of experimentation. Often you make mistakes. Because editing a bitmap image is so difficult, try to construct the image piece by piece so that you don't have to edit it. When you make a mistake, choose Edit | Undo or press CTRL-Z to undo your error (you can choose the command three times to undo three errors). Be sure to save the file often. That way, if you botch your graphic, you can close the file without saving it and reopen an earlier, more pristine version of the file.

Drawing Lines and Shapes

Drawing lines and shapes on your own isn't necessarily the best way to create a graphic in Paint. As the start of this chapter notes, you can find an image you like, click the PRINT SCREEN key to copy it to the Clipboard, and then choose Edit | Paste to copy the image into Paint. From there, you can start fashioning the graphic into something you can call your own. It might interest you to know, for example, that co-author Ron Mansfield, to create the images you see on the pages of this book, copied all the images into Paint using the PRINT SCREEN technique, then cropped the images using the Paint program as well.

See "Copying and Moving Shapes and Text" later in this chapter to learn how to do just that—copy and move stuff.

Still, even if you start by copying other work, you need to know how to draw lines and shapes if you want to do original work in Paint. These pages explain drawing lines and shapes.

Drawing Lines

Table 8.1 describes the buttons in the Tool box that you click to draw lines. After you click a button, drag onscreen to start drawing. Click a line-drawing button—Line or Curve—and then choose a thickness for the line on the Tool box menu. To draw a freehand line, click the Pencil or Brush button. The Pencil button is for drawing narrow lines. By clicking the Brush button, you can choose a line thickness and end for the line, either square or rounded. Click the Airbrush button to spray graffiti over your creations.

TIP

To draw straight lines at 45-degree angles, click the Line button and hold down the SHIFT key as you drag.

EXPERT ADVICE

To choose the width of lines, start by clicking the Line button, and choose a line width on the Tool box menu. Then choose whatever line- or shape-drawing tool you need from the Tool box and start drawing.

Drawing Shapes

Click the Rectangle, Polygon, Ellipse, or Rounded Rectangle button and start dragging to draw a shape. Table 8.2 explains what the shape-drawing buttons do. After you click a shape-drawing button, three options appear on the Tool box menu. Click the first to draw a simple shape in the color you choose in the Color box, the second to

TIP

To draw a square or circle, click the Rectangle, Rounded Rectangle, or Ellipse button and hold down the SHIFT key as you drag.

Button	Name	Use
	Pencil	For freehand drawing. You can't choose a line thickness with this option.
	Brush	For freehand drawing. Choose an option from the Tool box menu to choose a thickness for lines and whether the lines are square- or round-ended. When you click this button, the last six options on the Tool bar menu give you the opportunity to draw short 45-degree lines of 8, 5, or 2 pixels.
	Airbrush	For freehand drawing with a spray-can effect.
	Line	For drawing straight lines.
	Curve	For drawing curves. Draw a line first. Then click on the part of the line that you want to be the apex of the curve and start dragging.

Table 8.1: Tool Box Buttons for Drawing Lines

draw an empty shape, or the third to draw a shape filled in with the color you choose in the Color box.

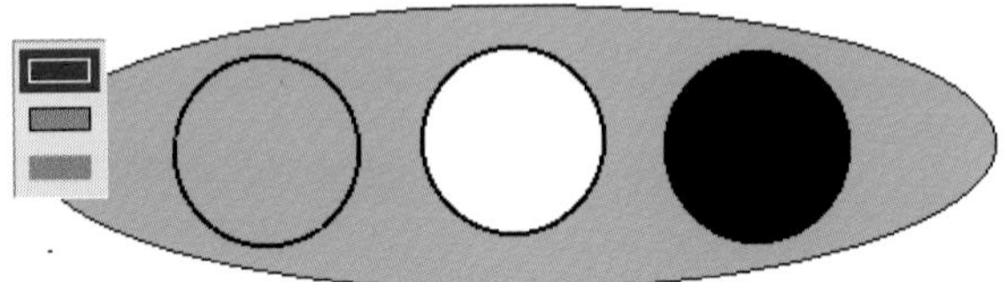

Selecting, Copying, and Moving Shapes and Text

Follow these steps to move or copy shapes or text:

1. Click the Free-Form Select or Select button. Click the Free-Form Select button to select far-flung items; click the Select button to select items that fit neatly in a rectangle.

2. Drag to draw around the thing or things you want to move or copy. A dotted line in rectangle form appears around the things you selected.

Button	Name	Use
	Rectangle	For drawing squares and rectangles.
	Polygon	For drawing many-sided shapes. Drag and click where you want each corner of the polygon to be. Then, to close off the polygon, double-click at the point where you want it to close.
	Ellipse	For drawing circles and ovals.
	Rounded Rectangle	For drawing squares and rectangles with rounded corners.

Table 8.2: Tool Box Buttons for Drawing Shapes

3. Gently move the pointer over a rectangle boundary. You see the four-headed arrow.
4. Either move or copy the item:
   - **To move it:** Drag the rectangle to a new location.
   - **To copy it:** Hold down the CTRL key as you drag the rectangle to a new location.
5. If the item you moved or copied overlaps another item, click the top or bottom option (probably the bottom) in the Tool box menu to tell Paint how to place the item in regard to the item it overlaps. The top option leaves white space around the item you moved or copied so it is opaque; the bottom option removes the white space to make the item transparent.

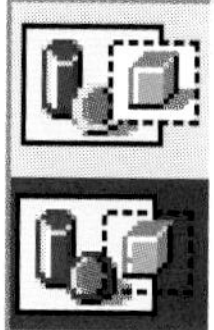

Colors for Text, Lines, Shapes, or a Background

Paint offers two ways to choose colors. Before you click the button you need to click to enter text, draw a line, draw a shape, fill in a shape, or fill in the background, do either of the following to choose a color:

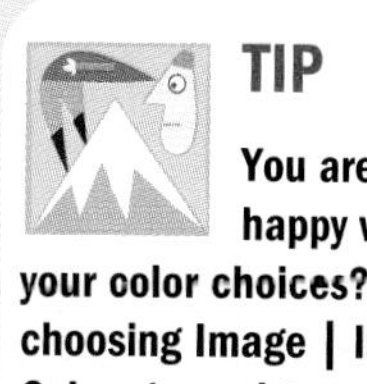

TIP

You aren't happy with your color choices? Try choosing Image | Invert Colors to assign each color its opposite.

- Select a color in the Color box.
- Click the Pick Color button and then click a part of your graphic to choose a color there. For example, if a rectangle is green and you want the same shade of green for a different item as well, click Pick Color button and then click the green rectangle.

To fill a shape or the background with a color, choose the color you want, click the Fill with Color button, and then click inside the shape or on the background. After you click the Fill with Color button, the cursor changes to a paint jar so you know that your next click will enter a color on the screen.

Erasing and Removing Parts of a Graphic

When it comes to erasing part of a graphic, Paint offers a bunch of different ways to do it. Which way is best? It depends on what you need to erase. Here are techniques for erasing and removing:

- **Use the Eraser tool** Click the Eraser/Color Erase button, choose an eraser size on the Tool box menu, and drag over the part of the graphic you want to remove.
- **Cut out part of a graphic** To erase a chunk of a graphic, select it and press the DELETE key or right-click and choose Edit | Clear Selection. (To erase an entire graphic, choose Image | Clear Image or press CTRL-SHIFT-N.)
- **Draw over the parts you want to erase** For fine work, draw over what you want to erase. Click the Brush button, choose a small line size on the Tool box menu, select a color that will hide what you want to erase, and start dragging or clicking.

TIP

When you are erasing little details, magnifying the image sometimes helps. Click the Magnifier button and choose magnification option on the Tool box menu.

Entering Text

TIP

To choose a font size different from the sizes shown on the Font Size drop-down menu, type in a size and press the ENTER key.

To enter text in a graphic that looks like that shown in Figure 8.3, click the Text button and drag to draw a rectangle onscreen. Then choose View | Text Toolbar, if necessary, to see the Text toolbar and choose a font and font size for the letters. Next, click in the rectangle and start typing. If you need to change fonts or font sizes, drag over the text you entered and make new choices on the Text Toolbar. To move the text, select it and drag it elsewhere (see "Selecting, Copying, and Moving Shapes and Text" earlier in this chapter).

As you enter text, remember the two drawbacks of entering text with Paint:

- You can't spell-check what you enter. Be careful to enter the text correctly.
- Text that appears in a bitmap graphic can't be read by Internet search engines. Normally, when you enter text on a Web page, search engines can index the text to help Internet searchers find the page. But as far as a search engine is concerned, text in a bitmap graphic isn't text—it's just a bunch of pixels.

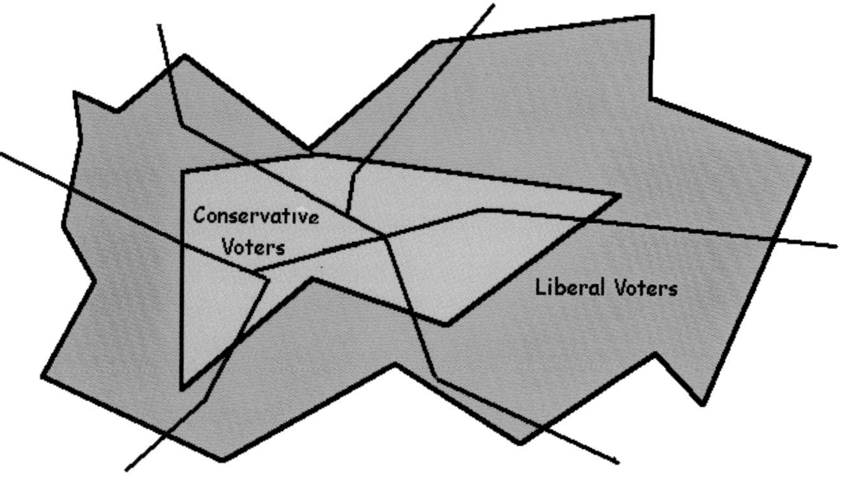

Figure 8.3: Click the Text button on the Tool box to make text part of a graphic

Bending, Spindling, and Mutilating Images

The Image menu offers a couple of interesting commands, Flip/Rotate and Stretch/Skew, for bending, spindling, and mutilating images. The commands are worth playing with. You never know what wild effects they will give rise to.

To try out one of the commands, select the part of the graphic you want to fool with and then follow these instructions:

- **Flipping and rotating images** Choose Image | Flip/Rotate. You see the Flip and Rotate dialog box shown on the left side of Figure 8.4. Choose a Flip or Rotate option to spin the image around.

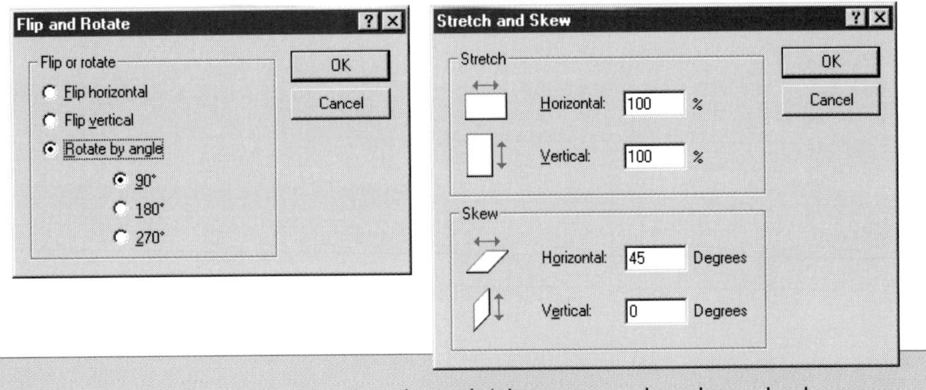

Figure 8.4: Try out the Flip/Rotate and Stretch/Skew commands and see what happens

- **Stretching and skewing images** Choose a Stretch or Skew command and enter a percentage or degrees figure in the Stretch and Skew dialog box, as shown on the right side of Figure 8.4. Stretch options make an image longer or shorter; Skew commands make it tilt.

Decorating the Windows Desktop with Your Own Images

On the File menu in Paint is a command called Set As Wallpaper (Tiled). Choose this command to decorate the Windows Me desktop with a bitmap image. You can create an image of your own for the desktop wallpaper or use an image you copied from the Internet or elsewhere. Follow these steps to decorate the Windows wallpaper:

1. Create the image you want to use.
2. Choose File | Save and save your bitmap image.

3. Choose File | Set As Wallpaper (Tiled). This command makes the bitmap image the background for the Windows Me desktop.
4. Click the Show Desktop button on the Quick Launch toolbar. What's this? The image you created appears on the desktop.

To go back to using an official Windows Me wallpaper for the desktop, right-click on the desktop and choose Properties. On the Background tab of the Properties dialog box, choose (None) or a different wallpaper design. Chapter 2 explains how desktop backgrounds work.

CHAPTER 9

Maintaining Your System and Making It Run Better

INCLUDES

- Surveying the Windows Me system tools
- Maintaining your system and making it run better
- Getting information about your system
- Updating your copy of Windows from the Internet
- Scheduling maintenance and other programs
- Restoring your computer system to an earlier incarnation

FAST FORWARD

Get More Disk Space by Removing Temporary Files ➥ pp. 210–211

1. Click the Start button and choose Programs | Accessories | System Tools | Disk Cleanup.
2. Make sure Temporary Internet Files and Temporary Files are checked in the Disk Cleanup dialog box, and then click OK.

Defragment the Hard Disk to Make Your Computer Run Faster ➥ pp. 211–212

1. Click the Start button and choose Programs | Accessories | System Tools | Disk Defragmenter.
2. Choose a disk to defragment and click OK.

Tell Windows How and When to Switch into Standby Mode ➥ pp. 214

1. Right-click the desktop, choose Properties, and click the Screen Saver tab in the Display Properties dialog box.
2. Under Energy-Saving Features of Monitor, click the Settings button.
3. In the Power Management Properties dialog box, choose your settings.

Check for and Repair Damage to Files on Disk ➥ pp. 214–216

1. Click the Start button and choose Programs | Accessories | System Tools | ScanDisk.
2. Choose a disk to check, choose whether you want to do a Standard or Thorough scan, and click the Start button.

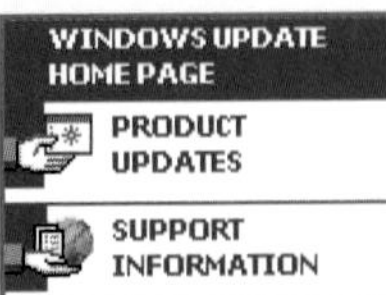

Make Sure Your Copy of Windows Me is Up-to-Date ➥ pp. 217–218

1. Click the Start button and choose Windows Update.
2. Go to the Windows Update site on the Internet and follow the instructions for downloading the latest edition of Windows.

Run Programs While You Are Away from Your Computer ➥ pp. 219–220

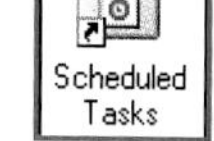

1. Click the Start button and choose Programs | Accessories | System Tools | Scheduled Tasks.
2. Double-click Add Scheduled Task in the Scheduled Tasks window (the first icon in the window) and answer the questions in the Scheduled Task Wizard dialog boxes.

Restore Your System to a Previous Incarnation ➥ pp. 221–222

1. Click the Start button and choose Programs | Accessories | System Tools | System Restore.
2. Make sure the Restore My Computer to an Earlier Time option button is selected and click Next.
3. Select a date on the calendar (dates in boldface offer restore points), select a restore point, and click Next twice.
4. Click OK in the Restoration Complete window after your computer shuts down and restarts.

A computer is like a high-strung English sports car. If you don't take the time now and then to maintain your computer, it starts to slow down. And if you ignore those strange noises and weird flickering lights, eventually your computer starts crashing. Then you have a real problem on your hands. When you need your computer most, it fails and stops running altogether.

Lucky for you, Windows Me offers a bunch of different ways to diagnose computer problems, maintain your computer, and make it run smoothly. This chapter explains how to play garage mechanic with Windows Me. You also learn how to schedule maintenance tasks so they can be done in your absence, update Windows Me by visiting a Web site on the Internet, and restore your computer to an earlier incarnation after you load new software but regret doing so.

Introducing the Windows Me System Tools

Windows Me offers many utility programs for making sure that your computer runs well. Most are found on the Programs | Accessories | System Tools menu. The programs that matter to most users (not network administrators or technicians) are explained throughout this chapter. Table 9.1 lists the programs, briefly explains what they do, and tells you how often to use them.

System Tool	What It Does	When to Use It
Disk Cleanup	Removes temporary files and files downloaded from the Internet from the hard disk.	Every week or so.
Disk Defragmenter	Reassembles parts of each file on disk so that each file is stored more efficiently in one place on disk.	When the computer runs slowly.

Table 9.1: The Windows Me System Tools

System Tool	What It Does	When to Use It
DriveSpace	Compresses files on disk to allow more free space for storing additional files.	Once, if ever.
Maintenance Wizard	Allows you to run Disk Defragmenter, Disk Cleanup, and ScanDisk automatically according to a schedule.	Make these settings once.
Power Management	Switches the monitor and computer into standby mode.	Make these settings once.
ScanDisk	Checks for and repairs damaged files and warped areas on the hard disk.	After a computer crash, frequent program failures, or a "bad sector" or "unable to read" error.
Scheduled Tasks	Allows you to schedule programs so they can be run automatically in your absence.	Daily or weekly, depending on which tasks are scheduled.
System Information	Presents information about your computer, its components, and its resources.	When you talk to a technician.
System Monitor	Lets you measure the performance of part of your computer system or network connection—your dial-up adapter, disk cache, or memory, for example	When you talk to a technician.
System Restore	Tracks changes to your computer system so that you can restore your system to a previous incarnation.	When you load new software or reconfigure your system and you regret doing so.
Windows Update	Takes you to a Web site where you can copy up-to-date Windows drivers and system files to your computer.	Periodically.

Table 9.1: The Windows Me System Tools *(continued)*

Maintaining Your System

Windows Me offers several different ways to maintain your system and make it run more smoothly. You can remove temporary files and other unneeded files, defragment a disk so files can be accessed faster, arrange for the monitor and computer to be turned off in your absence, and repair corrupted files. Better read on.

Disk Cleanup: Uncluttering the Hard Disk

Certain kinds of files have a habit of cluttering the hard disk and making the computer run slowly. *Temporary files,* for example, are a big culprit. When a computer crashes, Windows Me turns all unsaved files into temporary (.tmp) files so that you can recover the files later on. After a while, the number of temporary files adds up. And if you surf the Internet a lot, thousands of temporary Internet files (especially GIFs) collect like barnacles on your hard disk.

Lucky for you, Windows offers a special command for purging these files. Follow these steps:

1. Click the Start button and choose Programs | Accessories | System Tools | Disk Cleanup. You see the Select Drive dialog box.
2. If necessary, choose the drive that you want to clean up, and then click OK. A message says "Disk Cleanup is calculating how much space you will be able to free," and then you see the Disk Cleanup dialog box.
3. Select which kinds of files to remove (click the View Files button if you want to see which files will be deleted):

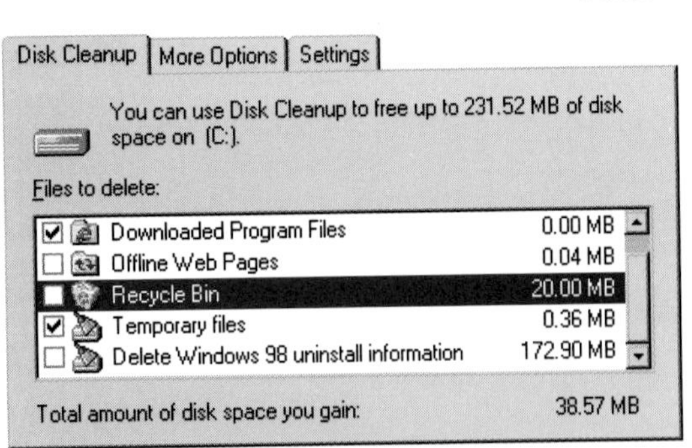

   - **Temporary Internet files** Definitely remove these. Your personalized Web-surfer settings remain intact when you remove these files.
   - **Downloaded program files** Get rid of them. These Java applets and ActiveX controls are just jet trash from the Internet.
   - **Offline Web pages** Keep them, more than likely. These are Web pages you stored for viewing when you are not connected to the Internet (see "Making Web Pages Available for Offline Viewing" in Chapter 6).

- **Recycle Bin** You can empty the Recycle Bin here if you want (see "Recycle Bin: Recovering Deleted Files and Folders" in Chapter 3 to learn about the Recycle Bin).
- **Temporary files** If your computer is running slowly, delete 'em.
- **Delete Windows Me uninstall information** When you upgraded from an earlier version of Windows, Windows Me stored this information in case you want to go back to the earlier version. If you are in Windows Me to stay, remove these files.
- **Temporary PC Health files** When you install new software, PC Health, a utility program, sometimes makes copies of installation files in case you need them later to restore your system. I'd keep these.

3. Click OK and then click Yes when Windows asks if you really want to delete this stuff.

Disk Defragmenter: Loading Files and Programs Faster

When you save a file, the new data you recently added gets placed on the hard disk wherever Windows can find room for it. Consequently, a file is stored in many different places on disk. If you've used your computer for a long time, files become fragmented—the bits and pieces are spread all over the disk and your computer has to work hard to assemble all the pieces when you open a file.

To make your computer work faster, you can *defragment* the files so that the various parts of each file are run together in one place on disk. Defragment your hard disk if your computer is running slowly. Defragmenting can take upwards of an hour, depending on how fast your computer is and how crowded the disk is. And you can't use your computer while it is defragmenting. I recommend doing it while you eat lunch.

Figure 9.1 shows how to defragment a hard disk. Be sure to close all open computer programs before you start defragmenting.

EXPERT ADVICE

Before you defragment a disk, remove the files and computer programs you don't need anymore. That way, you make defragmenting go faster. And while you're at it, you might run the ScanDisk utility as well to make sure that files, after they are defragmented, aren't copied to bad sectors on the computer's hard disk. ScanDisk is explained later in this chapter.

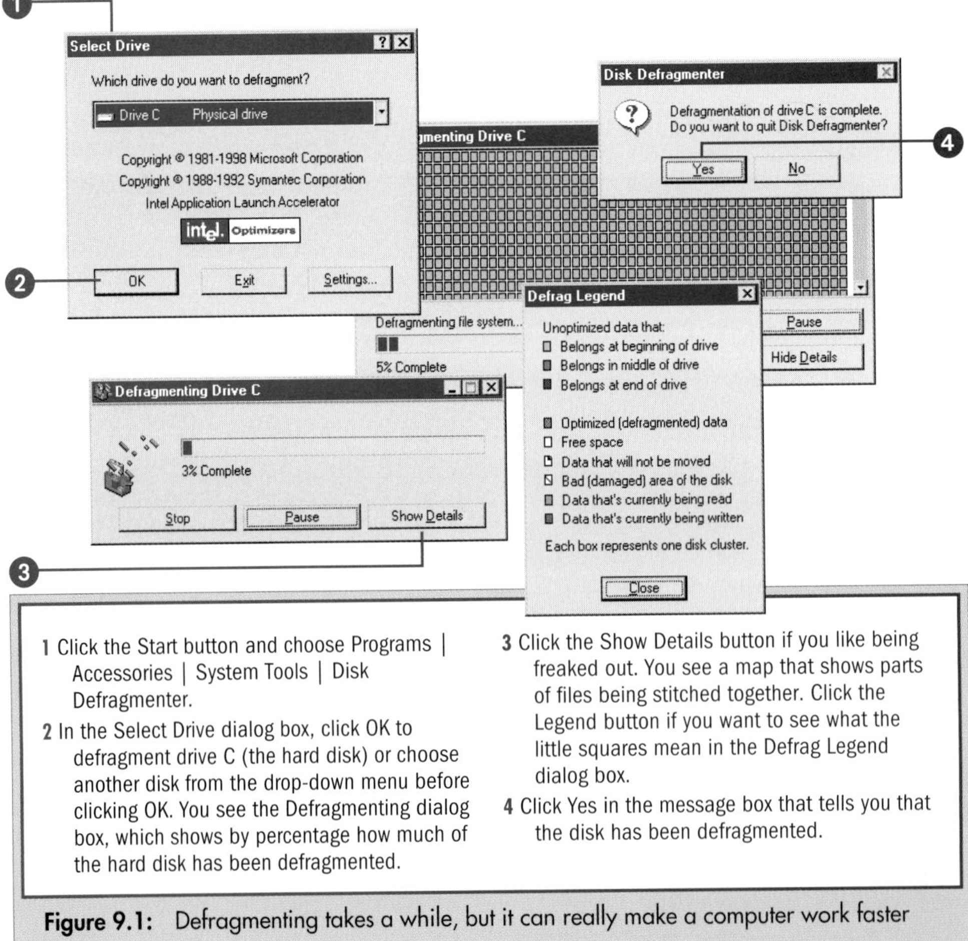

1 Click the Start button and choose Programs | Accessories | System Tools | Disk Defragmenter.

2 In the Select Drive dialog box, click OK to defragment drive C (the hard disk) or choose another disk from the drop-down menu before clicking OK. You see the Defragmenting dialog box, which shows by percentage how much of the hard disk has been defragmented.

3 Click the Show Details button if you like being freaked out. You see a map that shows parts of files being stitched together. Click the Legend button if you want to see what the little squares mean in the Defrag Legend dialog box.

4 Click Yes in the message box that tells you that the disk has been defragmented.

Figure 9.1: Defragmenting takes a while, but it can really make a computer work faster

Maintenance Wizard: Running Maintenance Programs Automatically

Maintenance Wizard is not so much a program as it is a convenient way to schedule three Windows Me maintenance programs—Disk Defragmenter, ScanDisk, and Disk Cleanup—in the Scheduled Tasks folder. After you are finished with the Maintenance Wizard, the three maintenance programs are listed in the Scheduled Tasks window and run automatically. Disk Defragmenter, ScanDisk, and Disk Cleanup are explained throughout this chapter. Look elsewhere in this chapter to see what the programs do and decide whether you want to run them automatically by scheduling them with the Maintenance Wizard.

Later in this chapter, "Scheduled Tasks: Running Programs in Your Absence" describes the Scheduled Tasks window and how programs can be run automatically.

Follow these steps to schedule Disk Defragmenter, ScanDisk, and Disk Cleanup so they run automatically:

1. Click the Start button and choose Programs | Accessories | System Tools | Maintenance Wizard. You see the first Maintenance Wizard dialog box.
2. Click Next to use the common tune-up settings.
3. In the next dialog box, choose when you want the maintenance programs to run, and click Next. You must be sure to leave your computer on during the hours you choose.

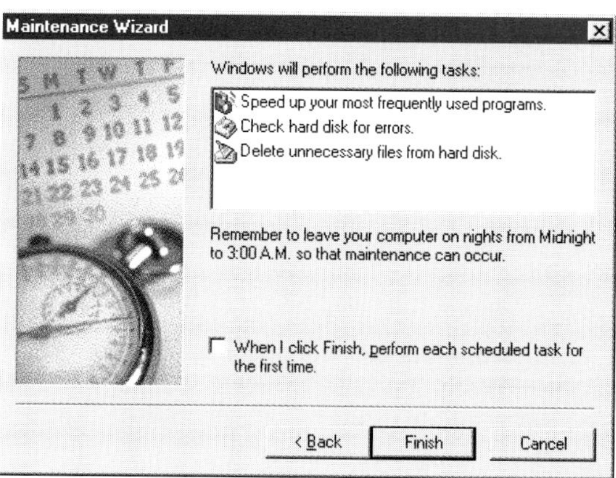

4. Click the Finish button (click the When I Finish check box as well to see exactly what a tune-up does).

To choose a specific tune-up schedule for each of the three utilities or to quit using one or all of them, open the Scheduled Tasks window by clicking the Start button and choosing Programs | Accessories | System Tools | Scheduled Tasks. Click the name of a maintenance program on the list and choose File | Delete to cancel it. To change a running schedule, choose File | Properties, click the Schedule tab, and enter a new schedule. Later in this chapter, "Scheduled Tasks: Running Programs in Your Absence" explains more about scheduling tasks.

Power Management: Saving Energy and Resting Your Computer

Most computers come with an energy-saving feature whereby the monitor and hard disk switch into standby mode after a certain amount of idle time has elapsed. In standby mode, the screen turns gray, the computer uses less electricity, and the computer gets a rest. To switch the monitor and computer out of standby mode, jiggle the mouse or press a key on the keyboard.

Figure 9.2 shows how to tell Windows Me when to switch the monitor into standby mode, when to turn off the monitor automatically, and when to shut down the hard disk as well.

ScanDisk: Repairing Damage to Files and the Hard Disk

ScanDisk checks the computer for damaged files and warped areas on the hard disk. It looks for files and parts of files that the computer has lost track of, files that were supposed to have been deleted, files that occupy the same space on the disk, and other anomalies. After ScanDisk finds these errors, it fixes them.

Run ScanDisk if a program fails frequently, if you see a "bad sector" or "unable to read" error, or if you see a bunch of gibberish after you open a file. Depending on which type of check you want—Standard or Thorough—ScanDisk can take a long time to search for and rectify errors. However, you can run the program

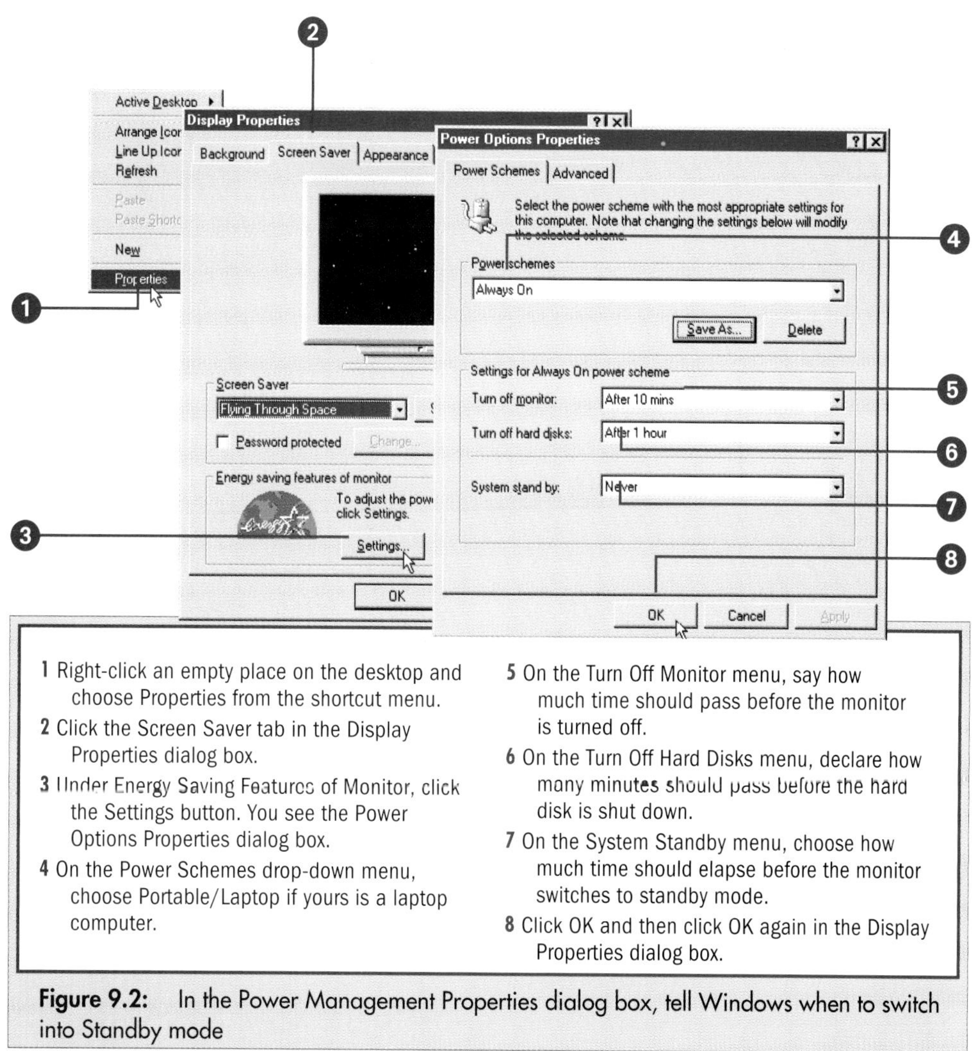

1 Right-click an empty place on the desktop and choose Properties from the shortcut menu.

2 Click the Screen Saver tab in the Display Properties dialog box.

3 Under Energy Saving Features of Monitor, click the Settings button. You see the Power Options Properties dialog box.

4 On the Power Schemes drop-down menu, choose Portable/Laptop if yours is a laptop computer.

5 On the Turn Off Monitor menu, say how much time should pass before the monitor is turned off.

6 On the Turn Off Hard Disks menu, declare how many minutes should pass before the hard disk is shut down.

7 On the System Standby menu, choose how much time should elapse before the monitor switches to standby mode.

8 Click OK and then click OK again in the Display Properties dialog box.

Figure 9.2: In the Power Management Properties dialog box, tell Windows when to switch into Standby mode

in the background while you do other work. Follow these steps to run ScanDisk:

1. Click the Start button and choose Programs | Accessories | System Tools | ScanDisk. You see the ScanDisk dialog box shown in Figure 9.3.

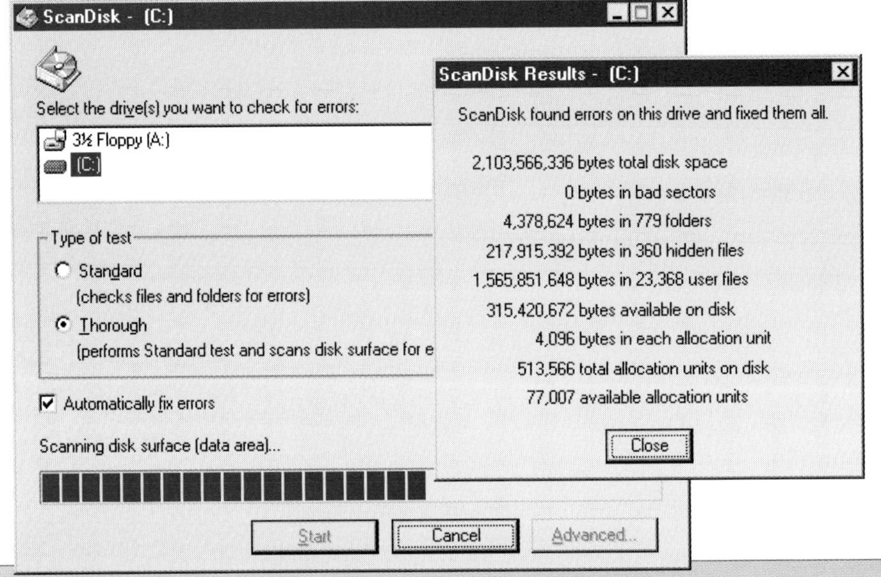

Figure 9.3: Use the ScanDisk program to check for damaged files and warped areas on the hard disk

2. In the ScanDisk dialog box, select a disk to check (probably your local disk, [C:]).
3. Choose which type of test to run:
   - **Standard** Checks for file errors and file-allocation errors.
   - **Thorough** Does what the Standard test does and also checks the actual surface of the disk for damaged areas that can't be relied upon for storing data. Run this test periodically, but not as often as the Standard test.
4. Make sure that the Automatically Fix Errors check box is checked and then click the Start button. When the test is done, the ScanDisk Results dialog box tells which errors, if any, were found and how the test was conducted.
5. Click Close in the ScanDisk dialog box.

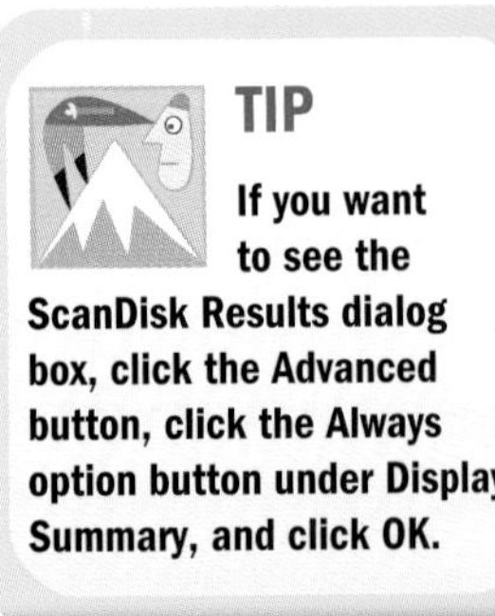

TIP

If you want to see the ScanDisk Results dialog box, click the Advanced button, click the Always option button under Display Summary, and click OK.

Getting Information About Your System

If your system goes south and you have to call a technician, they will ask all sorts of personal questions about your computer. How much RAM does it have? What kind of hard disk controller does it have? You can answer these questions and even find out from Windows Me if a device on your computer is not working by following these steps:

CAUTION

The System Properties dialog box offers buttons for removing and reconfiguring system devices. Don't do it! Don't do it unless you are foolhardy or you have, as Mark Twain put it, the confidence of a Presbyterian with four aces.

1. Right-click the My Computer icon on the desktop and choose Properties. You see the System Properties dialog box.
2. Visit each tab on the dialog box to see what you can see:
   - **General** Not much here that you wouldn't know already. The bottom of the tab lists how much RAM (random access memory) your system can draw upon.
   - **Device Manager** This tab is the interesting one. Click the plus sign (+) next to each device type, as shown in Figure 9.4, to find out more about it. You see manufacturer names and device types. By clicking a device and then clicking the Properties button, you can learn more about it. As the right side of Figure 9.4 shows, you can also learn from the Device Status box whether the device is working properly.
   - **Hardware Profiles** This is an advanced tab that has to do with system configurations and drivers. It's for professionals only.
   - **Performance** Here you see how much memory and virtual memory your system employs, among other things.
3. Click Cancel to close the System Properties dialog box.

Windows Update: Getting an Up-to-Date Copy of Windows

Windows Update

Registered users of Windows Me can go on the Internet and download the most up-to-date edition of Windows Me from the Windows Update site, a Web site that Microsoft maintains. At the

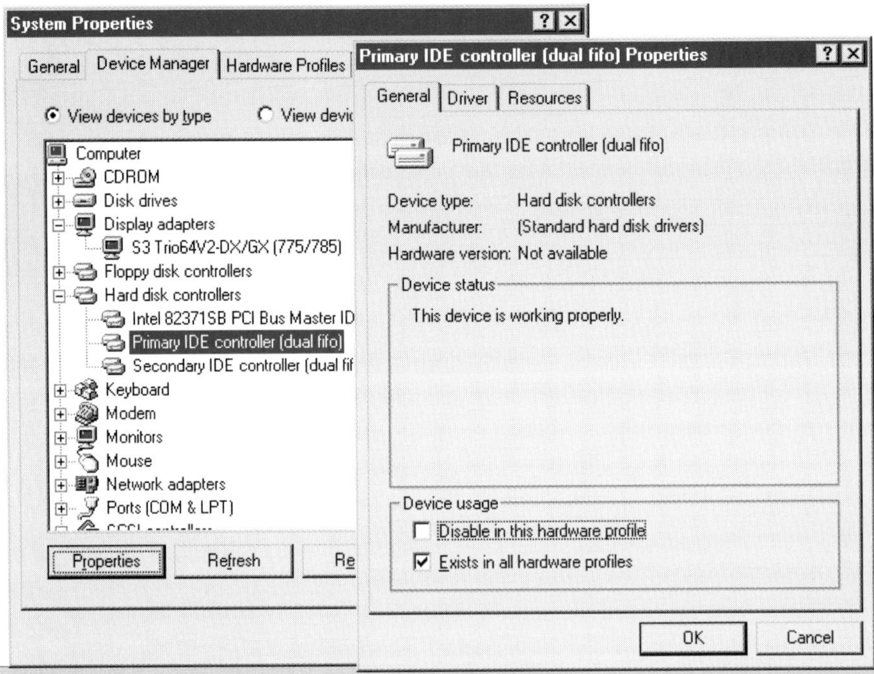

Figure 9.4: From the System Properties dialog box, you can tour the insides of your computer

site, you answer a few questions, learn what parts of Windows Me need updating, and get the opportunity to download new drivers and system files. Follow these steps to update your copy of Windows Me:

1. Click the Start button and choose Windows Update or Settings | Windows Update. Your Web browser starts so you can connect to the Internet.
2. Click the Connect button to go on the Internet. Soon you arrive at the Windows Update site (http://windowsupdate.microsoft.com).
3. Follow the instructions on the Web site for updating your copy of Windows Me.

Scheduled Tasks: Running Programs in Your Absence

To make sure that files get backed up and important tasks are done on a regular basis, you can schedule a program to run in your absence. For the plan to work, you have to leave your computer on overnight so the programs run when they won't distract you. Schedule tasks for the wee hours of the morning. I suggest choosing one night a week to run scheduled tasks. Turn off the monitor but make sure the computer is left on during Scheduled Tasks Night.

Earlier in this chapter, "Maintenance Wizard: Running Maintenance Programs Automatically" explained how to use the Maintenance Wizard to put Disk Defragmenter, ScanDisk, and Disk Cleanup on the Scheduled Tasks window.

Scheduling a Program to Run on Its Own

Follow these steps to schedule a program to run in your absence:

1. Choose Programs | Accessories | System Tools | Scheduled Tasks. You see a Scheduled Tasks window similar to this one:

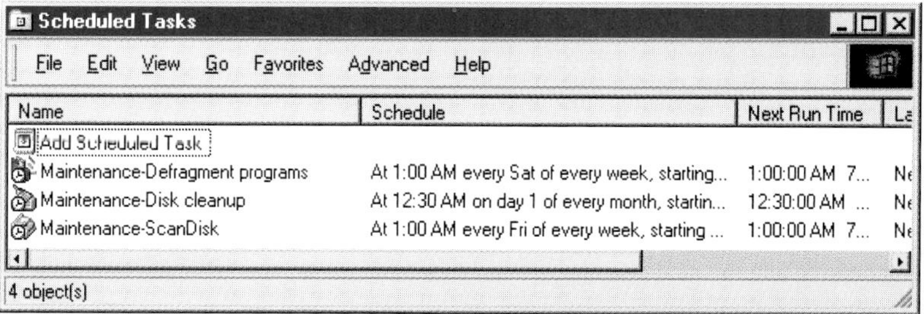

2. Double-click Add Scheduled Task, the first icon in the window. You see the first Scheduled Task Wizard dialog box.
3. Click Next. You see a list of the programs that are installed on your computer.
4. Scroll down the list, select the program that you want to run automatically, and then click Next. Obviously, you have to choose a program that can run without your assistance, since you will be napping when the program runs. Prime candidates for scheduling are backup and antivirus programs.
5. Choose when to run the program and click Next.

TIP

Choose When My Computer Starts to run the program each time you start your computer.

6. Enter the time of day, weekly frequency, and day of the week for the program to run, and then click Next.
7. Make sure your settings are correct in the last dialog box and then click Finish. A new task is entered in the Scheduled Tasks window. The window says when the program will run and when it will run next.
8. In the window, click the task you just scheduled and choose File | Run to make sure the task you created can indeed run correctly.

Changing the Schedule

Suppose you decide not to run a program automatically. For that matter, suppose you want to change schedules. Click the Start button, choose Programs | Accessories | System Tools | Scheduled Tasks, and do one of the following in the Scheduled Tasks window:

- **Unschedule a task** Click the program's name in the window and choose File | Delete.
- **Change schedules** Click the program's name and choose File | Properties. Then click the Schedule tab and enter new schedule settings.
- **Stop running all programs** Choose Advanced | Stop Using Task Scheduler. Choose this option, for example, when you go on vacation for a few weeks and turn your computer off. When you come back from Firenze, click the Start button and choose Programs | Accessories | System Tools | Scheduled Tasks. Then choose Advanced | Start Using Task Scheduler.

System Restore: Restoring Your System to a Previous Incarnation

Most people would like to turn back the clock now and then, and when a computer starts behaving sluggishly, everyone would like to turn back the clock. Everyone would like to have their old computer back, the one that worked well before new software, new system settings, or new hardware made the computer slow to a crawl.

To turn back the clock, Windows Me offers the System Restore utility. The utility tracks changes to your computer system by marking each change with a *restore point*, a record of your computer system as it stood at a certain point in time. When you want to restore your system to a previous incarnation, you choose a restore point. Restore points are created under these conditions:

- You install a new program
- You change system settings in Control Panel
- You delete a program file (an .exe or .dll file, for example)
- You run your computer for roughly ten hours
- You create a restore point on your own

Only system settings and system files are affected when you roll back your computer system. Word processed files, e-mail messages, and other files with commonly known file extensions are not deleted or altered. If you don't like your system after you roll it back, you can reverse the restoration. In other words, you can have your system as it stood before you decided to restore it. To store recovery files, the System Restore utility needs 200MB of free disk space.

EXPERT ADVICE

If you often tinker with your computer system, you may need more than the 200MB of free disk space that System Restore requires. To get it, right-click the My Computer icon on the desktop. Then, in the System Properties dialog box, go to the Performance tab and click the File System button. Finally, on the Hard Disk tab of the File System Properties dialog box, move the System Restore Disk Space Use slider to the right.

Restoring Your System

Follow these steps to restore your system to a previous incarnation:

1. Close all open programs.

TIP

System Restore does not tamper with files that have commonly known extensions or the contents of the My Documents folder. If you aren't sure whether a file's extension is "commonly known," move it temporarily to the My Documents folder.

2. Click the Start button and choose Programs | Accessories | System Tools | System Restore. You see the Welcome to System Restore window.
3. Make sure the Restore My Computer to an Earlier Time option button is selected, and then click the Next button.
4. Click OK in the message box that reminds you to close all open programs (and close them now, if you forgot to do so earlier).
5. Select a date on the calendar (dates in boldface offer restore points), select a restore point, and then click the Next button.

<			August, 2000			>
Sun	Mon	Tue	Wed	Thu	Fri	Sat
30	31	1	2	3	4	5
6	7	8	9	10	11	12
13	14	15	16	17	18	19
20	21	22	23	24	25	26
27	28	29	30	31	1	2
3	4	5	6	7	8	9

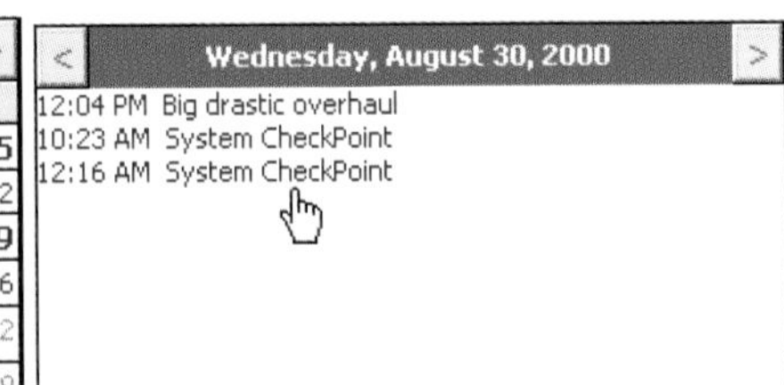

6. Click Next in the following window. System Restore restores your system to a previous incarnation. Sooner or later, depending on how much restoring needs to be done, your computer shuts down and restarts, and you see the Restoration Complete window.
7. Click OK.

EXPERT ADVICE

If System Restore isn't tracking changes to your system, right-click the My Computer icon on the desktop and choose Properties. Then go to the Performance tab in the System Properties dialog box and click the File System button. On the Troubleshooting tab of the File System Properties dialog box, uncheck the Disable System Restore check box.

Reversing a Restoration

Suppose you restore your computer to a previous incarnation but you aren't happy with the results. If that is the case, click the Start button and choose Programs | Accessories | System Tools | System Restore. In the Welcome to Restore window, select the Undo My Last Restoration option button and take it from there. System Restore creates a Restore Operation restore point whenever you restore your system. When you reverse a restoration, you are returned to the Restore Operation restore point—the state your computer was in before you restored it.

Creating Your Own Restore Point

Create a restore point on your own before you overhaul your computer or do something else drastic to it. That way, if you have to, you can restore your computer later on. Follow these steps to create your own restore point:

1. Click the Start button and choose Programs | Accessories | System Tools | System Restore.
2. In the Welcome to System Restore window, select the Create a Restore Point option button, and then click Next.
3. Enter a description of the restore point in the text box and click Next. Be sure to enter a description whose meaning you will understand later.
4. In the Confirm New Restore Point window, glance at your description to make sure it's right, and then either click the OK button to close the System Restore utility or click the Home button to keep the utility open and return to the Welcome to System Restore window.

New restore point:

Wednesday, August 30, 2000
12:04 PM Big drastic overhaul

CHAPTER 10

Sights and Sounds

INCLUDES

- Adjusting the volume of the sounds you play
- Recording and editing sound
- Playing CDs, music files, and video files
- Listening to the radio over your computer
- Building a media library of audio and video files on your computer
- Cropping and annotating images with Imaging

FAST FORWARD

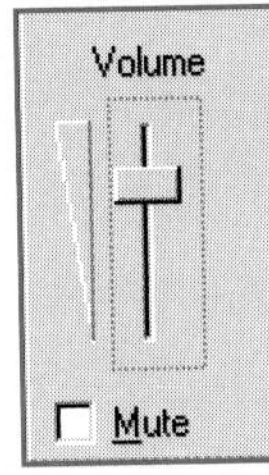

Control the Volume of Speakers and Other Sound-Producing Devices ➥ pp. 228–229

- Turn the volume knob on your computer monitor.
- Click the Speaker icon and drag the slider up or down.
- Double-click the Speaker icon and change settings in the Speaker dialog box.

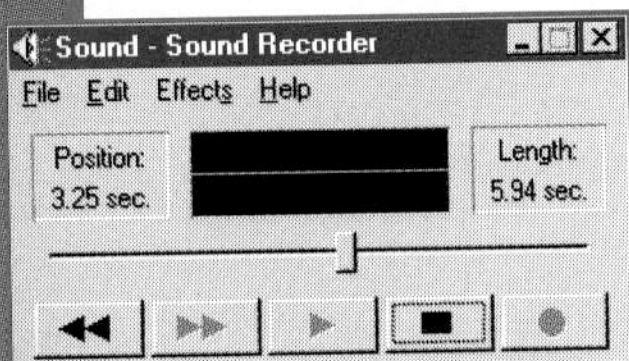

Record a Sound on Your Computer ➥ pp. 230–231

1. Click the Start button and choose Programs | Accessories | Entertainment | Sound Recorder. The Sound Recorder dialog box opens.
2. Click the Record button and start speaking.
3. Click the Stop button.

Play an Audio or Video File on Your Computer ➥ p. 232

- In Windows Media Player, click the Media Library button, locate the folder in the Media Library where the file is located, and double-click the name of the file.
- In Windows Media Player, click the Now Playing button, open the Playlist drop-down menu, choose a playlist, and double-click the file you want to play on the playlist.
- Locate the file in My Computer and double-click it.

Play a Commercial CD on Your Computer ➥ p. 232

1. Insert the CD in your computer's CD-ROM or DVD drive.
2. Click the CD Audio button in Windows Media Player. To hear a track, double-click its name.

Listen to the Radio over Your Computer ➥ p. 237

1. Click the Radio Tuner button in the Windows Media Player.
2. Open the Presets drop-down menu and select My Presets to see your list of radio stations, or select Features to see Microsoft's list.
3. Double-click the name of the station you want to listen to.

Create a Playlist and Add Files to It ➥ pp. 239–240

1. Click the Media Library button and then click the New Playlist button.
2. Enter a name for your playlist in the New Playlist dialog box and click OK.
3. In the Media Library, CTRL-click to select the files you want for your playlist.
4. Right-click and choose Add to Playlist on the drop-down menu, then select a list in the Playlists dialog box.

Crop Off Part of a Graphic File ➥ pp. 242–243

1. In Imaging, click the Select Image button and drag a frame around the part of the image you want.
2. Choose Edit | Select image.
3. Open a new image file and choose Edit | Paste.

It might interest you to know that the computer and the television are slowly merging into one device. In ten years, you will be able to watch movies and TV on computer monitors. Instead of visiting the local video rental store, you will download movies from the Internet when you want to watch a movie. You will be able to surf the Internet and watch television at the same time.

This chapter explains what you can do today to play video and sounds on your computer with Windows Media Player. As long as speakers are attached to your computer and your computer has a sound card and video capabilities, you can record sounds, play sounds, and play videos. This chapter describes how to do that and also how to edit digital photographs with Imaging, a program that comes with Windows Me.

Volume Control: Adjusting the Volume Levels

CAUTION

Sound and video clips consume a lot of space on disk. For example, a 60-second MPEG video clip that includes sound and music consumes about 7MB of disk space. If you want to experiment with video clips and sound files, make sure your computer has enough disk space, enough RAM, and an adequate video card to handle them.

These days, most computer monitors have a knob that you can turn to adjust the volume of sound coming from the speakers. And if the speakers aren't built into the monitor, you can usually control the volume of the speakers themselves. However, if your monitor and speakers don't have a knob, you can adjust the volume by clicking the Speaker icon in the lower-right corner of the screen (next to the clock). This icon looks like a bullhorn. When you click it, you see the Volume slider shown on the left side of Figure 10.1. Drag the slider up or down to adjust the volume.

Volume Control

You can also choose a volume level for the different sound and video devices installed on your computer. To do so, either

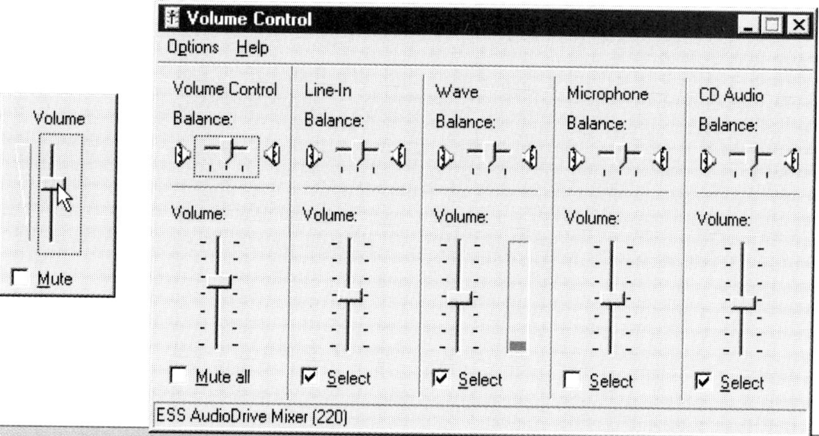

Figure 10.1: Click the Speaker icon and drag the volume slider to set the volume for the speakers (left); double-click the Speaker icon to control all volume settings (right)

double-click the Speaker icon or click the Start button and choose Programs | Accessories | Entertainment | Volume Control. You see the Speaker dialog box shown on the right side of Figure 10.1. Drag the sliders up or down to decide how loud the Windows Media Player and other sound-producing devices on your computer should be. While you're at it, notice the Balance sliders. Move them to adjust the volume of your computer's speakers.

TIP

If you don't see the Speaker icon, click the Start button and choose Settings | Control Panel. Then double-click the Sounds and Multimedia icon and, on the Sounds tab of the dialog box that appears, click the Show Volume Control on Taskbar check box.

EXPERT ADVICE

Sometimes the Volume Control dialog box doesn't offer sliders for controlling all the sound-producing devices on your computer. If that is the case, choose Options | Properties in the Volume Control dialog box. In the Properties dialog box, check the names of sound-producing devices you want to see in the Volume Control dialog box, and click OK.

Sound Recorder: Recording and Editing Sounds

Windows Me offers the Sound Recorder for playing, editing, and recording sounds. It goes without saying that to record live sound, a microphone as well as speakers must be connected to your computer. Sounds you record with Sound Recorder are saved as wave (.wav) files. Read on to learn how to record a sound, edit a wave file, and play a wave file with Sound Recorder.

Recording a Sound

Follow these steps to record a sound:

1. Click the Start button and choose Programs | Accessories | Entertainment | Sound Recorder. The Sound Recorder dialog box opens.

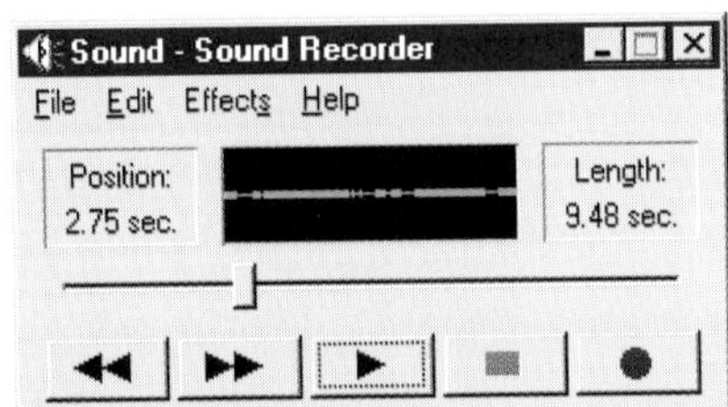

2. To choose a sound quality for your recording, choose File | Properties. You see the Properties for Sound dialog box.
3. From the Choose From drop-down menu, choose Recording formats.
4. Click the Convert Now button. The Sound Selection dialog box opens.

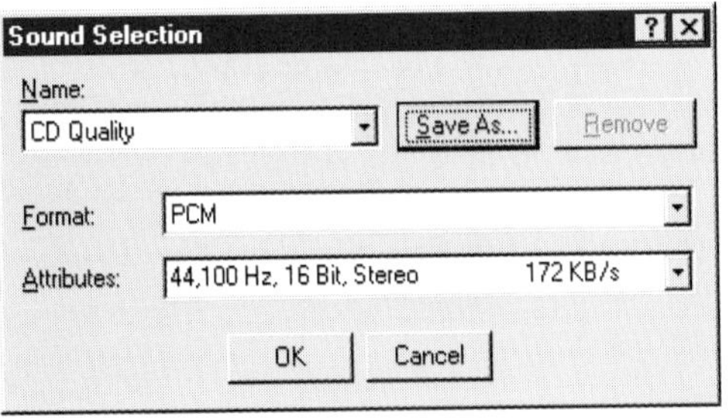

5. From the Name drop-down list, choose a sound quality:
   - **CD Quality** The highest quality sound, with the largest amount of space (172KB per second) required to store the sound on disk.
   - **Radio Quality** Medium-quality sound, with less disk space required (22KB per second).
   - **Telephone Quality** Low-quality sound with the least amount of disk space required (11KB per second).
6. Click OK to close the Sound Selection dialog box.
7. Click OK in the Properties for Sound dialog box.
8. In the Sound Recorder dialog box, click the Record button and start yapping, yammering, whistling, cooing, or making whatever sound you want to record.
9. Click the Stop button when you are finished.
10. Choose File | Save and, in the Save As dialog box, choose a folder in which to save the file, give the file a name, and click the Save button.

See "Windows Media Player: Playing Recordings and Video" later in this chapter to learn about the Media Player.

Play the sound you recorded either in Sound Recorder or the Windows Media Player.

Editing a Wave File

In Sound Recorder, wave (.wav) sound files can be cut and edited like video tape. In fact, with a couple of good wave files, you can pretend very easily that you are a record producer. Choose File | Open to open the wave file you want to edit, and then follow these instructions for editing your file in Sound Recorder:

- **Cut out the start or end of a file** Either play the sound or move the slider to the point before or after which you want to delete the file. Then open the Edit menu and choose either Delete Before Current Position or Delete After Current Position.
- **Insert one file into another** Move the slider to the point where you want to insert the file, choose Edit | Insert File, find and select the file in the Insert File dialog box, and click the

Open button. It goes without saying, but you can only insert another wave file into a wave file.

- **Mix sound files** Open one file and move the slider to the point where you want the second file to start. Then choose Edit | Mix with File, locate and select the other file in the Mix With File dialog box, and click the Open button.
- **Change the volume** To make a sound file louder or softer, choose Effects | Increase Volume (by 25%) or Effects | Decrease Volume.
- **Change the speed (and pitch)** To make voice recordings higher or lower, choose Effects | Increase Speed (by 100%) or Effects | Decrease Speed.
- **Add an echo effect** Choose Effects | Add Echo.
- **Reverse a sound** Choose Effects | Reverse.

Windows Media Player: Playing Recordings and Video

Windows Media Player is an all-in-one tool for playing sound recordings and video. You can even burn a CD with the Media Player. The following pages explain—take a deep breath before reading the rest of this sentence—how to find your way around the screen, play songs and videos from files on your computer, play a CD, listen to the Internet radio, put together a media library of your favorite songs and videos, make a playlist, and burn a CD with song files that are stored on your computer.

Finding Your Way Around the Windows Media Player

The Windows Media Player makes it possible to quickly find and play a song or video file that is stored on your computer. To start the Windows Media Player, do one of the following:

- Double-click the Windows Media Player shortcut icon on the desktop or the Quick Launch toolbar.

- Click the Start button and choose Programs | Accessories | Entertainment | Windows Media Player.
- Double-click a visual or audio file in My Computer.

Later in this chapter, "Putting Together a Media Library" explains how to assemble audio and video files for the Media Player menus. "Assembling a Playlist of Your Favorite Songs" explains how to create a playlist of your own.

Figure 10.2 shows the Media Player. By clicking taskbar buttons, you can do different tasks with the Media Player. On the bottom of the screen are controls for playing songs and videos. The fastest way to play a new song or video is to open the Playlist menu and choose a new playlist, as shown in Figure 10.2.

Click a button on the taskbar to tell the Media Player how you want to entertain yourself:

- **Now Playing** Shows videos (see Figure 10.2) and, when sound files are playing, "visualizations." See the next section in this chapter for more information on visualizations.

Figure 10.2: The Windows Media Player

TIP

What Microsoft calls *visualizations* appear in the Now Playing window when you play an audio file. If you find them distracting, choose Views | Now Playing Tools and uncheck the Show Visualizations command on the submenu.

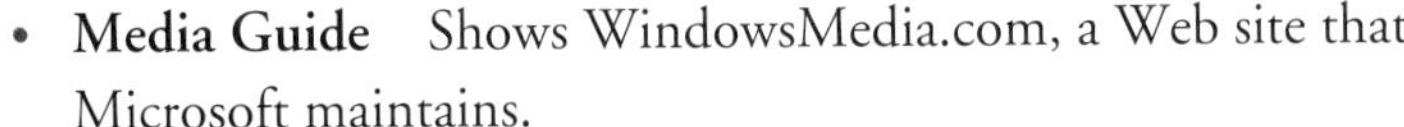

- **Media Guide** Shows WindowsMedia.com, a Web site that Microsoft maintains.
- **CD Audio** Lets you play CDs. See "Playing a CD on Your Computer" later in this chapter.
- **Media Library** Offers a means of building a media library of the songs and videos you want to play with Media Player. You can also choose files to play and create playlists starting here. See "Playing Songs and Videos" and "Putting Together a Media Library" later in this chapter.
- **Radio Tuner** Lets you tune in to radio stations over the Internet. See "Playing the Internet Radio" later in this chapter.
- **Portable Device** Offers a means of copying MP3, wave, and Windows Media files to a device such as an MP3 player.
- **Skin Chooser** Offers ways to change the appearance of the Media Player.

Want to tuck the Media Player into a corner of the screen while you do other things? Click the Compact Mode/Full Mode button. As shown in Figure 10.3, a compact version of the Media Player appears. To return to full mode, click the Compact Mode/Full Mode button again.

Playing Songs and Videos

The first step in playing a song or video is to find it. You can do that either by starting in My Computer or Windows Media Player:

- In Windows Media Player, click the Now Playing button. Then open the Playlist drop-down menu and choose a playlist (see Figure 10.4). The files in the playlist appear on the right side of the window. Double-click the file you want to play. (If you don't see the playlist, click the Show/Hide Playlist button.)
- In Windows Media Player, click the Media Library button. Then, clicking the plus signs to open folders, locate the file in your media library that you want to play, as shown in Figure 10.4. When you find it, double-click the filename. In a long list of files, click the Name, Artist, or Filename button at the top of the column to sort the files and thereby find the one you are

Figure 10.3: The Windows Media Player in compact mode

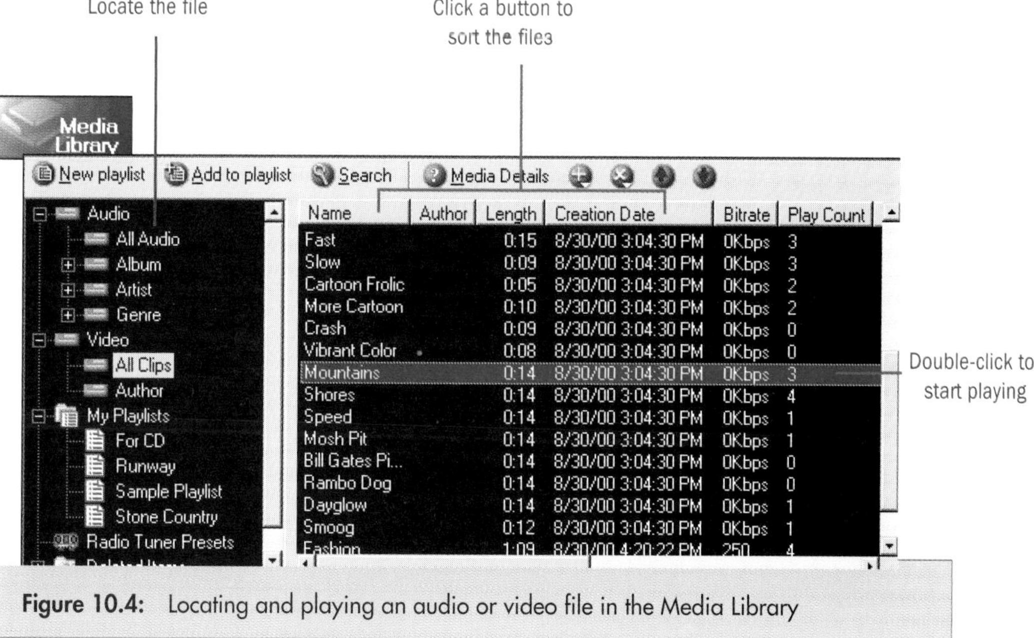

Figure 10.4: Locating and playing an audio or video file in the Media Library

looking for. Later in this chapter, "Putting Together a Media Library" explains how to assemble audio and video files on your computer so you can play files easily.

- In My Computer, locate the audio or video file and double-click it. Windows Media Player appears onscreen if it isn't already there, and the file starts playing.

The controls in the Windows Media Player work like the controls in a standard cassette tape player. Click the Play/Pause button to start or pause a file, the Stop button to...well, you know the rest—if you don't know the rest, experiment for a minute and you will know it.

While your audio or visual file is playing, select the Now Playing button and click the Show Equalizer & Settings button. Once there you can choose from among the settings listed below. To switch from setting to setting, click the Next Setting or Previous Setting button. You will find these small buttons directly above the Play/Pause button.

TIP

Click the Shuffle button or choose Play | Shuffle to play videos or audio files at random.

- **SRS WOW effects** Click the On/Off button to turn the effects on and then experiment with the TruBass and WOW controls. According to the company that invented this technology, you get a "psychoacoustic" sound when you play with the TruBass control. Wow!
- **Graphic equalizer** Play with the levels to adjust the sound of audio files.
- **Video settings** These are the same settings you find on a color TV: Brightness, Contrast, Hue, and Saturation. Use them to make videos more watchable.
- **Media information** Provides a description from the Internet of the audio or visual file you are playing.
- **Caption** Provides a description of the audio or video file that is playing.

Playing a CD on Your Computer

If your computer has a CD-ROM or DVD drive, you can play CDs on your computer. Insert the CD in the CD-ROM or DVD drive and click the CD Audio button in Windows Media Player. To play a track, double-click its name.

The Media Player maintains a database of CDs and recordings by popular musicians. In most cases, you can click the Get Names button to fill in the names of the tracks on the CD. Try clicking that button and clicking Next to go on the Internet and get names.

Playing the Internet Radio

Radio, you might be interested to know, is about to enter a new era, thanks to the Internet. Instead of being confined to nearby radio stations, you can listen to stations all around the world from your computer.

Click the Radio Tuner button in the Windows Media Player to play a radio station over your computer. On the Presets drop-down menu, select My Presets to see the list of radio stations you like, or select Features to see the list of stations Microsoft likes. On the list of radio stations, double-click the name of the station you want to hear. Figure 10-5 explains how to designate the radio stations you want to hear and put their names on the Presets list.

Putting Together a Media Library

A *media library* is a catalogue of the media files on a computer. After you create a media library, you can play audio and video files simply by clicking the Media Library button, opening a folder or two, and double-clicking a filename (see Figure 10.4 earlier in this chapter). What's more, to make it easier to locate files, you can create playlists after you have created a media library (see the next section in this chapter). The files are not assembled in one place when you create a media library. The library is really a map to different media files on your computer.

Windows Media Player has its own ideas about how to organize a media library. After you copy a file onto your computer, the Media Player classifies it for you. How does it do that? By comparing the filename to the names of files in its database. Music files, for example, are classified by album, artist, and genre. When the Media Player

TIP

In my experiments, Windows Media Player isn't very good at organizing files in the media library. However, that shouldn't bother you, because you can organize files yourself by creating playlists, as the next section in this chapter explains.

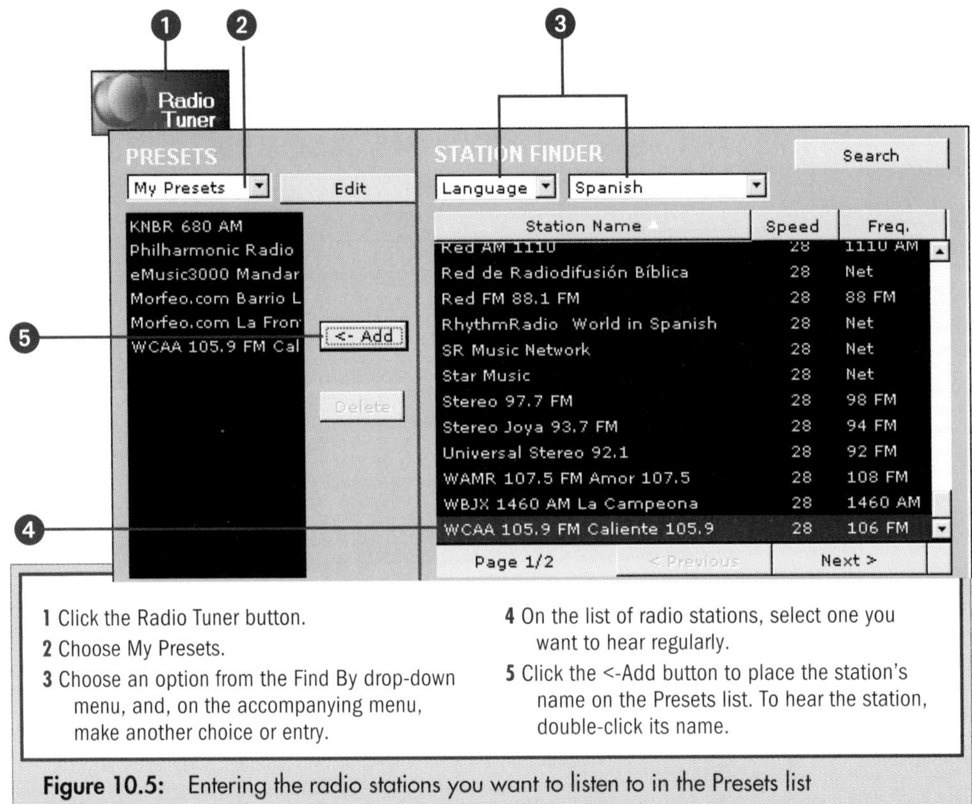

1 Click the Radio Tuner button.
2 Choose My Presets.
3 Choose an option from the Find By drop-down menu, and, on the accompanying menu, make another choice or entry.
4 On the list of radio stations, select one you want to hear regularly.
5 Click the <-Add button to place the station's name on the Presets list. To hear the station, double-click its name.

Figure 10.5: Entering the radio stations you want to listen to in the Presets list

doesn't recognize a file, it is catalogued under All Audio (if it is an audio file) or All Clips (if it is a video file).

Here are the three ways to build a media library on your computer:

- **Copy music from a CD** Insert the CD and click the CD Audio button. On the list of music tracks, uncheck the tracks you *don't* want to copy. Then click the Copy Music button. Files are copied to the C:\My Documents\My Music\Artist's name folder on your computer and are converted from CD audio track (CDA) to Windows Media audio (WMA) files.
- **Get files one at a time** Click the Media Library button and then either click the Add to Library button or choose File | Add to Library | Add File. In the Open dialog box, find

the audio or visual file you want, select it, and click the Open button.

- **Assemble files from your computer** Choose Tools | Search Computer For Media (or press F3). In the Search Computer for Media dialog box, choose a drive. Then click the Browse button and select a folder to start searching for files. Finally, click the Start Search button.

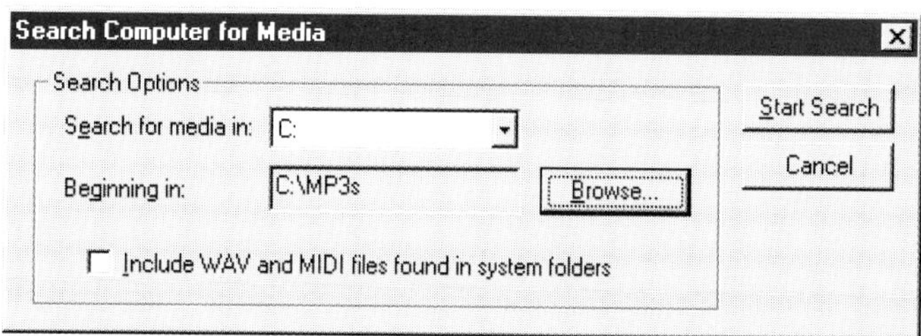

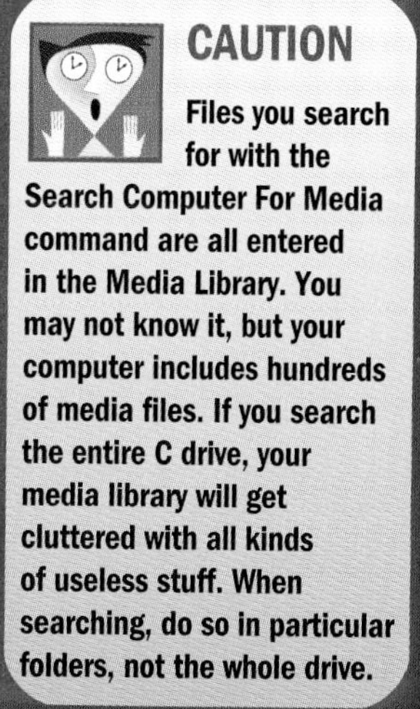

To change the name of a file or any other piece of information for that matter, right-click the item you want to change, choose Edit, and enter new information. To delete a file from the Media Library, right-click the file and choose Delete from Library on the shortcut menu.

Assembling a Playlist of Your Favorite Songs

A *playlist* is a collection of songs or video files that have been assembled in a list to make finding and playing songs or videos easier. As the section "Playing Songs and Videos" explained earlier in this chapter, you can click the Now Playing button, choose a playlist from the Playlist drop-down menu, see a selection of songs or videos on the playlist you chose, and double-click a song or video to play it.

Create a playlist for your favorite songs or videos by following these steps:

1. Click the Media Library button.
2. Click the New Playlist button. You will find it near the upper-left corner of the window.

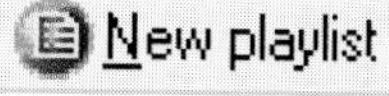

> **SHORTCUT**
>
> **To add several files at once to a playlist, CTRL-click to select the files, right-click one of the files, choose Add to Playlist on the drop-down menu, and select a list in the Playlists dialog box.**

3. In the New Playlist dialog box, enter a name and click OK. The name of your playlist appears under the My Playlists folder on the left side of the window (if you don't see it, click the plus sign beside the My Playlists folder).

Figure 10.6 demonstrates how to add filenames to a playlist. To change the order of files on a playlist, select the files one at a time and click the Up or Down button. Click the Delete button and choose Delete from Playlist on the drop-down menu to remove a file from the list.

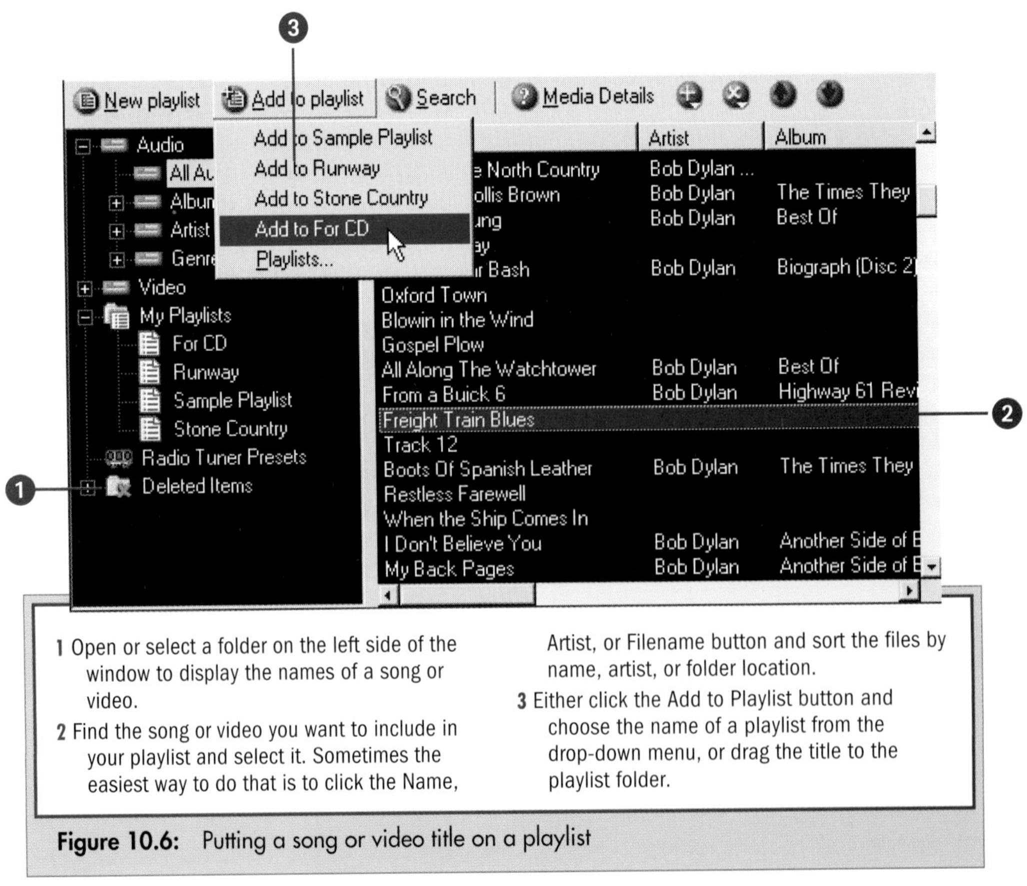

1 Open or select a folder on the left side of the window to display the names of a song or video.

2 Find the song or video you want to include in your playlist and select it. Sometimes the easiest way to do that is to click the Name, Artist, or Filename button and sort the files by name, artist, or folder location.

3 Either click the Add to Playlist button and choose the name of a playlist from the drop-down menu, or drag the title to the playlist folder.

Figure 10.6: Putting a song or video title on a playlist

Making Your Own CD

Yes, you can burn your own CD with the help of the Windows Media Player. To make the CD, you can use a CD-R or CD-RW. The following file formats can be copied to the CD: MP3 (.mp3), wave (.wav), and Windows Media (.asf, .wma, and .wmv). You can't remove songs from the CD, however, after you burn it, nor can you place more than 70 minutes of music on the CD. To copy the songs onto a CD, first gather the songs you want to copy on a playlist and arrange them in the order in which you want them to play. Then follow these steps to copy the playlist onto a CD:

TIP

When you copy MP3 files to a CD-R or CD-RW with Windows Media Player, Media Player converts the MP3 files to the CDA (CD audio track) format so that they can be played on household CD players.

1. Choose File | Copy to CD. You see the Playlists dialog box.
2. Select a playlist and click OK. The Recording in Progress dialog box appears as the files are copied to the CD.

Earlier in this chapter, "Assembling a Playlist of Your Favorite Songs" explains how to make a playlist.

Imaging: Annotating and Viewing Images

Use Imaging to view and manipulate scanned images and image files you've copied from the Internet. The program works with the graphic files listed in Table 10.1. Imaging is a fun little toy. Click the Start button and choose Programs | Accessories | Imaging to start the program.

File Extension	Format
.bmp	Windows Paint
.gif	Graphics Interchange Format
.jpg	JPEG File/Interchange Format
.pcx	PC Paintbrush
.tif	Tagged Image File Format

Table 10.1: Types of Graphic Files That Work with Imaging

On the menu bar are commands for zooming in and out, rotating images, and cropping images. You are invited to experiment with Imaging to your heart's content. As you experiment, click the Best Fit button or choose View | Full Screen to get a better look at images.

Cropping an Image

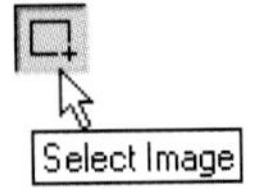

Cropping means to cut off part of a graphic. Most newspaper photographs are cropped. Photographers can't frame images just right every time around. To crop an image, click the select Image button on the Imaging toolbar and drag to form a frame around the parts of the image you want to keep. Then choose Edit | Select image (or press CTRL-SPACE), open a new image file, and choose Edit | Paste.

Annotating an Image

Following are instructions for annotating an image:

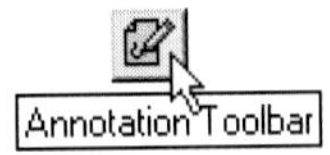

1. Open the image you want to annotate and click the Annotation Toolbar button. The Annotation toolbar appears along the bottom of the screen, as shown in Figure 10.7.
2. Click the Text button on the Annotation toolbar.
3. Click where you want the annotation to go and drag to create a text box to put the annotation in.
4. Type the annotation text.
5. Click the Straight Line button.
6. Drag to draw a line from the annotation to a part of the image.
7. To change the font or font size of the letters in an annotation or the thickness of a line, right-click the annotation or line and choose Properties. In the Properties dialog box, choose new settings.

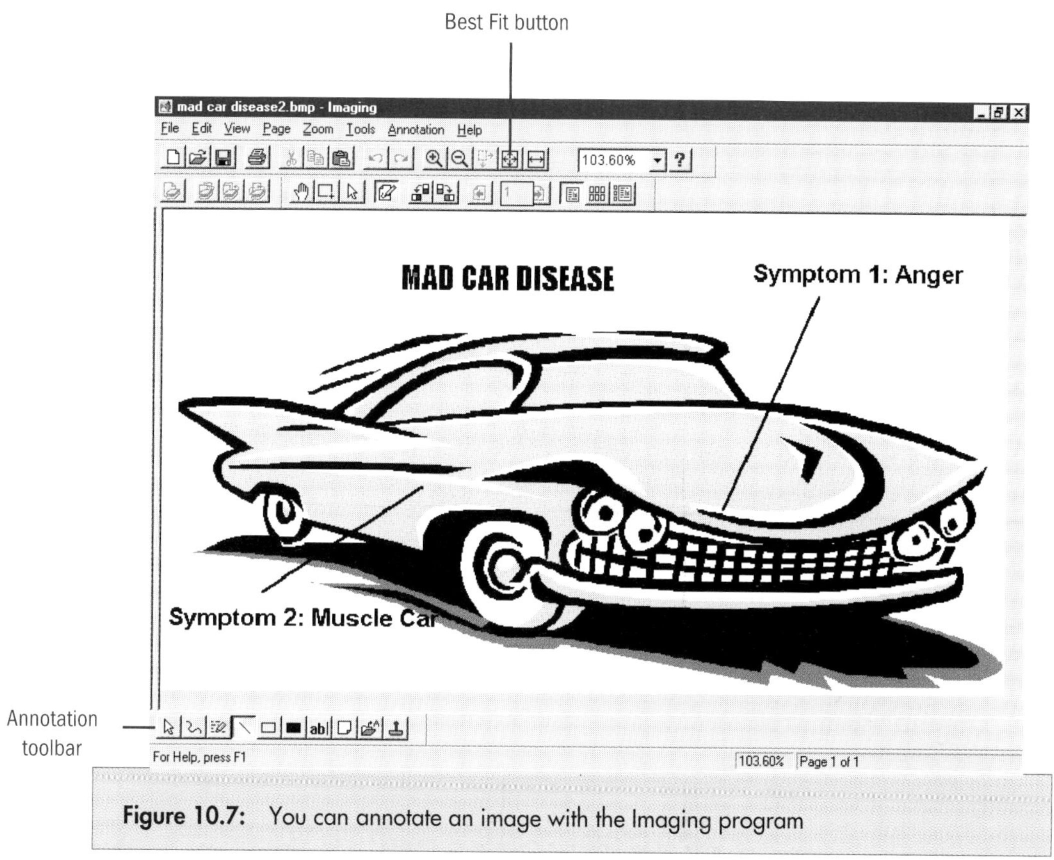

Figure 10.7: You can annotate an image with the Imaging program

To move an annotation or line, click the Annotation Selection button, click the thing you want to move, and start dragging.

APPENDIX A

Installing and Reinstalling Windows Me

This appendix explains how to install Windows Me as well as how to reinstall it when you want to add or remove some of the program's components.

To run Windows Me, your system must meet these requirements:

- At minimum, a 486 machine, although to run Windows well you should have a Pentium, or faster processor.
- At least 24MB (megabytes) of RAM.
- 240MB to 400MB of free disk space, depending on which parts of Windows Me you install.
- A CD-ROM or DVD-ROM drive

Installing Windows Me for the First Time

Installing Windows Me is actually very simple. You need a blank floppy disk with at least 1.2MB of disk space and about 30 to 60 spare minutes, depending on how many Windows Me components you want to install and how fast your computer is. The first time you install Windows Me, you get a standard installation with the default components. Afterward, you can reinstall the operating system and remove or add components (later in this appendix, "Reinstalling Windows to Add or Remove System Components" explains how). Follow these steps to install Windows Me:

1. Close all programs if any are running.
2. Insert the Windows Me CD in the CD-ROM drive. A message box tells you that the CD contains a newer version of Windows and asks if you want to install Windows Me.
3. Click Yes. You see the Windows Millennium Edition Setup Wizard dialog box.

If you don't see the message box or the Windows Millennium Edition Setup Wizard dialog box, either click Add/Remove Software in the dialog box or click the Start button and choose Settings | Control Panel, double-click the Add/Remove Programs icon in the Control Panel window, and click Install in the Add/Remove Programs Properties dialog box. Then click Next and click Finish.

4. Enter your Windows Product Key number and click Next.
5. Click Next in the Windows Me Setup dialog box. Windows runs some tests on your computer to see how much disk space you have.
6. Keep answering questions and clicking Next or OK.

In the course of the installation, you are asked to do the following:

"Create an Emergency Startup Disk" at the end of Chapter 2 explains what an emergency startup disk is.

- Insert a blank floppy disk in your machine in order to create an emergency startup disk.
- Tell Windows Me which country you live in.
- Restart your computer three times (be sure to take the emergency startup disk out of the disk drive before you restart the computer). Restarting your computer takes considerably longer than usual when you install Windows Me. Be patient.

When the ordeal is over, you can take a tour of Windows Me, although you don't have to take it right away. Take the tour whenever you want by clicking the Start button and choosing Programs | Accessories | Tips and Tour.

EXPERT ADVICE

As part of the installation procedure, Windows Me saves your old Windows system files in case you want to abandon Windows Me and go back to using the older version of Windows. See "Disk Cleanup: Uncluttering the Hard Disk" in Chapter 9 to learn how to remove old system files and save on disk space.

Reinstalling Windows to Add or Remove System Components

After you have used Windows Me for a while, you might discover that you need system components that weren't installed the first time around. Or perhaps you don't need some components and you would like to remove them to save on disk space.

Follow these steps to reinstall Windows Me and add or remove some of its components:

1. Close all programs if any are running.
2. Click the Start button and choose Settings | Control Panel.
3. Double-click the Add/Remove Programs icon.
4. Click the Windows Setup tab in the Add/Remove Programs Properties dialog box. As shown in Figure A.1, the dialog box lists all component categories. You can tell how many component options in each category are installed on your computer by looking at the check boxes:

   - **Check with no shading** All component options in this category are installed on your computer.
   - **Check with shading** Some component options in the category are installed.
   - **Empty check box** No component options in this category are installed.
5. Click a component category and then click the Details button. As shown in Figure A.1, you see a list of the component options in the category.
6. Scroll down the list and check or uncheck boxes to add or remove component options, and then click OK.

7. Repeat steps 5 and 6 to add or remove more component options from your computer.
8. Click OK in the Add/Remove Programs Properties dialog box.
9. Insert the Window Me CD and click OK in the Insert Disk message box.
10. Follow the onscreen directions to reinstall Windows Me.

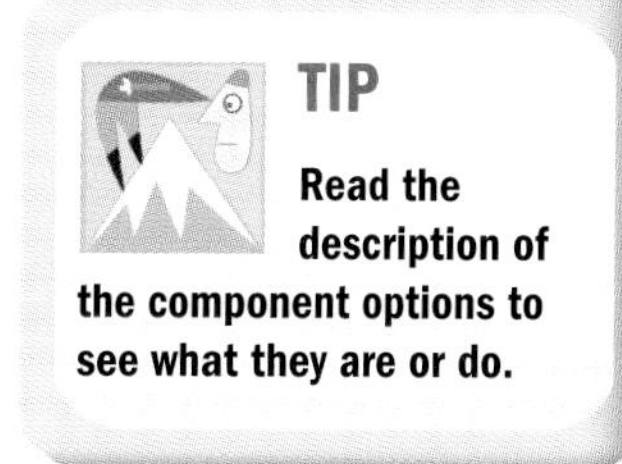

TIP

Read the description of the component options to see what they are or do.

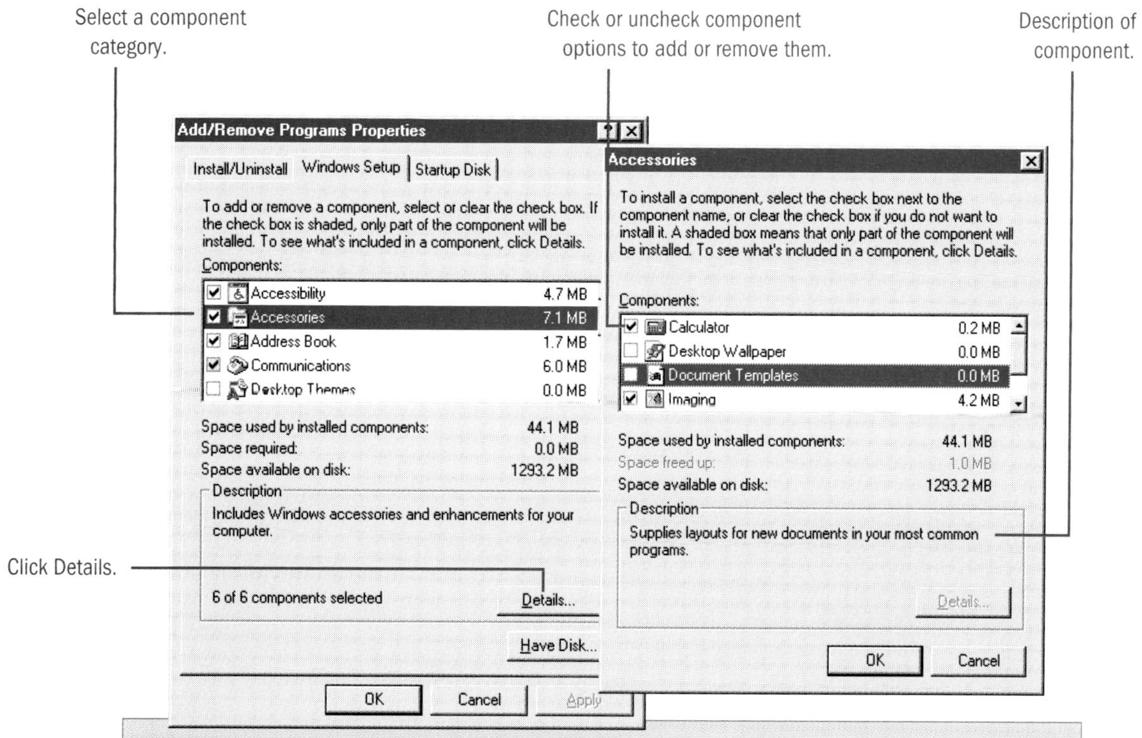

Select a component category.

Check or uncheck component options to add or remove them.

Description of component.

Click Details.

Figure A.1: Adding and removing Windows Me system components

Index

A

B

C

G

H

I

M

N

O

P

T

U

V

W